# FRAGMENTED FAMILIES

# *Fragmented Families*

## Patterns of Estrangement and Reconciliation

Ellen B. Sucov

~

southern hills PRESS

*Fragmented Families*
**Patterns of Estrangement and Reconciliation**
www.fragmentedfamilies.com

This book may be ordered through booksellers or by contacting:

Southern Hills Press
POB 7074, Jerusalem, 91070
Israel
www.southernhillspress.com

ISBN: 1-93388201-8

Typeset by Jerusalem Typesetting, www.jerusalemtype.com
Printed in the United States of America

"Everything has its season,
    and there is a time for everything under the heaven:
A time to be born        and a time to die;
    a time to plant        and a time to uproot the planted;
A time to kill        and a time to heal;
    a time to wreck        and a time to build.
A time to weep        and a time to laugh;
    a time to wail        and a time to dance.
A time to scatter stones  and a time to gather stones;
    a time to embrace        and a time to shun embraces.
A time to seek        and a time to lose;
    a time to keep        and a time to discard.
A time to rend        and a time to mend;
    a time to be silent        and a time to speak.
A time to love        and a time to hate;
    a time for war        and a time for peace."

*Ecclesiastes, 3*


"As in a fugue, two themes interweave in search of one another, unable to meet and yet linked in an inseparable association. Each of these themes is characterized by its key, in one case the major and in the other case the minor. The mood changes entirely according to the theme that is stressed, but whichever one is dominant, the other continues softly and never entirely disappears."

*Andre Neher: The Exile of the Word*

*This book is dedicated to the memory of
my father, my mother,
my sisters and my brother,
who come together for the first time
on these pages.*

# Contents

# APPRECIATION

*Fragmented Families* is about family conflict, estrangement, and reconciliation. I am responsible for formulating the concepts and for any limitations or faults you may find in this book. My beloved husband, Gene, provided the initial incentive to write. He gave me consistent support, constructive advice, and invaluable computer help while respecting my need for privacy and solitude. My daughter wrote significant portions of Chapter Seven and collaborated with me on the Coda. My son reviewed sections of the book and provided valuable advice. My eldest granddaughter read the summary I wrote for children and made helpful suggestions. Each of my grandchildren provided much joy and welcome distraction during the entire process.

Betsy Rosenberg, a gifted translator and poet, edited the early versions with great sensitivity and skill. Rolene Segal provided fruitful ideas for several portions of the manuscript.

I also wish to thank the following persons: Fran Ackerman, Malka Bina, Sarale Cohen, Joyce Driben, Moshe Kohn (*z"l*), Channah Niedorf, and Malka May. The storytellers shall remain anonymous, but I hope they know how much I appreciate their willingness to share their own family stories.

No words can express my boundless gratitude for the inspiration I have received from my revered teacher, Dr. Avivah Zornberg. Her wisdom has greatly enhanced my understanding of the levels of meaning that are inherent in the phenomena of estrangement and reconciliation.

A fine editor is a blessing. It was my good fortune to meet Dr. Ora Wiskind-Elper and convince her to edit the entire manuscript. Her superb linguistic skills, knowledge of Jewish concepts, and perceptive insights have enabled me to clarify my ideas and express them more cogently. Because she uses her red pen with such consummate gentleness, I never felt criticized or crushed, but rather, consistently enriched.

Endowed with boundless patience and a wealth of relevant information, Eva Weiss guided me through the labyrinth of hurdles related to the publishing process. Ben Hizak taught me many useful computer skills and helped me to organize the various parts of the manuscript with a minimum of frustration. The cover design was beautifully rendered by Moshe Zabari. Raphaël Freeman and Chaya Mendelson at Jerusalem Typesetting accomplished the typesetting of the text with remarkable speed and competence. Thank you!

# INTRODUCTION

Families are in continual transformation. They change and grow, expand and contract, move through crises, and resolve them. New members enter, old ones depart; the family survives. Some events are seen as vivid milestones, signaling substantial modifications in the family constellation. Others are more subtle: the youngest child leaves for college, a married daughter moves to a distant location, an uncle returns after a long absence. These events are usually perceived as benign and unremarkable. They may stir up a few ripples but cause no major upheavals in the course of family life. In sharp contrast, another type of event rips through the family like a tornado, generating great pain, anxiety, frustration, and rage. This is not a single event, but rather a sequence of interactions that mutter and buzz, erupt in angry confrontation, and culminate in rejection and cutoff. The elements that produce family conflicts are complex and multifaceted. Typically, some sort of crisis provokes one family member to sever his connection with others in the family. The ensuing fragmentation brings about radical changes in the life of the family and presents extraordinary challenges to family members, all of whom are inevitably identified in terms of the conflict. One will be cast into the role of "victim," another will be seen as an "enemy," someone else will feel as if he or she has been neglected, rejected, betrayed, or exploited. Others will be observers, watching from the sidelines. The situation invariably requires each person to learn a new repertory of emotional response, to find new ways of coping with the reality of an unfamiliar, highly charged emotional climate. This book will describe a wide spectrum of these events, illustrate their various permutations, and discuss how families deal with them. It will also offer suggestions for strategies that may help to heal the fragmentation and restore the family to wholeness.

## Author's perspective

It is April 2004. Sunlight glimmers on a distant hill, reflecting from the roofs of temporary shelters for Ethiopian immigrants. The hill overlooks Bethlehem on one side and the new city of Jerusalem on the other. In the park beneath our windows, children are playing, their nannies chatting in Russian. Fragrant roses, jasmine, and clusters of purple pansies are blooming along the winding paths. Observing this tranquil scene, I feel a sense of incongruity. The Hebrew news is on the radio, reporting another suicide bomber, another retaliation. I'm at home in Israel. Here, eruptions of family conflicts have persisted for thousands of years, remnants of ancient rivalries between Isaac and Ishmael, Joseph and his brothers, Arabs and Jews, Jews and other Jews. Here in Jerusalem, where I live for six months each year, I am writing about family conflict.

I am a psychologist, retired from a university faculty in the United States. My orientation to psychology is based on phenomenology, the branch of psychology that is concerned with the essential meanings of human experience. Phenomenological psychologists use descriptions rather than measurements to understand human behavior. We look at the context of experience and try to discover the connections between different types of life events and the meanings that people attribute to them. In my work, I focused on the development of young children and adolescents in the context of their families and communities. Utilizing various theories of family systems, I learned how to interpret the complex interactions that occur in families. My initial interest in family dynamics may have been sparked by the sudden death of my father when I was ten, leaving me, my mother's only child, to grapple with a very conflicted family situation. But the mood and color of my thinking has been influenced more by the many years I devoted to the study of music. There are parallels between the complexities of family life and the melodies, harmonies, and rhythms in music. For me, families are like an animated contrapuntal system with themes that appear and fade, rhythms that surge, quicken, and diminish, soothing sounds alternating with sharp dissonance. In families, as in counterpoint, rules are made and broken; patterns of interaction are sometimes discernible, sometimes obscure. Just like the cantatas of Bach, families resonate with moments of passion and great joy and with episodes of bitter pain and anguish.

My mother was the youngest child and the only daughter of her aging parents. I am uncertain about the place of her birth. She claimed to have been born in a small town in Pennsylvania, but she had no birth document and I suspect that she was brought to America as a babe in her mother's arms. Her Orthodox Jewish family came from a *shtetl* in Lithuania where they had survived more than one pogrom. From fragments of stories my cousins told, I gather that my grandfather was a sober, observant Jew, determined to uphold the laws and commandments of his forefathers. The rest of the family was eager to assimilate, to become Americans. There is one terrifying story, a secret kept hidden, which illustrates their struggle. One of my mother's brothers, anguished over a failure or transgression, journeyed to the country farmhouse of his elder brother and hanged himself on a tree in the front yard. This ultimate expression of cutoff, when the family had not yet gained a foothold in the strange new world, must have been a terrible shock. My mother never discussed this episode, so I am left to wonder how my grandparents, who died before I was born, survived the grief and the shame. Some years later, frustrated in his efforts to remain an "old world" Jew and appalled at his assimilated family, my grandfather cut himself off from his wife and adult children and moved to an Orthodox old-age home in New York City. He died there, alone and forsaken by the rest of the family. It was on this shaky foundation that my mother set out to find herself and to shape her own identity.

Rabbi Nachman of Bratslav said: "Whoever is able to write a book and does not, it is as if he has lost a child." This book is a "child" of my mature years, coming to fruition at an age when most people have completed their work. The topic was inspired by a conflict that erupted more than seventy years ago, when one large branch broke off from my father's family tree. The drama began two years after his first wife died, when he married the woman who would become my mother. His second marriage set off a wave of opposition and rejection by his children, a teenaged son and two older daughters. During my childhood, I had a vague sense of a brother and sisters but no connection with them. For more than forty years, I felt only bewilderment and resentment toward that entire segment of the family. I referred to them as the "enemy camp" and never intended to initiate any contact with them. My mother had expressed alternating feelings of regret and outrage at their determination to exclude us. She died without any expectation that the rift would ever be mended.

Fifty years later, the conflict was resolved and the broken branch was partially repaired. The process of connecting with my estranged siblings was challenging, intimidating, often frustrating, but ultimately rewarding. Chapter Five contains a detailed description of the estrangement and the subsequent process of reconciliation with the cut off branch. This book is an extension of the exploration of my own family history.

When I began to organize my ideas and collect stories, my intention was to produce a book for family therapists, psychologists, and other professionals who work with troubled families. As the book progressed, the focus of my life shifted. Now I am the grandmother of Israeli children who are growing up in an atmosphere of traditional, Orthodox Judaism. Here in Jerusalem, I have become deeply engrossed in various aspects of religious study. As my interests, curiosity, and commitments turned more frequently to Jewish topics, I realized that my perceptions of family conflict would be seen through a Jewish lens. Many of the narratives I have collected are about Jewish families. In the course of hearing and writing their stories, I have come to see that religious tradition plays a vital role in the lives of families, even when they claim that such influence is irrelevant or trivial. No matter how assimilated, no matter how alienated from their religious tradition, a remnant adheres to their psyche, an imprint of what Rabbi Adin Steinsaltz has called the "essential Jewish archetype." There is a reciprocal interaction between cultural tradition, religious heritage, and family relationships, each one influencing and shaping the others. These dynamic connections are reflected in many of the stories in this book.

## Overview

My topic is estrangement in the family. The lingering echo of a door slammed; the click at the other end of the phone followed by silence; a letter "returned to sender." An enraged voice screaming "Get out of my house!" or "Get out of my life!" Forty years of alienation between brother and sister. A rebellious daughter declared "dead" by her parents. This is my topic. The stories I have chosen to tell, the way I have elaborated the themes, and the readers to whom I am speaking – all of these reflect who I am and how I have come to understand this topic. The use of "I" and occasionally "we" throughout these pages reflects these present realities: I the writer, you the reader, and "we," those of us who have "been there," who have experienced the upheavals and anguish of estrangement in the family.

This book opens with general descriptions of family dynamics and the types of provocations that are likely to lead to conflict and estrangement. Reflecting my conviction that "family" is a multidimensional phenomenon, the first three chapters introduce the salient features of each dimension. Chapter One highlights the structural, emotional, and behavioral elements that are inherent in the form and content of every family system. Chapter Two focuses on the cultural and religious aspects of family life. To support my contention that historical events and religious traditions influence family interactions, I examine those factors that have had significant impact on the expression of particular emotions and behavior. Although the discussion centers on the Jewish experience, my formulation can serve as a template for readers whose identity is based on different religious and cultural legacies. In Chapter Three, I address the dimension of ultimate values, the moral and ethical aspects of family life as they are depicted in sacred literature. Interpretations of narratives and discussions of legal issues based on themes from the Hebrew Bible are presented to illustrate specific aspects of family conflict.

Shifting from sacred to secular literature, Chapter Four contains excerpts from fiction, drama, and biography. These narratives depict the perspectives of opposing positions in the escalation of family discord. They capture the complexity of these estranged relationships and in some cases, chart the pathways to the cessation of hostilities.

The next four chapters form the heart of this book. They contain stories of real families who have experienced the pain of estrangement. While protecting the anonymity of persons who shared their stories, I have tried to preserve the vividness of their bitter disputes. Some of these families are still in the midst of the struggle; a few have found ways to rebuild connections and achieve closure. The story of the fifty-year cutoff in my own family is documented in detail. My intention is to present the sequence from alienation to resolution as one model of how the healing process can be accomplished.

The final chapters speak of reconciliation and its manifestations. Two contrasting versions of reconciliation are described, with all the obstacles and detours, the agony and the exaltation that accompanied them. For readers who are struggling with crucial questions about their own family conflicts, I suggest strategies for reaching solutions. The book concludes with a dramatic story of the escalation of a bitter conflict in which a cutoff was averted and a fragmented relationship was repaired and strengthened. But not all conflicts are resolved. Despite honorable intentions, the path to a "happy ending" is often elusive and unpredictable. During the process of writing this book, my own perceptions of the phenomenon have changed. I have come to realize that estrangement can be seen, not only as a locus of anger and retaliation, but also as an opportunity for self-understanding. The task of exploring one's family, examining its splintered parts, and clarifying one's own role as a family member is a crucial step in personal development, whether or not the effort leads to reconciliation. Hopefully, the conclusions I have reached will encourage you, the reader, to map out your own pathway and discover your own solutions.

**Confidentiality of names**
The families who are described in this book are alive and real. The relationships and family process are depicted accurately, as one or more family members described them to me. To ensure confidentiality, all of the stories have been modified and the names, places, and other details have been altered. If you, the reader, recognize certain family patterns, you are probably correct, since many of the elements are universal and familiar. If you think you can identify an individual person or a specific family, you are probably wrong. It's all made up, except for the parts that are true.

# CHAPTER ONE

# The Multiple Dimensions of Family

## Prelude

*"Everything has its season, and there is a time for everything under the heaven."* But how do we understand the "season" for estrangement? When is the time to scatter, to break, to hate, and to cut off from one's own family? And how can the fragments be restored to wholeness? Is it possible to heal the wounds, to mend the broken parts? How can a woman reconcile with a brother who has shunned her for forty years? Can we learn to make peace with alienated parents, with children who have banished us from their lives? Will we ever be able to laugh together and embrace one another?

In the Random House *Dictionary of the English Language*, the word "family" has fifteen definitions: parents and their children; all persons who are descended from a common progenitor; a major sub-division of a species of plants or animals; a local unit of the Mafia. A more emotionally laden definition is given by Anita Diamant in her novel, *The Red Tent*. She speaks of Jacob's biblical family as "a sticky web of loyalties and grudges." All of these definitions have a common thread of meaning: they express a bond of relatedness, a set of similar qualities. To introduce the theme of estrangement, I propose this definition:

> *A family is any group of persons closely related by blood, mar-*
> *riage, or choice, as spouses, parents, sons, daughters, siblings,*
> *uncles, aunts, cousins, grandparents, and in-laws, whether*
> *dwelling together or apart, respected or rejected, estranged*
> *or reconciled.*

The phenomenon of family estrangement is infinitely complex and elusive. The main task of this book is to describe the entanglements and the rifts, the tensions and upheavals that disrupt the continuity of family bonds. Like a contrapuntal fugue with multiple voices, all the parts of the family may, at times, be joined together in harmonious progression. At other times, they move along separately. One part may transpose itself into a different key and jab at the others in sharp dissonance. Within the family, each person has a distinctive voice, sequence of development, his or her own life, but each of these lives is inextricably bound up with the others. For long periods, some voices may not be heard at all, yet they remain in the family as a muted echo.

To delineate the process of estrangement in family relationships, I will propose a multidimensional model with three distinct levels. As in a fugue, no dimension stands alone, and the whole can be understood only when we are tuned in to the manifold realities that shape and color the dynamics of family life.

The first level consists of the structural, emotional, and behavioral elements in the family system. This dimension includes the size and shape of the family and the patterns of births and deaths. Here, too, are the vital relationships between those in the same generation (siblings) and those in different generations (parents, children and grandchildren, spouses and their in-laws). This dimension reverberates with the dynamics of family life, the expectations, frustrations, love and anger, attachments and separations that express the emotional tone of the family. It is at this level that family therapists and family theorists work.

The second level is the historical legacy, the events and processes that have shaped the family through time. These include the family's religious, cultural, and ethnic heritage, the patterns of migration and settlement, the catastrophes and triumphs that occurred in previous generations, the rituals and traditions that have been handed down. The sum of these elements constitutes the collective memory of the family. At this level, we find the writings of anthropologists, family sociologists, and historians.

The third and most basic level is the realm of ultimate values, the foundation of ethical standards and moral behavior. For some families, this foundation is clearly defined. For example, Orthodox Jews perceive the Torah and its commentaries as a fundamental source of truth, a divinely given set of laws and commandments. Every act and thought, every aspect of family life, emanates from this basic source. Christian readers may cite corresponding sources of wisdom that provide guidelines for virtuous behavior.[1] Persons who do not affirm traditional precepts will construct a scale of values that reflects their own constellation of beliefs. For many families, this effort is visible and pervasive. For others, the process is less obvious, humming under the surface. Those who focus on this dimension include Bible scholars and philosophers of religion and culture, as well as authors who specialize in religiously inspired advice to families.

This book contains many stories about estrangement in families. In every case, the multiple dimensions of family life will be operating, but each family expresses them in unique ways. The following sections present the components of the first significant dimension, the family system. We will begin by describing the structural elements and emotional forces that are implicated in the phenomenon of estrangement.

THE FIRST LEVEL: THE FAMILY AS A SYSTEM

The term *system* is rooted in Latin and Greek words that mean "to place together." A system unites and organizes separate elements into a whole. The unity of the system implies that each of the elements serves the needs of the entire system; no part is independent of the others. In a family system, there is an observable pattern of interaction among the members. The behavior of each person influences all of the others. A change in one part of the family produces compensatory changes in the other parts.

Family therapists can choose from a wide variety of theories to interpret the behavior of their clients. One approach that is particularly relevant to the phenomenon of estrangement is "Bowen Family Systems Theory."[2] Initially conceived by the psychiatrist Murray Bowen, the theory was subsequently elaborated by his colleagues.[3] Now widely used to interpret behavior in many different types of families, the theory consists of eight concepts.[4] The main emphasis is on the nature of attachments and separations, the turbulence that erupts in triangular interactions, and the projection of guilt, blame, and anxiety from one generation to another. The core concept is the "differentiation of self," which Bowen defines as the degree of autonomy a person is able to achieve in the face of pressures to be enmeshed and dependent. "Differentiation" is measured in terms of the level of emotional reactivity, that is, the intensity of feelings that are aroused in one family member by the behavior of another. The less differentiated person has a limited repertory of responses. He is at the mercy of his fears, compulsions, instincts, and aggressive drives. The more differentiated person can think about how he wants to respond and choose among various alternatives. He can use his intellect to analyze the situation, but he can also respond emotionally without losing control. Each of the concepts in Bowen's theory is implicated in the process of estrangement. A conflict between family members can be seen to reflect all of the structural and emotional factors that characterize that particular family. True to the nature of systems, every family member has a role in the conflict. No one exists in isolation from the others.

STRUCTURE AND SIBLING POSITION

The term "structure" is used to describe a constellation of interrelated parts. It can refer to many different entities. For example, we speak of the "structure" of an atom, a corporation, a political party, a bridge, and a family. Bowen and his colleagues use special diagrams to depict the structure of any individual family, that is, the number of related persons, their birth order, marriages, divorces, and deaths.[5] The diagram depicts the persons in each generation, beginning with the nuclear family, the parents and their children. It becomes more complicated when adult children marry and in-laws enter the fold, or when stepfamilies or other adopted relatives are added. In the extended family, there may be multiple branches and several generations, thus increasing exponentially the number of emotional attachments and potential separations.

Walter Toman is a psychologist who pioneered the idea that sibling position is a major factor in the dynamics of every family. Using data from interviews with several hundred normal families, he constructed profiles of the characteristics of ten sibling positions and the significance of each position. His profiles describe, for example, the situation of being the firstborn versus the youngest son, or a girl who has sisters compared to one who has brothers, or the role of an only child.[6] The profiles are not intended to be precise for every person, but rather to indicate general trends and patterns of behavior exhibited by siblings in various roles. In the unfolding of a family conflict, sibling positions – and the meanings attached to them – are often implicated in the escalation of tensions.

EMOTIONAL PROCESS

The expression of *emotion* is a complex, multifaceted phenomenon. It cannot be adequately represented in a diagram, although there are symbols in the genogram that depict some of the more emotionally laden events, such as cutoffs. Every family has its own unique textures, intensities, and moods; each member has his or her own convictions about how family members should behave. Tensions escalate when basic beliefs and values are ignored, when power is challenged, loyalty denied, or trust betrayed. Conflict is likely to erupt in a family when one child is favored over others, aged parents are neglected, or cultural traditions are not respected. The emotional climate of a family is significantly affected by a silent, sullen father or a mother who is alienated from her own siblings. Threats, power plays, promises not kept: these are all elements in the emotional climate.

Every family develops its own patterns of closeness and distance. In an optimal family environment, there is a flexible alternation between attachment and separation so that each person can retain a sense of autonomous identity while sustaining connections with other family members. The spectrum of possible positions ranges from excessive enmeshment and dependency to alienation. The emotional component of these positions may not coincide with their outward manifestations. Estrangement does not imply a lesser degree of emotional involvement; to the contrary, it is often a sign of intense, unresolved animosity. In one family, a mother and her adult daughter have not spoken to each other for several years, but they are not indifferent to each other. Rather, they continue to be stuck together by the glue of anger and blame. In another family, a woman was humiliated by her brother and has not spoken to him in forty years, but she reacts emotionally to any reminder of him. She tends to relate to all men as if they were her brother. A son may claim to be "liberated" from his parents and refuse all contact with them, but he continues to act out the role of rebellious child. All of these people are still emotionally enmeshed with their alienated relatives, despite the vast distance between them in terms of physical contact, geographical location, and the duration of the estrangement.

Excessively close, dependent ties between two family members are likely to erupt in anger when one person perceives the other as an accessory or an appendage to himself. The "otherness" of the other is then seen as a threat, something foreign and disposable. When I need the other person to take care of me, protect me, or confirm my identity, I feel anxious and deprived when she does not comply. This sense of vulnerability lies at the heart of many conflicts between family members. If the other person does not fulfill my expectations or meet my needs, I may feel justified in dismissing that person, cutting her off. The variety of emotional

6

reactions is infinite, but the constellation of provocations that lead to estrangement in a particular family is unique to that family.

DEVELOPMENTAL PROGRESSIONS: THE FAMILY LIFE CYCLE

We are born and nurtured, we develop, mature, and die within the sphere of our families. Each stage of the life course is characterized by specific tasks that correspond to the age of each person and his or her role in the family. Within each stage, the roles of males and females are defined, clarified, revised, and sometimes reversed. We learn how to give and receive, work and play; we experience the most significant achievements and losses, all in the context of the family. At every stage, the family's agenda changes. Its members adjust their goals and priorities to fit the family's changing needs, or they refuse to do so and move out of the family orbit. There is a reciprocal relationship between family time and historical time. As the family grows from one stage to another, its members are simultaneously confronting and dealing with events in the extended family, the neighborhood, the community, and the larger world. The family system moves through time; time moves through the family.

Family therapists have formulated various conceptual frameworks for understanding the family life cycle. In dealing with the problems presented by many different types of families, they have learned to recognize certain general developmental patterns. One source identifies nine stages.[7] In this section, we will summarize the main tasks of these stages. Later, in the stories of estrangement, we will notice how the family's developmental pathways are implicated in the emergence of conflict.

THE FIRST STAGE: Infancy (birth to age 2). The beginnings of empathy and emotional attachment. The infant learns to receive nourishment and recognize its sources. He achieves upright posture. Soon, with the help of parents and siblings, he can face the world and respond to it.

THE SECOND STAGE: Early childhood (age 2 to 6). The child masters a wide range of skills. She begins to speak and communicate with parents and siblings as well as with persons in the extended family. She experiences the tensions of interdependence: giving and taking, winning and losing.

THE THIRD STAGE: Middle childhood (age 6 to 12). The child expands his knowledge base, builds up his physical skills, and extends his social milieu beyond the boundaries of the family. He begins to develop ethical and moral standards.

THE FOURTH AND FIFTH STAGES: Pubescence (age 11 to 14) and adolescence (age 13 to 21). During this period, the child becomes a young adult as she moves through the transformations of puberty and the stresses of adolescence. She charts her own directions and begins to form a sense of herself that is separate from her family. Growth spurts that erupt during this period may become breeding grounds for future conflict. Those parents and siblings with strong needs for closeness and conformity can sense the impending separation from more independent, rebellious youth. There is a lurking temptation to reject and eject those who are different. This tendency must be balanced by the more constructive task of sustaining familial connections while shaping one's own identity.

THE SIXTH STAGE: Early adulthood (age 21 to 35). The young person creates meaningful relationships with persons outside of the family. The obligations of marriage and parenthood may be undertaken, or other kinds of commitments may be chosen. A work role is defined; networks of colleagues and friends are expanded and consolidated.

THE SEVENTH STAGE: The middle years (age 35 to 55). During this period, earlier gains are confirmed, repudiated, or transformed. There may be radical shifts in one's role as a result of a new job, a divorce, remarriage, the creation of a stepfamily. The person learns to cope with major transitions such as the launching of children and the "empty nest."

THE EIGHTH STAGE: Late middle age (55 to 70). Retirement from the workplace requires adjustments at home. There is now a sharper awareness of one's mortality. Knowledge and information are transposed into wisdom as one reassesses values and priorities. The person learns to relate to adult children, redefines sibling connections, and mourns the death of parents.

THE NINTH STAGE: Aging. This period holds the potential for creativity as well as for decay. Older persons often experience a heavy accumulation of grief and loss. They may also have the gratification of seeing their family grow and flourish. The activity of retrospection can lead to a meaningful review of one's life and accomplishments. This stage offers opportunities to reconnect with estranged relatives and repair damaged relationships. Some old people are afflicted with the burdens of illness, mental deterioration, anxiety, and regret. Others are blessed with the resiliency to cope with loss, achieve new insights, and accept the inevitability of death.

As a person grows through each of the stages, family members respond with varying degrees of encouragement, protection, opposition, or indifference to the challenges presented by that person. The family life cycle is like an ongoing fugue, a multi-voiced sequence of simultaneous progressions. Additional factors amplify the complexity. Socioeconomic status, religious convictions, cultural and ethnic identification, patterns of health and illness, and the consequences of world events are only a few of the realities that influence how families grow and change. When we study the process of alienation among family members, these multiple realities appear and reappear. Like the sounding of musical themes in an infinite variety of contexts, family developmental patterns reflect an endless array of possible configurations.

DYADS: TWO-PERSON INTERACTIONS

Every family constellation includes various two-person relationships: two voices that speak and reply, confront and negotiate, love and sometimes detest each other. In each of these dyads, emotional threads bind one to the other. What does each person expect or demand from the other? When demands are not met, how does each of them respond?

The "dance of anger"[8] usually originates between two members of the nuclear family: a parent pitted against a son or daughter, a woman feuding with her brother. There are many variations on this theme. When two relatives face off against each other, where is the concentration of emotional intensity? If basic values are scorned, promises broken, or trust betrayed, who retaliates? How is punishment imposed, and what is the outcome? In every family with an estranged member, there will be a different set of provocations and reactions. Two-person relationships are never static; they are in a continuous state of flux. Each person monitors the other for evidence of change, signs of "too little," "too much," or the wrong kind of attachment. When the relationship is relatively calm and balanced, adjustments seem natural. But if one person begins to exert excessive demands on the other, the level of anxiety rises and the sense of equilibrium is disturbed. When the family includes a prodigal, a rebel, black sheep, scapegoat, addict, eccentric, or any of the roles that are likely to cause trouble, relationships will inevitably be put off balance. In the stories of real and fictional families, we will see the unfolding of some of these patterns. As the "dance of anger" is set in motion, the entire family system is disrupted. The eventual outcome depends on many factors, but a solution will require the willingness of the original protagonists to address the problems and find new ways to resolve them.

### TRIANGLES: THREE-PART INTERACTIONS

Triangular patterns are much more complicated than two-part interactions. According to Bowen Theory, triangles are a basic ingredient in the escalation of conflict. When a third person intervenes in a feud between two family members, the emotional atmosphere becomes more turbulent. What is the sequence in the activation of a triangle? In every dyad, there are ambivalent needs: for closeness on the one hand and autonomy and distance on the other. These alternating currents of attachment and separation are always reverberating, between persons in the same generation, such as two sisters, and between generations, such as mother and son. One person may yearn for more closeness, the other for more distance. One may complain of being smothered, while the other feels ignored or unappreciated. Then the dyad is out of balance; reciprocity turns into animosity. When the tensions escalate to a level that is intolerable to one or both persons, the system is ripe for a third party to enter the scene and a triangle forms. The third person may try to repair the rift between the two or take sides with one against the other. In some families, there are recurring patterns of triangles that persist across two or more generations. A conflict between mother and father over how to protect a vulnerable child can infect other relationships: for example, the husband, wife, and grandmother. The forms and content of triangular relationships reflect countless variations. To understand their significance in an individual family, we need to pay attention to the role of the third party in the escalation or the reduction of tensions and consider how the process affects others in the family.

PROVOCATIONS AND CONFRONTATIONS:
ESCALATING EMOTIONAL INTENSITY

What are the characteristics of a fragmented family? When relatives are alienated, the usual points of contact are broken and the lines of communication are tangled or severed. The participants are locked into a permanent state of hot or cold war, unable or unwilling to use conventional forms of communication for confronting and resolving the issues. Estrangement can occur between persons who live in the same house as well as between those who live a continent apart. The emotional components vary, depending on the individual personalities and the family dynamics in any given situation. One psychologist has compiled a sourcebook of case studies that use Bowen Theory to describe how family therapists cope with conflict and emotional upheavals in their own families.[9] A more recent publication by the same author expands the parameters of Bowen Theory and provides detailed examples of its application to the phenomenon of cutoffs.[10]

What are some of the patterns that culminate in estrangement? We can identify a few of the more common ingredients, but no listing or description will encompass the full range of dynamics in families with a rejected member. In the stories of real families and in the examples from literature in Chapter Four, you will find illustrations of many of these patterns.

A major upheaval may be sparked when one family member rejects values and beliefs that are seen as crucial to the family's identity or survival. Strong religious convictions are among the most prominent issues in the eruption of conflict. These may include secular parents who face off against their religiously observant adult children, or, at the other end of the spectrum, children raised in a traditional, devout home who rebel and become secular, antireligious, or perhaps even worse from their parents' point of view, indifferent. Similar reactions can be seen in families when a son decides to convert to another religion, or a daughter "marries out." Outrage may be evoked by a choice of lifestyle that contradicts the expectations and values of the family; for example, when a son announces that he is homosexual and living with a same-sex partner. A cutoff can also occur as a response to high-risk or deviant behavior, a pattern that a "hippie," an adventurer, or an addict may follow. In some families, the choice of a particular profession or work role is crucial to their sense of prestige, so a son or daughter who takes a different path may be seen as rebellious or indifferent to the family's priorities. Contradictory political beliefs, especially in the midst of a volatile political atmosphere, can set off sparks in the family. In many situations, there is no obvious motive. As you will see in some of the stories, parents may not understand why their adult children sever connections with the family. Often, we do not have the answer to "why?"

When one family member fails to meet another's crucial needs or challenges his beliefs about decisive issues, reactions may be expressed in a variety of ways. In some situations, they are conveyed sharply and explicitly, as, "You are no longer my son! I don't ever want to see you again!" Or they may be understated and condescending, as, "You're a grown woman now. You don't need me to be your big brother anymore." The process of rejecting a family member can be set in motion by an apparently trivial event: a gift not offered, or a perceived insult. Turmoil may explode suddenly, like an erupting volcano. One story of an aborted wedding ceremony describes the chaos that broke out when a family secret was divulged by a wedding guest. In another family, a daughter blamed her mother for the father's suicide and ignited a sequence of bitter estrangements in the family. Whatever the reasons or the perceived "causes," in every family in which estrangement occurs, the emotional climate will be transformed.

The phenomenon appears in many guises and forms. For some people, separating from the family is the only way to resolve an impasse, achieve some distance, and begin to create a new sense of self. Perhaps this is the motivating factor in the process of "cool-off" I have observed in several families. An adult son or daughter will move out of the family milieu and maintain brief, non-committal communication with his or her parents. The contacts may be infrequent and unpredictable, as for example, only email. The parents feel destabilized; their questions go unanswered, and their confusion grows with time. One bewildered mother asked her daughter to explain what went wrong and was told, "If you don't know by now, I certainly won't tell you!"

Conflicts are often provoked by the introduction of a new element that alters the structure of the family, especially when the change is seen as a threat to the family's solidarity. For example, some families cannot tolerate a remarriage or a divorce. The fifty-year cutoff in my own family was set off by my father's second marriage, an event that was seen as outrageous and unacceptable by his adult daughters. Similarly, a schism may occur when someone refuses to accept an adopted child as a legitimate member of the family, or rejects a child who is handicapped. Another potentially inflammatory situation occurs when one person is unwilling to share responsibility for a family member who is ill or needy. We will examine the virulent conflict that erupted in the family portrayed by Arthur Miller in his stage drama, *The Price*. The brothers were mired in a morass of rivalry, misunderstandings, and recriminations, exacerbated by their aged father's frailty. The estrangement persisted long after his death.

Family disputes can become full-scale wars when there are competing claims for money, possessions, and property. Battles over the provisions of a will may focus on money as the visible agenda, but there are usually other, more potent issues submerged in the background. These include the favoring of one child over another, the failure to keep a promise, acknowledge a favor, or pay a debt. In Chapter Seven, we will encounter two situations in which sisters battled over a disputed inheritance. As we follow their struggles, we can almost taste the bitter fruits that were produced by their conflicting claims.

Many topics are beyond the scope of this book. Appalling battles are waged in the sphere of family business, when relatives compete for power, promotions, or profits. The act of suicide is one of the most extreme expressions of cutoff. Its profound ramifications call for special attention and study. Multiple challenges confront persons who are caught up in a contentious divorce that is complicated by the presence of stepchildren from more than one marriage. In many cases, there are no solutions to the crisis that erupts when a son or daughter chooses a partner who is not accepted by the family. Each of these situations is extremely complex, requiring a whole book of its own.

Individual family members react to provocations in a variety of different ways. In some fortunate families, the protagonists struggle with the contradictions and work through the tensions, eventually arriving at a compromise that allows the family to remain intact. In other situations, the emotional reactions build up and explode. Opposing factions take up sides, split wide apart, and generate estrangements that pollute the emotional climate for years to come.

## LETTERS OF INDICTMENT

A "poison-pen letter" is a document, usually anonymous, that contains accusations, denunciations, and vitriolic attacks on another person. We shall speak here of a different kind of "poison-pen letter" in which the sender is clearly identified. The letter is addressed to a family member who is perceived to be guilty of numerous offenses. In some cases, it comes after a long period of estrangement; in others, it serves as the initial blow in an impending battle. The content is phrased to convey the sender's pain and suffering; his intent is to evoke remorse in the other person – a sibling, parent, or other relative. Such a document may expose long-forgotten misdeeds that are likely to undermine the recipient's image of certain family members. It may include the revelation of a closely-guarded secret that now, concretized in written form, explodes like a bombshell. The recipient may be shocked, enraged, incredulous, or deeply hurt when he or she reads the letter.

One woman described her reaction to finding such a letter in her mailbox. Her relationship with her older brother had been marked by intermittent hostility and alienation for many years. Now these siblings are approaching old age; they live on different continents. Their parents, long deceased, took up various roles in the conflict, sometimes as distant observers, other times as defenders of one or the other of their contentious adult children. The brother's letter is ten pages in length, single-spaced. It contains a litany of grievances and a list of offenses he accuses his sister of perpetrating during a period of more than six decades. The letter had an overwhelming effect on its recipient, opening old wounds and arousing intense feelings of resentment, frustration, and despair.

The person who receives a "poison-pen letter" from a family member can choose among various options. She can respond in kind, returning blow for blow, justifying her own rage and providing examples of the anguish her accuser has caused in their relationship. After writing that letter, she can send it immediately or put it away, giving herself time to consider the best course of action. Another possibility is to ignore the provocation and refuse to reply, assuming that the storm will probably dissipate and retaliation would only exacerbate the problems. Or, she could compose a letter in which each of the offenses is re-framed, described from the point of view of the recipient. Yet another option is a "sugared-pen letter" that disregards the accusations and recalls only the positive moments in their past. Such a response would relate instances of generosity and mutual respect and would be geared to defusing the hostile atmosphere. Still another possibility is to ask for forgiveness. This option is the most difficult to follow and requires considerable preparation. In some families, it can bring about a dramatic transformation. In others, it fails to elicit a reciprocal response or it may even intensify the sender's anger. If you have been the recipient or the author of such a letter, please read the final chapters in this book and carefully consider the implications of your action before deciding on your next response.

### ACTIVE AND PASSIVE FORMS OF ESTRANGEMENT

How are we to understand the experience of persons in these two "opposite" positions: the one who cuts himself off, and the one who is rejected, banished, disinherited? Consider some of the following permutations of estrangement. Each of these situations depicts a distinct role or position in a family conflict.

*A defiant young woman cuts off from her mother, whom she accuses of "every bad thing."*

*A blind baby is rejected by her grandparents, who cannot tolerate the presence of a sightless child in their family.*

*A man takes sides with his wife and they both cut off from his sister, citing a litany of slights and insults.*

*A proud woman incurs the unremitting wrath of her son-in-law for ridiculing and demeaning his mother.*

*A young woman from an Orthodox Jewish family announces that she will marry a Catholic man. She is banished from the family and declared "dead" by her parents.*

*A woman is deprived of a significant portion of her inheritance by her mother, who changed her will in favor of a younger sister. The bereft woman vows never to speak to her sister again.*

In every story of family conflict, there are main protagonists as well as observers or secondary players. When we analyze the patterns, we will discover at least three distinct positions. First, there is the person who initiates the cutoff, who severs himself from the family. Then, there are the relatives whom he rejects, the unwilling victims. And third, the persons who act to banish an offending relative, declare her to be an outcast, "dead" to the family. In the wake of the banishment, the secondary players take up different roles. Some join in the blame and fury; others may sympathize with the cut off person. In every fragmented family, the dynamics will reflect these complex patterns of action and reaction. There is no single truth. Rather, we can discern relative truths, or *relatives'* truths. The estrangement will be experienced differently by each of the protagonists and by the observers in the extended family. Reflecting now on the family stories that were told to me, I feel sympathy for the plight of the ones who were rejected, but I can sense the overtones of other voices, nuances, and points of view that were not expressed. The themes and variations are endless.

GENDER AND ESTRANGEMENT

A woman cuts off all communication with her sister. A man is rejected by his dying father. Wife, mother, brother, father: the protagonists in a family drama are gendered, and their gender is a significant aspect of the phenomenon. Every family has its own convictions about the roles of men and the roles of women. A father's expectations of what his sons should do are likely to be different from his expectations of daughters. The obligations undertaken by a woman in caring for her aged, ill parents may not be the same as those acknowledged by her brother. Every culture, ethnic affiliation, and religious group has its own definitions of the proper roles for men and for women. In religious codes of law, gender roles occupy a prominent place. When these assumptions are ignored or rejected, conflicts erupt.

How is gender implicated in the process of estrangement? The stories in this book tell of women and men who have cut themselves off from relatives. In selecting the stories, I did not focus specifically on gender issues, but in retrospect, I realize that most of the stories were told to me, a woman, by women. If the topic were to be addressed and interpreted by a man, would the stories and the storytellers be different? Perhaps a masculine voice would emphasize different themes. Each question about gender leads to another. Do men react to different kinds of provocations? Are women more likely to repair rifts and forgive offenses? Male readers may find meanings in these stories that are different from those seen by female readers. If we view family conflicts through the lens of gender differences, we would focus on the roles that are played by the male and the female protagonists and consider how those roles contribute to the course of the conflict and its aftermath.

One author conducted in-depth interviews with men and women to clarify differences in their perceptions of relationships.[11] She concluded that gender is a significant factor in the way we experience attachment and separation. Each sex is more likely to perceive a danger that the other does not see. Men tend to avoid closeness; women fear separation. But the differences are more complex and subtle than simply a preference for one modality over another. When men speak about the meaning of a particular relationship, their descriptions emphasize notions of power and control, exemplified by the image of hierarchy. In other words, men wish to be situated at the top, and fear that others will get too close. For women, the web is the primary image. They long to be at the center of connection and worry about being too far out on the edge.[12] These distinctions may be seen to influence the way some men and women generate and respond to conflicts in the family.

## THE PERMANENT SEVERING OF FAMILY TIES

In every ethnic group and social context, there are extreme situations that may require radical separation from a family member; for example, a dysfunctional family in which there has been severe abuse or neglect, incest, alcoholism, addiction, or other criminal behaviors. Counselors who work with clients from these families may advise them to cut off from their family of origin in order to preserve their sanity and build a more healthy sense of self. In these situations, there is often no possibility of healing or growth without a complete separation from the contaminated family environment. However, although the intention is to separate forever, we can never be certain that the severing will be final. When one's family is involved, there is always a shred of hope that the destructive elements can be transformed, that the persons will eventually work out a compromise or a partial resolution.

Some cultures have developed their own ways of dealing with family members who cannot be contained within the setting of the family. One example is the story of a young man in Japan who went berserk and killed eight children. According to the suspect's father, his son had been "abnormal" from birth. He had been hospitalized for mental illness but "released too soon." The father explained that thirteen years ago, he and his son had gone through a process known as *kando-suru* – the severing of ties between parent and child, releasing each of them from obligations to the other.[13] Western cultures have not developed a parallel ritual to mark the necessary severing of family ties.

## NEED FOR RITUALS

In the natural sequence of family life, rituals accompany each of the life cycle events and major transitions. These rituals convey the significance and the emotional components of the occasion.

When a death occurs in the family, relatives and friends gather at the funeral to express their grief, share recollections, and provide support to cope with the loss. A wedding ceremony is a clearly defined ritual that marks a significant change in the family: a new member is entering the fold. For each of these occasions, there are special words and phrases that have common meanings: expressions of sympathy, congratulations, or affirmation.

In stark contrast to the "natural" life cycle events, there are no rituals or ceremonies for an estrangement. Often, the ones who remain "inside" the family are reluctant to speak of the person who rejected them or to seek help for their sense of loss. There is an uneasy silence, a covering up of the tension. Silence may reflect an effort to suppress the shame, confusion, frustration, rage, or any of the other emotional by-products of the estrangement. The absence of ritual isolates the protagonists and deprives them of a modality for sharing their anguish. Frequently, they are left alone to deal with the fallout from the conflict. In the concluding sections of this book, we will describe some strategies and rituals that family members may use to break through the silence and transform the patterns of alienation.

TIME AND PLACE

In every family where an estrangement has occurred, the story includes a time and a place. "It happened one month after her father took his own life." Or, "He ordered his stepfather out of his house just after the twins were born." These are objective "facts" about the situation, placing it in a temporal-spatial framework. But there are also other, more subjective aspects of time and place that mark these situations. We can notice not merely when and where the cutoff occurred, but how it affects the family's sense of time passing. For example, when the seasons change, memories of the absent person may be evoked. One father recalled, "I remember that we used to go camping with him early in the fall." A mother reminisces: "…After the first snow, my daughter would get such awful colds, and I would take hot chocolate up to her room and read stories..." After the cutoff, the seasons continue to change and the snow falls, but the estranged person is missing from that temporal framework. This is not the season for camping or caretaking; it is the season for regret, recriminations, and weeping.

The time line of the family moves on. There are comings and goings, births, funerals, weddings, family reunions. At each of these events, some relatives attend, others are absent. There are questions, expressions of genuine curiosity, pointed barbs. The estranged person is conspicuously absent from the photos. The family portrait without Ruth will be an enduring reminder of the estrangement.

When a cutoff occurs abruptly, there is a sharp break in the sense of time. Suddenly, everything has changed. The past is no longer only "past," but a kind of black hole that looms up again and again. The reverberation of the door slamming has faded; the bitter accusations no longer pierce the air, but now what? What happened? When did our relationship begin to fall apart? And what about the future? Plans are put on hold. There is a vacuum in the space where that person used to be. Until the crisis can be integrated and the emotions can be tempered, there is a sense of being in limbo. In some situations, the process of restoring equilibrium can take a very long time.

A cutoff that evolves gradually is different from one that explodes in a spasm of sudden rage. When a previously sanguine relationship becomes clouded, signs emerge in a series of subtle innuendoes, snide comments, or silence. Like a storm that gathers its power over a long distance, the hostility builds slowly. Some family members may be sensitive to the changes in the atmosphere. Others deny or ignore the mounting tensions; they assume that life will go on as usual. It is only when the tumult comes to a head, when the complaints and accusations burst forth that the temporal flow is interrupted and the storm erupts in all its fury.

Parallel to the temporal aspect, there is a spatial component in the process of cutoff. If the estranged person is in the same city, his parents and relatives may "bump" into him at unexpected moments. There is inevitably an embarrassed silence, a moment of confusion. Is there a greeting? Do they pretend not to recognize each other? One father calls it a "sighting" when he catches a glimpse of his estranged daughter in the supermarket. If the other person is a continent away, does the sense of "distance" differ from a situation in which he or she is living in a nearby suburb? Some families do not know the whereabouts of the estranged person. Is it possible to sustain an image of him in a non-place? In the house where he once lived, does his room remain empty, or has it been converted to a different use? Who occupies the place at the table where she always sat, and how does the family relate to that space? How do they deal with the possessions she did not take? Do they continue to look at her photos, or store them away in a dark closet? These are some of the dilemmas that continue to prickle in families who are left behind in the wake of estrangement. The spatial and temporal reminders of the estranged person will persist. In each family, they will reverberate with their own unique meanings.

## SOUNDS AND SILENCE

The jolting impact of a door slammed; a dish shattered against the wall. Her son's voice screaming: accusations, denunciations, tantrums, threats. These are the sounds of rage; they are the prelude, or the accompaniment, to estrangement. The long months, perhaps years of silence. No chatter, banter, idle talk. No inquiry about his mother's terminal illness. No comforting presence at her sister's funeral. No phone call, no familiar voice. I wait for a response to my letter. There is no response. This is the silence of estrangement.

When family members initiate the process of reconciliation, one of the first signs is the beginning of speaking. This is not the *resumption* of speaking, but a new, different kind of speaking. These new sounds emerge from a deep well of hope. They herald change and growth. At first, they may be tentative, a duet with only one voice. It's risky to open old wounds. With reassurance, the new sounds gather momentum. For some fortunate people, they take wing and soar. The atmosphere is permeated with the anticipation of a renewed connection. The sounds of healing may continue to hum for a long time.

## Social, cultural, and religious factors

The elements of family dynamics are universal; they constitute the basic ingredients of family life in every culture and society. The tensions between attachment and separation, power and passivity, loyalty and betrayal, old values and new commitments, all of these competing forces are found in families everywhere. However, the meanings that are conferred on them differ from one cultural context to another. Persons draw on the available cultural resources to define their relationships with significant others. These resources have evolved in the course of countless historical processes that contribute to the cultural, ethnic, and religious identity of individuals and families. How one group perceives "family loyalty" may be significantly different from another group's perception of the same concept. The provocation for a cutoff in a devoutly religious family may not be the same as in a secular family. The motives, process, and outcome of family conflict among Italian Catholics may be significantly different from those among South Carolina Baptists. Many of the families described in this book are Jewish. Their family dynamics may display features that are shared by all ethnic groups, but their values and social interactions will be influenced by factors that are uniquely Jewish. When we listen to the stories of families with estranged members, we should pay attention to the role of religious convictions and cultural affiliations. The binding and breaking of family ties will inevitably reflect the impact of these crucial influences. In the following chapter, we shall examine the second dimension in the evolution of family conflict: the cultural, religious, and historical legacy.

# CHAPTER TWO

# Family Assets and Vulnerabilities

*"Very deep is the well of the past.*
*Should we not call it bottomless?..."* [1]

## Prelude

Imagine that you could move backward in time, speak with your grandmother's grandmother and gaze at her face as she responds to your questions. What would she tell you about the daily life of her family, the crises they confronted, the rituals for their holiday celebrations, the prayers chanted at her father's funeral? Suppose you could trace the wanderings of each generation in your father's line, going back to the period of the first millennium. Imagine the multitude of places they inhabited before reaching the place you now call home.

Our perceptions and behavior reflect the legacy of our family's past. Remnants of the past adhere to our present actions, as well as to our future aspirations. William Nerin says that we learn five fundamental skills from our family of origin: a pattern of relating to others, a set of rules to live by, a constellation of meanings about life experiences, the ability to handle threats, and the resources to cope with loss, illness, hardships, and calamities.[2] This basic knowledge is profoundly influenced by the cultural, ethnic, and religious orientation of the family. "Ethnicity," "culture," and "religion" are distinct but overlapping concepts, each referring to a specific claim of affiliation and a common heritage. Like all families, the families described in this book have been shaped by their past, by the historical legacies of their members.

### THE SECOND LEVEL: CULTURAL AND RELIGIOUS FACTORS

Let us consider how these terms, *ethnicity, culture,* and *religion,* are implicated in the phenomenon of family conflict. An ethnic group is a body of people who affirm their common ancestry or geographic origin, and who are regarded by others as a distinct group. *Ethnicity* signifies a quality of personal identity that is transmitted by the parents, shared by the family, and reinforced by the community. The contours of your face, the way you prepare food for family meals, the political system you support, all of these reflect your ethnic heritage. *Culture* is the sum of the products, rituals, patterns of behavior, and ways of life that are developed by a particular ethnic or societal group and transmitted from each generation to the next. The constellation of kinship in my family, the work roles my parents chose and the languages they spoke, the clothes I wear and the books I read, these and countless other elements express my cultural milieu. *Religion* is a constellation of beliefs and practices that are imbued with divine authority. Religious meanings determine the parameters of moral and ethical behavior. Every religious orientation develops its own distinct configuration of ultimate values that influence how its adherents perceive reality and respond to it. The family is the primary repository and transmitter of the religious archetype. Parents teach and demonstrate basic convictions; the children imitate and adapt, modify or reject them. In the life of every family, traditions, values, and beliefs can serve as incentives for harmonious relationships. Conversely, they can become provocations for rebellion and bitter antipathy. In the following sections, I intend to demonstrate that ethnic, cultural, and religious issues often lie at the root of family conflict.

## IDENTITY SYSTEM

The three terms, ethnicity, culture, and religion, constitute what has been called an "identity system." The essential feature of an "identity system" is a group's allegiance to a specific constellation of beliefs and symbols. In any social group, a distinct set of meanings adheres to the behavior of its members and influences their linguistic expression, kinship patterns, rituals and customs, all the things that *matter* to them. We can visualize this configuration as the "vital organs" of the group, the elements that are essential to its identity. These elements will invariably influence the way people relate to their families. Every "identity system" has a historical dimension and a developmental progression; that is, a distinct genesis and an identifiable sequence of growth. When the system persists over many centuries, the meanings of its symbols become engraved on the identity of its people and are repeatedly reinforced by rituals and traditions. Although similar patterns of family dynamics may be observed in many different cultural groups, each distinct identity system develops its own unique set of assumptions regarding the appropriate ways for a family to function. Family members draw from a deep well of implicit knowledge to make crucial decisions about how to educate the children, cope with adversity, and mediate disputes between relatives. In your family, the manner of carrying out these vital functions will be different from mine, colored by your personal beliefs and cultural traditions.

The anthropologist Edward Spicer has studied a number of these systems and noted that some are more durable and more persistent than others.[3] He points out that the quality of persistence refers not merely to the duration of the group's life span but also to the durability of its identity and the continuity of its symbols, beliefs, traditions, and rituals. Spicer cites Judaism as a prime example of a "persistent identity system." For 3,500 years, Jews have been exiled, forcibly converted, threatened with annihilation, and "reconstructed" from within, but the core of identity remains.

With remarkably few exceptions until the nineteenth century, Jews have resisted assimilation. How is such a system sustained over long periods of time, despite all the obstacles? Spicer identifies specific "areas of common understanding" – a shared language, a commitment to similar moral values, and a clearly defined social organization. My mother's family represented a typical model of this system. Her parents lived in a *shtetl*, a small village in Lithuania that contained all of the essential elements, as did virtually every Jewish community in many parts of the world. They spoke Yiddish and prayed in Hebrew; they observed the commandments and practiced the same rituals as other Jews in far-distant locations. Wherever Jews lived, the core of identity held fast. But in my family and in countless others, the same heritage that had kept them together became the wedge that divided them. After they immigrated to America, new patterns were created when some parts of the family rebelled and turned away while others cleaved to the tradition.

Similar patterns may be observed in other ethnic, religious groups. Whenever a minority community dwells in the midst of a stronger majority, the minority group either consolidates its strengths and endures, or assimilates into the larger whole. The tension is always strung out between two poles: to remain the same or to become like the "others." The case of the Jews is especially compelling, perhaps because of the relentless series of calamities that has afflicted them. Dominated by stronger powers that controlled their daily lives, Jews have always been a minority group. Without military capability or the means to mobilize for self-defense, they have repeatedly been pressured to assimilate or forced to convert. During their long presence in the Diaspora, Jews have invariably lived in the midst of other ethnic and religious communities while remaining on the periphery of those communities. In the course of time, they mastered certain skills that are unique to this kind of precarious existence. They learned to blend in with their alien surroundings, to become *like* the majority groups without being absorbed by them. Anthropologists have studied such disparate Jewish communities as a Moroccan town[4] and a city in New Zealand.[5] Similar patterns in countless other communities have been described in personal memoirs.[6] In every example, Jews lived out their lives next to the mainstream culture but always on the delicate edge. They mastered the art of blending in with their alien surroundings, assuming many of the outer trappings of the majority group. At the same time, they remained utterly distinct and different, maintaining their own language, rituals, social institutions, and legal structures.[7] This double identity resulted in an ambivalent way of life that persisted, despite all the obstacles. Such a prolonged, insecure existence imposed a heavy emotional burden, a burden that continues to be felt within the context of family.

What behavior patterns are likely to emerge in families who must survive in such a stressful emotional atmosphere? I suggest that this kind of vulnerability fosters excessive closeness and dependency on one's own people. Threats from outside invariably sharpen the boundaries between us and the others. In order to cope, the pervasive sense of insecurity must be submerged or denied because of the danger of exposing weakness. Rather, the tensions build up and explode within the realm of the family, with the people who are closest to us. The experience of my mother's family mirrors this process. When they emigrated from Lithuania to America, my grandfather insisted on remaining an "old world Jew," resolutely clinging to his rituals and beliefs. Younger members of the family, confronted by a plethora of new possibilities, were eager to assimilate, learn English, wear modern clothing, and embrace the American way of life. But remnants of traditional religious beliefs continued to intrude on their budding independence. When confronted with such crucial questions as whom to marry, how to observe life-cycle events, and where to be buried, their ambivalence became the focus for heated arguments. Caught on the horns of opposing forces, the family was simultaneously settled and unsettled, together and fragmented. Disputes erupted, not only between generations but also between siblings as to what they would cherish and what they would discard.

Similar stresses arise in immigrant families from other ethnic and religious groups. Conflicting priorities invariably create tensions between those who wish to preserve the past and those who rush headlong into the future. Each person is compelled to confront essential questions: Who am I, what do I affirm, and where do I belong? Under what conditions do my various identities coalesce, and how do I define my role as an individual in my family? With so many profound uncertainties, the potential for conflict escalates into reality.

## JEWISH IDENTITY

I have chosen to focus on the parameters of my own religious affiliation, Judaism, to demonstrate how one's ethnic-cultural-religious orientation can color the behavior and emotions of persons and families. While I give special emphasis to the Jewish viewpoint, I believe that the ideas expressed here will be relevant to the experience of families with other cultural and religious affiliations.

Gestalt psychology teaches us that every phenomenon has a "figure" and a "ground." The figure cannot exist without the ground and their significance can only be understood in terms of reciprocal interaction. In the previous chapter, we focused on the "figure" of the family, its structure and process. Now, we will explore the "ground," the historical legacy and cultural context. In the following sections, we will examine the imprint of historical factors on the lives of Jewish families and discuss how cultural-religious meanings are transmitted from one generation to another; that is, how the "persistent identity system" is preserved. My intention is to demonstrate that family conflict arises out of this "figure-ground" configuration, the mutual influence of family dynamics and its cultural-historical-religious context.

Who is a Jew? To understand how the Jewish past can influence us in the present, we must first identify the distinguishing characteristics of a Jewish person. Most of us acquired an understanding of our religious affiliation as it was taught and modeled by our parents. In adulthood, some of us have affirmed and strengthened those early perceptions; others have modified them, still others have denied and rejected them. We trust that the way we eventually choose will be correct and authentic, for us.

Jean-Paul Sartre, the French philosopher, said that Jews are those people who are considered by others to be Jews, regardless of their religious beliefs or ethnic allegiance. But this description fails to express the complex reality of Judaism. The following definitions focus on the separate domains and their salient characteristics. These distinctions seem most authentic to me, but others may wish to define the boundaries differently.

"*Halakhic*" or legal definition: According to traditional Jewish law, a Jew is any person born to a Jewish mother or one who undergoes a process of conversion under the aegis of an Orthodox rabbi.

An *Orthodox* Jew subscribes to the principles of Judaism and is committed to observing the 613 commandments, as articulated in the Torah, the "Five Books of Moses." For such a person, the Jewish Bible, its commentaries and the codification of its laws are the primary sources of knowledge, authority, and practical guidance. The traditional Orthodox (some call it "classical") position assumes that a Jew is accountable to God in every aspect of his or her life. Within the domain of Orthodoxy, there is a continuum of belief and observance, to the extent that the most rigid adherents, the *haredim*, would question the authenticity of some "modern" Orthodox practices. All Orthodox Jews, however, affirm the divine source of the Torah and perceive themselves as eternally bound to the one God by the original covenant, the *brit* that was promised to Abraham and his descendants.

In the wake of the emancipation and enlightenment movements in nineteenth century Europe, various groups broke away from "classical" Judaism and developed their own ideologies and practices. These included, but were not limited to *Conservative, Reform, and Reconstructionist Judaism*. Each of these denominations advocates different ways of affirming one's Jewish identity while acknowledging the full force of modern ideas and events. Their adherents practice varying degrees of observance, depending on the weight they give to the commandments and the traditions. Even within the same faction, there are differences between the beliefs held by one synagogue group and another, and between one time period and another. "Reform," with the largest number of congregants, continues to flourish and, true to its own precepts, to change. The identity of a Reform Jew may be primarily defined by his affiliation with a particular synagogue as well as a strong commitment to community service. According to the original Reform "platform," religious laws may be reinterpreted, modified, or discarded, depending on one's perception of their relevance to contemporary life. The main point is to revise religious practice so that it is compatible with current social realities. Reform Jews are unlikely to observe religious precepts that would set them apart from the mainstream of contemporary society. In recent years, however, many Reform congregations have embraced more traditional expressions of religious practice. Some members welcome these trends, while others view them as unacceptable, a return to the restrictive patterns that were discarded by the original founders of Reform.

*Secular or humanistic:* Secular Jews may choose to affiliate with Jewish organizations or work for Zionist causes. In Israel, they are likely to identify themselves primarily as Israeli citizens and secondarily as Jewish. In the Diaspora, secular Jews may be strongly attached to the majority culture and essentially assimilated, seeing their Jewish identity as a marginal aspect of their lives. Or, they may affirm Jewish values through participation in the activities of "Humanistic Judaism," which emphasizes the brotherhood of all peoples and the primacy of basic human rights. Secular families who have distanced themselves from religious beliefs and practice are likely to deny that religion has any influence on their values and behavior. However, since the vast majority of Jews are only two or three generations removed from the time when religion formed the central pillar of family life, we can speculate that religious currents are still murmuring under the surface, even though they may not be conscious or acknowledged.

One additional category has been given the name *"half-Jewish."* A book with this title describes the attitudes and perceptions of persons who are "half," that is, offspring of one Jewish parent, or who choose to identify themselves as "partially Jewish."[8] Countless numbers of people, with their divided allegiance, are creating new models of family identity. These families must learn to navigate through the cross-currents of conflicting convictions that are expressed by in-laws and extended family members.[9]

For some people, these definitions refer to discrete entities, separated from one another by clear demarcations. For others, the various categories and the boundaries between them are seen as blurred and overlapping. Compounding the complexity, each of these denominations divides into additional factions and branches with their own corresponding beliefs and convictions. If there is one common denominator, it is the fervent adherence to one position or vehement opposition to a conflicting set of beliefs. Those who identify with one of these categories will express values, expectations, and commitments that are congruent with that position. The lives of their families will be colored by their convictions. The main point in understanding the religious component of family conflict is the intensity of emotion that each position is likely to generate. For Orthodox Jews, keeping the commandments and living according to Jewish law is a binding obligation. Some families will reject or even banish members who decide to abandon the tradition. Others may express pain and regret but sustain their connections with the rebellious members. In some secular families, a son who chooses to become Orthodox or a daughter who marries an Orthodox man may be ostracized for betraying their parents' values. In other situations, one person's decision to embrace religious traditions will have a constructive, creative influence on the life of the family. Variations on these themes are depicted in the stories that appear in later chapters of this book.

## CULTURAL ISSUES AND FAMILY THERAPY

Therapists who work with troubled families have noted the influence of ethnic and religious factors on the types of problems presented by family members. "There is increasing evidence that ethnic values and identification are retained for many generations and play a significant role in family life and personal development throughout the life cycle."[10] Awareness of these values is part of the therapist's knowledge base. One team of therapists [11] identified four main patterns in Jewish families:

1. The family is the central anchor for all experience. Closeness and mutual dependency are seen as survival strategies and are highly valued. The stereotype of the controlling Jewish mother is one aspect of the dominant role of family in the lives of Jewish people.

2. Suffering and persecution are defining features of life, ever present in memory and always potentially repeatable.

3. Intellectual achievement is a predominant value, with professional competence and success in business as parallel, sometimes conflicting, aspirations.

4. Emotional reactivity is dramatic, intense, and uninhibited. The verbal expression of emotions is encouraged and expected.

These patterns are not so remarkable, and they are not unique to Jewish families. Other ethnic groups would claim at least some of these characteristics. What makes them specifically *Jewish*? The essential point here is the *meaning* that Jewish persons attribute to them. Within the context of historical events and cultural patterns that contribute to the Jewish archetype, each of these assumptions has been imbued with special significance for Jewish persons and families.

The *Forward* is a Jewish newspaper that was originally published in Yiddish, now in English. It contains a column called "Ask Wendy," a contemporary version of the earlier, groundbreaking advice column "A *Bintel Brief*" (a bundle of letters) that first appeared in the same newspaper in 1906.[12] Here is a question and answer from a recent column:

> "*I am not Jewish, and I hope that this question will not sound anti-Semitic. I have had a number of Jewish friends, and it seems to me that so many of them have siblings who don't speak to each other or are on difficult terms with their parents or children. My "significant other" happens to be Jewish and is not on speaking terms with either of his brothers or his daughter. While I know these things happen, do you think such family rifts happen more often among Jewish families?*" The letter was signed "*Worlds Apart.*"

Here is Wendy's answer:

> "*...In my experience, WASPS and Catholics... hail from cultures that are more reserved. Displays of emotion and frank discussions about matters of real import are likely to be discouraged. In contrast, Judaism is known to be an exegetic tradition – one that pulls things apart, debates interpretations, splits hairs, and argues. Different cultures, different individual dynamics, different coping mechanisms – they all boil down to one thing, as the comedienne Paula Poundstone so aptly put it: 'I'm in therapy, because I come from a family.'*"[13]

The implication of Wendy's reply is that Jewish families are, in fact, particularly vulnerable to conflict. My reply would have a different emphasis. I would argue that Jewish families may be "worlds apart" from other families, not simply because they are more vulnerable to conflict, but because the provocations for conflict have uniquely Jewish meanings. I would suggest that the roots of the Jewish experience extend far deeper and wider than Wendy's reply indicates. The rest of this chapter is a discussion of the historical background and cultural context that are reflected in the manifestations of conflict in Jewish families.

HISTORICAL EVENTS AND PATTERNS

An overview of Jewish history would identify particular types of events and processes that appear and reappear in many different periods and locations. Each of them may continue to exert a potent influence on family dynamics, even though their significance may be denied or unconscious. All of them, in one way or another, have been incorporated into the Jewish psyche as part of the "persistent identity system." The point I wish to emphasize is that the fundamental beliefs and meanings derived from one's cultural-religious orientation affect the way we perceive our obligations, define priorities, react to provocations, and seek peace in the family.

## 1. Expulsion and exile

More than two thousand years ago, the small Jewish nation was expelled from its ancestral home on the eastern shores of the Mediterranean Sea and scattered over the face of the earth. Until our own time, the descendents of those original exiles had no military power, political autonomy, economic stability, or permanent territory. Jewish history reflects a relentless succession of upheavals and banishments. In virtually every place where Jews have settled, they have experienced the trauma of expulsion and dispersion.

Various reasons – social, religious, political, economic – have been cited to justify the ejection of Jews at different periods. The motive behind all the expulsion decrees, however, was hatred, inflamed by the fear that Jews would undermine the beliefs of the majority or weaken the power of the establishment. The displacements invariably resulted in an enormous loss of property and status as well as profound damage to body and spirit. Deprived of all sources of protection and self-defense, fleeing Jews were often the victims of plunder and murder. For the survivors, forced exile meant massive upheavals in the cultural and social patterns of Jewish communities.

Expulsion may be considered one of the decisive factors that has shaped the reality of Jewish family life and influenced the thought, behavior, and emotions of Jews everywhere. The "wandering Jew" has been permanently scarred by these repeated traumas. Even today, after several generations of comparative security, the emotional patterns and dynamics of family life continue to be affected by so much loss and suffering. No matter how safe their situation may appear on the surface, the collective memory of Jews continues to be burdened with a sense of insecurity. As a people, Jews have always been a passive minority, forced to obey the dictates of ruling powers. Until the establishment of the State of Israel in our own time, Jews were prohibited from mobilizing resources for self-defense or empowerment. For more than two thousand years, the Jewish people have managed to survive in the Diaspora. Except for a small Jewish presence in Palestine that struggled to endure under Christian or Muslim rule, they had no constant place to call "home." The dream of a secure homeland has been a major force in the minds and hearts of Jews everywhere, from the beginning of their history.

Let us consider how this pattern of repeated displacements manifests itself in the lives of families. Narratives of the experiences of Jews expelled from Spain, from other parts of Europe and from Muslim lands describe their broken dreams and terrible anxieties, their frustrations and, for some of the survivors, their triumphs.[14] Features that are characteristic of Jewish families, such as close, dependent connections between family members and highly charged emotional reactions, can be seen as the natural consequence of countless forced expulsions, or what I would call "separation saturation." Repeatedly separated from loved ones, buffeted by recurrent bouts of anxiety, frustration, and rage, all of this played out in alien environments with hostile onlookers, these elements have combined to produce an abiding antipathy to separation. The trauma of exile has generated two contradictory tendencies. One is the compelling need to preserve and protect the remnants of the previous life, to cling to those artifacts, beliefs, and rituals that serve to connect the familiar past with the unknown future. The other is to adapt and change, to learn new behaviors and to accommodate to unfamiliar environments in order to survive. The ambivalence generated by these paradoxical positions, to preserve ancient patterns and to create new ones, has influenced the behavior and relationships in Jewish families throughout their history.

## 2. Persecution and pogroms

*Pogrom* is a Yiddish word derived from the Russian term for an organized massacre marked by destruction, looting, rape, and murder. The term was initially used to refer to attacks against Jews in Russia in the late nineteenth and early twentieth centuries, carried out by Christians while the local police and military establishment looked on or, as frequently occurred, collaborated with the instigators. Pogroms usually erupted during periods of political crisis and social upheaval. Since Jews were always unarmed and powerless, they were invariably selected as a convenient target for frustration and rage. Additional waves of persecution occurred during the same period as an expression of anti-Semitic sentiments in Germany, Austria, Romania, and the Balkan countries. There were similar outbreaks of persecution of Jews in Arab countries, especially in Morocco, Algeria, and Persia (Iran). Over a period of hundreds of years, major pogroms and isolated attacks struck Jewish communities, killing and maiming countless numbers of people. Jewish history reflects a cycle of catastrophes that have affected virtually every generation in every location. Undeniably, the most devastating trauma occurred in our own time. The Holocaust, a cataclysm of violence involving millions of families, continues to impact on the lives of the third and fourth generations of survivors.

We can imagine the dreadful sense of fear and helplessness that resulted from these repeated episodes of persecution. In many cases, families were splintered when a parent was killed and children fled to distant relatives. Others attempted to find safety by assimilating into the surrounding community. Surviving families who had no escape routes would inevitably close ranks, encourage mutual dependence, and develop closer bonds. Today, there is scarcely a Jewish family in the world that does not have a pogrom or comparable disaster in its family history. The physical scars from these afflictions may have healed, but the unconscious residue continues to affect the emotions and attitudes of Jews everywhere. Many survivors have developed an extra supply of stamina, resourcefulness, and resilience to compensate for the pain and terrible anxiety. This cacophony of powerful emotional elements continues to resound in the memory of Jewish families.

### 3. Segregation: the ghetto and the mellah
The segregation of Jewish neighborhoods may have originated in Jews' own preference to live where they could observe traditional customs and laws without interference. Religious practices were concentrated in the synagogue, study hall, marketplace, cemetery, *mikvah*, (ritual bath) and welfare organizations. The traditional structure of the Jewish community has been one of the prominent features in the persistent identity system. It was natural for Jews to create neighborhoods that clustered around these locations.

As early as the fourth or fifth centuries, the first coercive and oppressive forms of segregation appeared, as Christians began to isolate and humiliate the Jews. In the Middle Ages, Church councils published decrees that prohibited Jews from living in Christian neighborhoods. Jews were identified by special badges, colors, or clothing. By the year 1600, the institution of the ghetto was established throughout Italy and quickly spread to other Catholic countries. Papal decrees defined the rules to be applied to ghetto dwellers, including the size and boundaries of their living space and the professions Jews were allowed to practice. Laws were invoked to prohibit marriages and regulate the size of Jewish families. These laws had the effect of separating family members and forcing relatives to re-locate to faraway places in order to marry and create families of their own.

In Muslim countries, there was a parallel pattern of segregation of Jews, but with different regulations and restrictions.[15] In Morocco, the term *mellah* referred to the Jewish quarter in various cities. From the fifteenth century, these areas were isolated, walled, and clearly separated from the Muslim inhabitants. In many Muslim countries, Jews and Christians were perceived as a contaminating presence. They were prohibited from living in any town with a sacred shrine or a landmark that had special religious significance. Jews in Arab lands were never given opportunities to assimilate into the host culture, as they were in some European communities. They were called *dhimmis*, an Arabic term that defines the legal status of non-Muslims. *Dhimmis* lived under the patronizing "protection" of their Muslim rulers and were treated as subservient, inferior, and humiliated outsiders. They were required to pay a special tax and wear certain distinctive clothing, silly hats, or odd colors. Some Muslim rulers prohibited any visible sign of religious practice and forbade the construction of synagogues. The legal status of Jews in Muslim lands was always tenuous; their security was constantly threatened. Their sense of identity was permeated by the *dhimmi* image, an oppressed and segregated minority.[16]

How did the ordeal of segregation and isolation affect the psyche of a people? One obvious consequence was to become dependent on one's own kind, to maintain clear boundaries between "in" and "out" groups and to avoid antagonizing the "others," the majority. Inevitably, the pressures generated close emotional ties among family members and expectations that all relatives would behave the same way. In those precarious social settings, alienation from one's family was dangerous, sometimes fatal. Family connections served as a lifeline. To be separated and cut off was tantamount to disaster. While those patterns may have been useful as coping strategies in previous periods and places, they take on radically different meanings when they are repeated in contemporary family life. In today's Jewish world, with permeable boundaries and wider horizons, close family attachments may be felt as obstacles and hooks rather than lifelines. Separation and distance are seen as liberating, healthy values. When some family members demand closeness and others resent it, resistance erupts and family bonds may splinter.

## 4. Emancipation and Enlightenment

Emerging in the eighteenth century, two interrelated historical movements, "Emancipation" and "Enlightenment," have had a lasting impact on the attitudes and behavior of countless Jewish families. The yearning for personal and political sovereignty swept through many different ethnic communities in Europe. The fervor of those repressed people inspired revolt against ruling powers and, in some countries, led to the establishment of new forms of government. For Jews, "emancipation" meant a lessening of many of the restrictions and inequities that had imposed heavy burdens on them. With the new freedom, Jews in some locations were recognized as equal to other persons and were granted the rights and duties of citizenship. In the early stages of the emancipation movement, the struggle for freedom went hand in hand with the readiness to assimilate. It was only later, in the last decades of the nineteenth century, that the movement became associated with nationalistic yearnings for autonomy. With the upsurge of Zionist aspirations, some Jews turned their energies to the task of creating a homeland in the land of Israel. However, emancipation also gave Jews new opportunities to mingle with the majority culture and "be like everyone else." In many cases, it encouraged conversion and intermarriage, two radical events that led to the fragmentation of families and the severing of connections between traditional segments of the family and those who chose to move "out."

For those Jews who settled in Muslim countries, there was no comparable movement toward emancipation; that is, Jews had few if any opportunities to achieve real political or social equality. Yemen, which won its independence between the two world wars, never granted equal legal status to Jews. Other Arab states granted some forms of entitlement to Jews, but these were all rescinded when Israel achieved its independence. Beginning in 1948, new forms of segregation and persecution were imposed, accompanied by violent reactions to the establishment of the Jewish state. The vast majority of Jews in Arab lands found themselves in mortal danger. Emigration became their only sensible option, initiating yet another wave of upheavals and displacements in the lives of thousands of Jewish families.

The second major movement that emerged in European Jewish communities during the eighteenth and nineteenth centuries was the "Enlightenment" or *Haskalah*. This movement was fueled by motives that pointed in one direction, toward assimilation and secularization. Those who embraced the *Haskalah* were anticipating a new kind of freedom, away from the restrictions imposed by religious belief and toward a secular culture. The followers of this movement vehemently opposed the observance of religious laws, the study of Talmud, and the practice of traditional customs. Jewish education, previously limited to religious topics, was expanded to include a wide range of secular subjects. Linguistic assimilation was admired and pursued. The language of choice became the vernacular: German, Russian, whatever language was spoken by the majority group. Education for girls was encouraged. Non-traditional clothing and styles were adopted. These were radical innovations, intended to replace religious traditions with secular cultural values.

The Enlightenment movement first appeared in France and Germany. It gathered momentum as it spread to other countries in Western and then to Eastern Europe, where it influenced hundreds of Jewish communities in Russia. Families were sharply divided in their reactions, with some members enthusiastically embracing the new ideas and others emphatically rejecting them. During this same period, other movements emerged, within Judaism as well as outside of it, that promised a better life (or, depending on one's point of view, threatened to dilute the strength of the tradition). The main point is that all of these changes caused turmoil in those families where opposing factions took up sides. Ultimately, some broke away. In the works of many Jewish writers of that time, particularly the stories of Sholem Aleichem and Der Nister, we see vivid examples of the effects of these movements on Jewish families: intense conflict between generations and the dissolution of traditional family patterns.

## TRADITIONS, RITUALS, AND FAMILY CONFLICT

Historians choose many different ways to depict the history of a particular period or nation. One scholar, Huston Smith, focused on the differences between the world's great religions and their respective development. In his analysis of the Jewish perspective, he notes that other peoples experienced similar social and political upheavals, but the outcomes were always different. What is distinctive about the Jews? He suggests that, "what lifted the Jews from obscurity to permanent religious greatness was their passion for meaning."[17] This is not to imply that other religious traditions are devoid of meaning. Rather, what sets Jews apart is their obsession with ideas and experiences that are characteristically Jewish. Since ancient times, sages, rabbis, and their students have delved deeply into the possible meanings of each section, word, letter, dot, and space in the Torah. Jewish scholars continue to contemplate the nuances in every biblical law and its application to countless practical situations. They dwell on the significance of decisive historical events and recall them in daily prayers and holiday liturgy. They pore over ancient texts and contemporary interpretations to elucidate the proper functions of family relationships. They analyze the emotional forces that bind persons together and rip them apart. And incessantly, echoing the voices of the prophets, they ponder the meaning of the Divine Presence in daily life. This vast storehouse of meaning has been preserved and enriched over the centuries through rituals and particular behaviors. In the following section, we will examine an array of these traditions to see how they may be implicated in the phenomenon of family conflict. The list is not definitive or complete, but it is sufficient to make the point: "Jewishness" is a reality that influences relationships in Jewish families.

## 1. The issue of gender: feminine and masculine identity

In the second chapter of *Genesis*, God speaks: "It is not good that man should be alone. I will make him a 'helper as his partner,'" in Hebrew, *ezer k'negdo*.[18] A different edition says "a compatible helper for him."[19] There is much disagreement as to the actual meaning of this phrase. One source[20] identifies four different interpretations of gender that may be derived from the original texts in *Genesis*: the female is subordinate, the male is subordinate, they are vying for power, or they are complementary, sharing responsibilities. How can these contradictions be understood, and what is their implication for Jewish families today?

Throughout the ages, scholars have struggled with the ambiguities inherent in gender roles. Their questions lead to more questions about the contrasting, often conflicting, natures of man and woman. They plumb the depths of the classical sources to review and reinterpret previous definitions.[21] How have the roles of women been perceived in Judaism? In our own time, Jewish feminists, as well as traditionalists, are creating new answers to ancient questions. Various customs and laws have defined the roles of men and women in the four main realms of activity: home, work, community, and synagogue. "Judaism postulates innate gender differences and is sensitive to their specific, non-interchangeable character. Traditional Jewish society is based on the essential dissimilarity of the sexes."[22] Contemporary feminist scholars argue against many of these traditions. Citing countless examples of the subjugation of Jewish women, they call for sweeping changes in the way gender is configured in Jewish life.[23] The enforcement of sharp divisions between the functions permitted to men and to women is being challenged by some and defended by others. In our own day, controversies continue to seethe regarding the proper role of men and women in contemporary Jewish life.

One collection of essays examines the lives and writings of Jewish women in different periods and settings.[24] These writings describe how women have endured and even thrived in the male-dominated, patriarchal system that has characterized traditional Judaism. A potent source of a woman's influence is her power to determine the religious affiliation of her children. According to Jewish law, every child born to a Jewish woman is Jewish. During the early years of a child's life, the mother is the primary educator, thus ensuring that she will have a vital part in the child's development. Women are partners in the task of preserving the "persistent identity system." In their roles as housewives, mothers, teachers, and authors, they help to maintain the essential balance between accommodation to the Gentile milieu and commitment to the religious Jewish tradition. In the midst of rapid social, political, and economic changes, it has often been the women who have sustained the continuity of the family. When individual family members threaten to reject the prevailing values, who rebels, and who punishes them? In the stories of Tevye and his rebellious daughters,[25] it was the father who banished them from the family. The mother stood by and mourned her losses. But it was the young women who were rebelling against the tradition, cutting off from their family of origin in order to create new forms of family life and new patterns of relationships.

Since the period of the Enlightenment and the subsequent waves of emigration to the New World, the old values have been undergoing complex transformations. For a significant number of contemporary Jewish families, roles are not so clearly defined. Many of the traditional gender distinctions no longer hold. The resulting ambiguities require men, as well as women, to carve out new forms of identity. Without the guidelines of a firm religious foundation, this task is more complex. We can speculate that the inevitable competition may provoke conflict in the family as well as in other domains. As we meet the protagonists in the stories presented in this book, we will find gender issues as the background, and sometimes the focus for conflict.

## 2. Scholarship, learning, and language

The study of the Torah, the Talmud, and their commentaries is one of the fundamental religious obligations in Judaism. The highest praise is reserved for those scholars who master the most complex *halakhic* (legal) interpretations. A tractate of the Talmud lists the most important commandments, such as honoring one's parents and performing acts of charity, and concludes, "the study of the Torah is equal to them all."[26] From the earliest periods of Jewish history, great centers of Jewish learning were established. During the first five centuries of the Common Era, thousands of dedicated students learned Torah in the *batei midrash*, the study halls of Palestine and Babylonia. Subsequently, virtually every Jewish community has included a site specifically designated for prayer and study.

From the beginning, the commitment to the study of Torah has had two related goals, at times congruent, but often competing. For some scholars, the act of study, the abstract, intellectual process itself, is considered to be a religious obligation of the highest order. For others, the intellectual effort is a bridge to action; learning Torah and its commentaries is the preamble for all subsequent ethical behavior. The adherents of the first goal, study for its own sake, were often at loggerheads with the defenders of the other view, study for the purpose of action. Controversies over the rationale for learning have persisted to the present day and are still being argued among contemporary scholars and rabbis. In the context of family, these ancient tensions may be transposed into disputes between parents and children regarding the content and process of education or the value of one career choice over another.

The tradition of Torah study as a lifelong pursuit is an obligation, not only for scholars and rabbis, but for all Jewish males. In Judaism, there is no exclusive status of clergy as the preeminent teachers. Everyone, that is, every man, is expected to study and master aspects of the sacred texts. The teaching of Torah became the guarantee of a father's immortality. "He who teaches his son, it is as if he had taught (not only) his son, but his son's son, and

46

so on to the end of all generations."[27] In the Middle Ages and well into modern times, families engaged tutors to supplement the teaching of the father and to provide their sons, and sometimes their daughters, with instruction in the sacred texts. The rabbis believed in the psychological value of verbal expression and advised that Torah study should not be a silent, purely mental exercise. They insisted that the words of the text should be uttered aloud, customarily with a chant, and preferably with a *havruta*, a study partner who will scrutinize and argue the concepts. Perhaps this enduring tradition to study aloud and to debate each point is reflected in the tendency to place such high value on verbal expression. It may also be one of the factors in our predilection to talk back, to "let it all hang out."

In Jewish communities everywhere, shared language has been a consistent element: Hebrew for the articulation of prayer, Aramaic for Talmudic discourse. In virtually every community, people would learn to converse in the vernacular, whether Polish, Hungarian, Arabic, Farsi, or English, and they would use the distinctively Jewish language – Yiddish or Ladino – to communicate with fellow Jews. For thousands of years, language has been the connecting thread, linking Jews from locations that were far apart geographically, culturally, and chronologically. A family's language history will be an accurate indicator of who they were and where they came from. In our own time, a woman from an assimilated, secular family who marries a man with Yiddish-speaking, traditional parents may discover that their differences go far beyond the choice of words.

Jewish communities everywhere are reacting to the implications of the high rates of intermarriage and the concomitant enticements of secular culture. Reflecting these concerns, Jewish day schools have been established and the study of Hebrew encouraged. Verbal agility is highly praised. Jewish parents place heavy emphasis on higher education and academic excellence. In former times, the primary role of the father was not to attain wealth, power, or fame, but to accumulate knowledge and impart it. Now, traditional values tend to be ignored. Instead, parents strive for success in professions and business. Excessively high expectations place heavy burdens on the sons and daughters who are groomed to follow in the footsteps of their high-achieving parents, or even to surpass them. The competition that is set up between fathers and sons, brothers and sisters provides yet another ingredient in the stew pot of family tensions. While the high value given to learning and achievement serves to ensure continuity of an ancient tradition and encourage individual success, it can also provide the springboard for conflicts, rivalry, and alienation.

### 3. Genealogy and the attachment to roots

*"This is the book of the generations of Adam..."*[28] These words introduce the first formal telling of genealogies in the Hebrew Bible, from the founding father through a series of generations, until the birth of Noah. It is one of many such lists in the Bible. The recording of genealogies is an ancient tradition, reinforced by practical necessity. Only by demonstrating one's connection with a particular family or clan could a person claim the privileges that had been assigned to that group. Genealogical lists in ancient Israel were known from the time of the First Temple (950 BCE) and from accounts of priestly families in biblical writings. After the Babylonian exile and the return to Zion, those who claimed to be descended from priests were searching for proof of their pedigree. Without evidence, they could not qualify for service in the Temple. Purity of descent was significant not only for priestly families. Genealogy also played a role in the struggle for secular power among many prominent families. Even royal houses had to provide proof in order to defend and strengthen their status. Other families needed to demonstrate their identity before they could claim property that had been abandoned at the time of exile. The emphasis on purity of lineage led to much competition and conflict between certain groups who claimed higher status or superior connections. The Talmud makes frequent reference to families and individuals who quarreled over such claims: "When men quarrel among themselves, they quar-

rel over birth" (*Kid.* 76a). The sages warned that a man should not marry a woman who was "inferior;" that is, from a group with lower status. They insisted that, "a family once mixed up, remains so."[29]

How are these ancient patterns relevant to family dynamics in our own time? Most people are not aware of the historical process; how, then, can it continue to shape our lives? We can speculate that the values and prejudices that were established and maintained during past generations have crept into the mindset of Jewish people and continue to influence us, whether we are conscious of them or not. The family is like a tree, with roots extending deep into its past. Patterns that have been reinforced for many generations continue to affect how we feel, think, and behave, especially in relation to the people who are closest to us. Conflicts erupt over a son or daughter's choice of a marriage part-ner if parents perceive the choice as degrading. Emotions escalate when a family member rejects long-established beliefs, or when his behavior threatens the continuity of family traditions.

The significance of genealogy has emerged with renewed vital-ity in our own time. Beginning in the last decades of the twentieth century and continuing in the new millennium, a novel challenge has seized the imagination of Jewish families. "Jewish genealogy" has become a favorite pastime for thousands of people in many parts of the world. Currently, there are more than eighty "Jewish Gen" societies, located in virtually every country where Jews live. The search for roots has yielded amazing discoveries. Each year, countless numbers of families return to the sites of their grand-parents' birth. They examine documents, explore ancient Jewish cemeteries, and ask provocative questions about themselves and their ancestors. Before and during World War ii, in virtually every Jewish community in Europe, the "Final Solution" was carried out by the Nazis and their local collaborators. It culminated in the extermination of millions of families. The hope of locating survivors and discovering the fate of lost relatives has intensified efforts to find traces of family. More recently, in the aftermath of the Cold War, families from the USSR have been reunited with long-lost relatives in the West. For many people, the search has succeeded not only in confirming the birth and death dates of relatives or discovering the grave of a grandfather. More importantly, some of the inquiries have led to the source of long-buried family secrets and multigenerational family feuds. Relatives who have been estranged or lost for decades have found each other. In some cases, they have confronted and resolved long-standing disputes. If you have tried to imagine the family life of your grandmother's grandmother and if you are lucky enough to discover documents that reveal aspects of her life, the reality of your family history will suddenly become more vivid. Learning about the conditions and events that affected the lives of our predecessors can provide valuable resources for understanding patterns in our own lives.

### 4. "Yichus" – pedigree and stigma

The Hebrew/Yiddish word *yichus* may be translated as "descent" or "pedigree." It has also come to mean a sense of pride in one's ancestry or a claim of special status because of the presence of prominent persons on one's family tree. From the twelfth century, the term assumed a particular meaning in the lives of Jewish families in Eastern Europe. Dynastic connections not only protected the family against suspicion of stigma but also provided its members with various privileges (*zechut avot*, or "rights of forefathers"). Family dynasties were often traced to a single founder who was known for his extraordinary scholarly achievements. Many people believed that one pious person could transmit his sanctity to his descendants. The concept of *yichus* has also been extended to include families with great wealth, especially when they are generous in contributing to charitable causes. These families are perceived to be highly prestigious; they are respected and admired by others.

The concept of *yichus* has psychological as well as social significance. In families who claim special status because of the founder, there are always "insiders" and "outsiders." Members devise behavioral norms for the insiders and maneuver to keep outsiders out. Preferential treatment is given to those with the highest status, while others are ignored or shunned. *Yichus* may be a critical factor when a son or daughter is anticipating marriage, or when a person is cited for a special function or role in the synagogue. Ancient writings contain references to the importance of family status.[30] In many communities today, failure to respect the significance of *yichus* in one's family history is seen as an insult and, in extreme situations, as a threat to the honor of the family.

### 5. Food and dietary laws

In all societies, eating is one of the essential modalities for initiating and sustaining human relationships. Children learn the beliefs and practices of their parents through repeated experiences of eating with the family. The table is the setting in which individual personalities develop, kinship obligations emerge, and the customs of the group are reinforced.[31] In every culture, food and drink have immense emotional significance. No important occasion occurs without a meal. It is not surprising that a comprehensive volume of advice on how to run a traditional Jewish household concludes with a collection of the author's mother's "plain, basic holiday recipes."[32]

For many people, the choice, preparation, and presentation of food are clear indications of the family's religious and ethnic affiliation. We are what we eat. The Jewish dietary laws have played a central role in the lives of Jewish families for thousands of years. Stated in the Bible and interpreted and elaborated by rabbis and scholars, specific rules determine the types of foods that are permitted and the procedures for preparing them. Jewish dietary laws are classified as *chukkim*, or divine statutes. Scholars have suggested a variety of possible reasons for their prominence in Jewish observance: they promote hygienic conditions, connect the people to ancient traditions, reinforce a sense of aesthetics and order. Some say they are intended to keep Jews apart from other groups. The bottom line is that they are divine commandments and require no further justification.

The Hebrew term *kashruth* pertains to that which is "fit" or "proper." The laws of *kashruth* identify the animals, birds, and fish that observant Jewish persons may and may not eat. Regulations also determine how food should be prepared. Animals must be ritually slaughtered according to the law. Meat must not be cooked or eaten with milk or other dairy products. Portions of the Oral Law specify the number of hours that must elapse between the consumption of meat and dairy foods. These laws also provide guidelines for determining the products that can be used, the arrangement of the kitchen, and the correct procedures for supervising foods prepared in kosher restaurants. Additional legal statutes pertain to fasting on specified days and not eating leavened bread during Passover. For observant Jews, these laws are binding and meaningful. Failure to obey them is considered a serious offense.

Beyond the realm of formal legal precepts, innumerable customs guide the preparation and consumption of food in Jewish families. For every holiday and life-cycle event, special foods are presented, using favorite recipes that were handed down from previous generations. Especially important are the foods and wine used for the Sabbath, the prayers that accompany them, and the ceremonies that are observed. Food preferences vary from one ethnic group to another, such as between Ashkenazim (Jews from Europe) and Sephardim (from Spain and Muslim countries). These differences may become provocations for conflict when members intermarry, or when families compete for the "best" dishes.

In the twentieth century, two parallel trends could be seen in Jewish communities around the world. On the one hand, Jews have been known to endanger their lives by their faithful adherence to the dietary laws. Although the laws of *kashruth* are allowed to be broken in order to preserve life, under conditions of terrible deprivation during the Holocaust, some observant Jews chose to starve rather than eat non-kosher food. On the other hand, Reform Judaism introduced the concept that the dietary laws, among other elements of the *halakhah*, have become "outmoded" or "obsolete." Many modern Jews have willingly given up the dietary restrictions and now eat "like everyone else." Along this wide spectrum, individuals and families take up every conceivable position, from strict adherence to flexibility and accommodation.

For most people, the "right" way to eat is the way one's own family eats. The family's decision to assimilate or to remain visibly Jewish is reflected in the food that is served at their table. Serious conflicts can erupt in families where the eating patterns are called into question. The son of a secular family becomes Orthodox and announces that if his parents will not observe the laws of *kashruth,* he will never eat at home again. A woman marries a non-Jewish man and must decide whether or not to invite her parents to a Christmas dinner. An Orthodox man is invited to a Reform synagogue for a family bar mitzvah. For the sake of family solidarity he comes, but eats nothing. He is appalled when he sees the platter of shrimp on the luncheon buffet. There are countless examples of such awkward situations, where the potential for conflict is especially high. When someone in the family rebels and renounces parental values, the table is one of the most likely places for the battle to be waged.

## 6. Jewish time: The calendar, life cycle events, and holidays

Throughout history, the repeated occurrence of exile and persecution has colored many features of family life. Perhaps because Jews have been displaced for so long and uprooted so often and so violently, they have learned to create a sense of continuity in time rather than place. For more than two thousand years, Jews have shared a common calendar but no common homeland. One's sense of "Jewishness" is expressed through events in time: religiously defined rites of passage, the commemoration of significant historical events, and the celebration of Jewish holidays. The Jewish mission became the "creation of a spiritual calendar constructed of timeless moments, sacred events, and religious imperatives, these largely ordered by the cycles of time, the passing of season, and even the hours of each passing day."[33]

The Jewish calendar has its origins in the Torah. Its center-piece is the Sabbath, *Shabbat*, the seventh day of the week. The Sabbath has its own laws and customs, which are scrupulously observed by Orthodox Jews. The special days of the festival cycle are not random moments scattered through the year, but significant events that draw their power from Divine laws. Michael Strassfeld[34] has suggested that the Jewish holidays are like lodgings for travelers, providing rest and retreat from the mundane world. They also serve as a point at which persons can take their bearings, reinforce memories of the past, and confirm their most crucial beliefs. The observance of *Shabbat*, the annual festivals, and the religious rites of passage help to keep them in touch with the temporal dimensions of their lives. The festivals illuminate the great human themes of nurturing, shelter and security, destruction and renewal, freedom and bondage, the earthly and the transcendent. Life cycle events emphasize the role of the family in the experience of each individual. By sanctifying special moments, hours, and days, Jews have created stability in time as an antidote to the trauma of recurring spatial upheavals.

For observant Jews, each of the major life cycle events is structured according to specific legal requirements. Birth, baby naming, *brit* or ritual circumcision, *pidyon ha ben* (the redeeming of the firstborn son), bar and bat mitzvah, weddings, funerals and mourning rituals – each of these has its own laws, temporal framework, and shared religious significance. All of these events are essentially family-centered; they provide special occasions for the family to mark its connection with Jewish history and celebrate the continuity of the Jewish people. These same events, however, can also serve as the basis for arguments and estrangements. The way a particular ritual is observed by one's parents may be significantly different from the way one's in-laws observe it. The wholehearted celebration of a holiday by one segment of the family may be rejected or ignored by members of another branch. Who is invited and who is left out, who is honored by a prestigious assignment, what style of clothing should be worn and what kind of food is served, each of these issues can be a catalyst for bonding or a potential source of conflict.

One example of a time-ordered tradition with great emotional significance is the injunction to recite the *Kaddish* prayer every day during the eleven months following the death of a parent. For many Jewish men, "saying *Kaddish*" is a sacred obligation, a clear affirmation of God's power to create life and ordain death. Those who choose not to observe this tradition may incur the wrath of those who do. Surviving family members may view its absence as a denial of the honor to be given to a deceased parent or a blatant rejection of one's religious heritage. In a secular, assimilated family, a son who chooses to observe this obligation may be viewed as superstitious or reactionary.

A male infant is born to a Catholic mother and her Jewish husband. The entire family becomes embroiled in the controversy over if, how, and when to circumcise the baby. Each of the parents and each of the grandparents have a different opinion, all of them pulling in another direction. No one can agree on one acceptable source of advice: rabbi, priest, or physician. There is no satisfactory solution and the problem lingers, leaving a residue of rancor throughout the family.

It is part of the richness of Jewish tradition that any holiday, any observance of a life cycle event can have multiple meanings for different people. Each family will observe (or ignore) these events in its own distinct way. Some will focus on the religious aspect, others on the food, and still others on the opportunity for a family gathering. For some families, these events are truly *smachot* (joyful occasions). For others, they are a source of tension, disappointment, and frustrated expectations. As we shall see, people use holidays and life cycle events for many different purposes: as the venue for settling old scores, a springboard to cut off, or a golden opportunity for reconciliation.

### 7. The concept of *shlom bayit*, family solidarity
Jewish literature contains countless references to the concept of *shlom bayit*, peace in the home. Honoring one's parents and

preserving family solidarity is considered a divine commandment. The Hebrew word for marriage is *kiddushin*, or sanctification, emphasizing the holy aspect of marriage and family. The Jewish home is the most vital factor in the survival of Judaism and the preservation of the Jewish way of life, even more than the synagogue or the school. "Woe to the father who has banished his children from his table; and woe to the children who have been banished from their father's table."[35] We can read this statement as an injunction to preserve family solidarity. Its original Talmudic source refers to the trauma of exile, in which the Father is God and the children are His banished people.

In the Hebrew Bible, family solidarity is frequently stressed,[36] and harmony among family members is highly valued.[37] Brothers were obligated to avenge each other's murder[38] as part of their duty in the role of *goel* ("defender" or "redeemer").[39] Another aspect of this responsibility was the requirement to ransom a family member who had been taken captive or had gone into servitude as the result of financial adversity.[40] According to Jewish tradition, children who do not behave respectfully toward their parents are guilty of committing a sin. *Derech eretz*, or honorable behavior, is owed to parents because they, like God, have a share in the making of the child.[41] The Fifth Commandment is the basis for a mountain of writings on the subject of honoring one's parents. Children are required to "revere their mother and father" and to "respect their father and mother." The order of these phrases and the meanings of each word are discussed in great detail in Talmudic literature.[42] Observant Jews who allow a dispute between parents and children to destroy the solidarity of the family are aware of the seriousness of their transgression. Others who are marginally Jewish may not realize the religious significance of their acts, but their guilt and anguish may have roots in the deep well of unconscious cultural memory.

Some narratives have the power to portray the deepest meanings of human experience. The following condensed version of an old Jewish folktale expresses the spirit of *shlom bayit* in its most profound sense.

*There was once a field owned by two brothers. One of them had a wife and children; the other had no wife and no children. They lived together in one house and they tilled the land they had inherited from their father.*

*During one wheat harvest, they bound up stalks and made two equal piles of the grain they had reaped, and they left them there in the field. That night, the brother who had neither a wife nor children decided that his brother had more need for the grain, so he took from his own pile and added it to his brother's pile.*

*At the same time, his brother thought that the solitary brother deserved more grain than he, so he and his wife secretly added to the other's pile. Next morning, both men were astonished to see that their piles were equal as they had been at first. This pattern was repeated: each night they did the same thing, and every morning they found that the piles were equal.*

*Then they decided to investigate. When each of them saw what the other was doing, they embraced and kissed. And they gave thanks to God who had given them a brother who did such good deeds.* [43]

The brothers in this story reflect the quality of *chessed*, a Hebrew term meaning "loving kindness" or generosity of spirit. It is this quality that supports and preserves *shlom bayit*, the solidarity of the family. In some families, bitter conflicts have obliterated the expression of *chessed*. If the protagonists can join in a process of reconciliation, the atmosphere of loving kindness may be revived.

### Concluding thoughts: optimizing assets

The elements described on these pages constitute only a portion of the rich heritage of the Jewish people. They were selected because of their pervasive influence on the emotional life of families. In addition to these factors, countless other experiences contribute to a person's self-image as an individual and as part of a family group. Home remedies for illnesses, books that were treasured by previous generations, patterns of naming children, expressions and gestures used by parents and grandparents: all of these are part of the legacy of a family. They contribute to a shared history.

Jewish persons who acknowledge little, if any, connection to their religious tradition may consider these ideas irrelevant to their experience. For them, the ancient laws may not be seen as binding, nor are the rituals observed or respected. But regardless of a person's determination to sever himself from his roots, remnants of the past will continue to echo in the unconscious memory. "Despite the vast range of ways in which a Jew can alienate himself from his past, he nevertheless retains a metaphysically, almost genetically, imprinted image of his Jewishness. The unique paradigm or prototype persists."[44] Invariably there will be a moment of truth when the power of the past breaks through. Beginnings and endings can be especially potent experiences in the lives of families. When a parent dies or a baby is named, some people experience a crisis of identity. At such moments of high emotional intensity, the potential for conflict is particularly high, as opposing factions in the family face off against each other.

In the legacy of every cultural or religious group, the elements that constitute its history may be seen as assets or liabilities, depending on how they are perceived and lived. Individual families incorporate some aspects of their heritage as sources of strength, while others use them as provocations for conflict. By recognizing the pressures that compel us to over-react, leap into disputes and cut off, we may be able to avoid the worst-case scenarios. With this knowledge, we can draw on the resources that optimize our strengths and contribute to a more harmonious family environment.

Within the traditional Jewish archetype, the fundamental source of our strength is the Bible and its commentaries. The Torah, the Hebrew Bible, provides the foundation for the Jewish identity system. For those who acknowledge its power, the Bible is the connecting link to the past and a reliable blueprint for the future. All of the historical patterns and traditions described on these pages have their origins and inspiration in the Torah. The meanings of exile, the roots of scholarship, the genealogical patterns, the blessings and the curses, the significance of holidays and life cycle events, all of these are found in the texts of the Bible. Its commentaries provide a deep well of insights into the complexities of family life. As we explore the manifestations of conflict, rivalry, estrangement, and reconciliation in biblical families, we may discover patterns that come close to home.

CHAPTER THREE

# Sources of Ultimate Values

---

*"...Everything holds together in Jewish history – the legends as much as the facts. Composed during the centuries that followed the destruction of the Temple in Jerusalem, the Midrash mirrors both the imagined and the lived reality of Israel, and it continues to influence our lives."*[1]

---

**Prelude**

The third and most basic element in the delineation of family dynamics is the dimension of ultimate values, the foundation of ethical standards and moral behavior. Inseparable from the structure and process of family life and its historical and cultural patterns are the guidelines that determine our beliefs and behavior. Every religious denomination and cultural group has developed its own sacred literature. For Jewish families throughout the ages, the Torah and its commentaries have stood as this vital foundation. These sacred texts continue to be "their law and lore, their culture and code of practice, their way of life and world view, even if only in the sense that (they are) the center from which (some of them) have diverged."[2]

In the Pentateuch, the Five Books of Moses, we find prototypes of the conflicts, loyalties, estrangements, and reconciliations that constitute the basic ingredients of family life. Here also are the laws and traditions that teach us how to live in a family. These texts endure as an abiding legacy. The early Sages understood their fundamental significance: woven into the narratives and reflected in the legal statutes are the strengths and vulnerabilities that define the human condition. Countless scholars have analyzed the texts to clarify the parameters of proper human behavior. The challenge for later biblical commentators was to study the previous interpretations, struggle with the contradictions, develop their own conclusions, and inspire their students to continue the work. In this chapter, we will undertake a small portion of this task.

### THE THIRD LEVEL: THEMES OF ESTRANGEMENT IN SACRED LITERATURE

Two main categories of biblical texts are particularly relevant to our understanding of family conflict and its psychological dimensions. The first category consists of narratives. These are concentrated in *Genesis*, in the stories of the patriarchal family and the events in their lives. The second category, legal obligations and commandments, appears throughout the Bible and was codified over a span of centuries in the body of law known as *halakhah*. Many of these sources are contained in *Leviticus*.

In attempting to understand the biblical texts, scholars have recognized at least four levels of meaning: *pshat*, the literal or surface meaning, the homiletic level (*drash*) that lies just beneath the surface, the allegorical level (*remez*), and the hidden or mystical dimension (*sod*). The surface meanings correspond to the body, the deeper meanings to the soul of the narrative. They all complement and clarify each other. It is the task of Bible commentators to uncover and illuminate these levels of meaning. Avivah Zornberg has defined this task as a way to reveal the *unconscious* level of biblical discourse.[3] According to Zornberg, interpreting sacred texts is a special way of listening to the inner voices, gaining access to ambiguous themes and extracting new meanings from them. In music, it would be like hearing the harmonics, the breath and the heartbeat beneath the melody.

*Midrash*, the act and process of biblical interpretation, is a Hebrew word derived from the root "to search out." In popular usage, it has come to stand for a wide range of biblically inspired literature. Wiesel uses it in the widest sense as "interpretation, illustration, creative imagination." Simi Peters defines the term more explicitly as a unique method of interpreting "*TaNaKh*" (Torah, Prophets, Writings) that was formulated by the rabbis of the Talmudic period.[4] Subsequently, a great flowering of commentaries emerged that were based on those early insights. During the period between 400 and 1200 CE, a scattered array of oral teachings – sermons preached in synagogues and lectures given by sages – was organized, edited, and put into writing. Those texts were based on ideas and methods that had been developed earlier. Authentic biblical commentaries derived from *midrash* must conform to specific rules and guidelines. One requirement is a thorough knowledge of all existing writings and interpretations on a given topic. Using this vast accumulation of knowledge, each scholar then applied his own unique experience, cultural tradition, and historical context to elucidate individual portions of sacred text. The collection of writings based on authentic *midrash* is thought to have been completed by the twelfth century. However, the Bible continues to serve as an inexhaustible resource. Many contemporary authors have preserved the ancient tradition by mining the depths of biblical texts for their inspiration. Thomas Mann produced some of the most extraordinary examples of this genre. The Bible has the glorious and uncanny ability to speak to us with many voices. Some of us may hear the commanding voice of God thundering down through the ages. Others examine the commentaries in their original languages and thus participate in a dialogue with preeminent rabbis and sages. I have searched for interpretations that can be integrated into a psychological frame of reference. The sources I have chosen originated in Jewish tradition, but I trust that readers who identify with different ethnic and religious histories will find parallel resources in their own sacred literature. Each of us, by means of careful, respectful study of sacred texts, can discover valuable clues for understanding fragmented families.

## PART ONE: DISCORDANT FAMILIES IN *GENESIS*

The Book of *Genesis* presents an awesome progression of expulsions and separations. Each episode initiates a transformative process for the person and a new sequence of historical events. Adam and Eve are evicted from the Garden of Eden. Cain is sent to wander the face of the earth. Noah leaves dry land and sets out on the unstable realm of water. Abraham, obeying God's command to go (*lech lecha*), embarks on a journey that requires a "strange order of abandonments,"[5] first his birthplace, then his homeland, and finally his father's house. Ishmael is banished from his father's presence. Jacob flees from the wrath of Esau. Joseph is betrayed by his brothers and carried off to Egypt. Each of these events requires a radical breaking-away from a familiar milieu, a severing of attachments. Each of these persons must deconstruct what has been known and move on to create a new self and a new paradigm of reality.

The first series of narratives in *Genesis* develops in a distinct progression, from the darkness of chaos to the emerging forms of creation; from the primeval saga of the first man and woman to Noah's redeeming presence; from the whirlwind of the deluge to the covenant of the rainbow. Then, Abraham appears. The transition from these episodes to the patriarchal narratives reflects a shift of focus from cosmic events to a single family. For God the Creator, the selection of Abraham and his family represents a renewed attempt, after the Flood, to establish an ongoing relationship with mankind and with individual persons. When the emphasis shifts to Abraham, a new tone is sounded and the centrality of the family is affirmed. If Abraham and his descendants accept God's teachings, they will bring blessings to all the families of the earth.[6]

The biblical family is a closely ordered, patriarchal system in which ultimate authority is vested in the father. The husband may have more than one wife; brothers are closely connected to each other and to the father. The firstborn son has privileges relating to succession and inheritance. In the *Genesis* narratives, many of the family relationships appear to be discordant or dysfunctional. Each of the patriarchs experiences the loss or separation from an older brother. In every generation, from Abraham to Joseph, the expected order of succession is subverted and conflicts erupt between siblings. Woven into the tangled web of the family, there are ambiguities, deceptions, rivalry, and retribution. Despite all the tensions and upheavals in the lives of these parents and their progeny, the family survives and flourishes.

We will consider specific interpretations of the following scenarios:

**Cain and Abel.** A man murders his brother and suffers the consequences.

**Ishmael and Isaac.** The sons of the Patriarch Abraham are favored and protected by their respective mothers, each of whom claims that *her* son is the rightful heir.

**Jacob and Esau.** A family with twin sons: one is favored by his mother, the other by his father. Jacob succeeds in convincing his father Isaac to bestow on him the mantle of succession while Esau is rejected and scorned, leading to a bitter estrangement between the brothers.

**Joseph.** The beloved son of Jacob is envied and despised by his brothers. They abandon him in the wilderness and deceive their father about his fate. After many years and wondrous adventures, Joseph and his family are reunited.

## 1. Cain and Abel

> *...When they were in the field, Cain rose up against Abel his brother, and killed him.*[7]

The world's first family consists of Adam, his wife Eve and their two sons. Some versions give them additional children: two daughters who were said to be twins of the sons.[8] The murder occurs in the second generation of the human race and represents the ultimate, most terrifying form of estrangement. "It is the curious and frightening tale of two brothers who, jealous of each other's belongings, memories, and solitude, are unable to co-exist in a world they are still alone to possess."[9] Is this a story of two brothers competing for favor or is it a timeless myth that contains the archetypal elements of all family conflicts? Competition between brothers appears throughout ancient mythologies and persists to the present day, in every place and culture. In the narratives of the Patriarchs, estrangements between brothers occur in each generation. Like many of the others, the struggle between Cain and Abel does not lead to a resolution.

Why are we confronted with this terrifying tale of fratricide so early in *Genesis*? What does it intend to teach us? Scholars recognize two different types of biblical dialogue, vertical and horizontal. The vertical dialogues are between persons and God; the horizontal ones are between two persons. When we examine the chapters of *Genesis*, we find both types of dialogue on virtually every page. The pattern is invariably the same: the text tells us that one spoke to the other, followed immediately by what they said. This sequence can be seen in dialogues between all the main protagonists, between Adam and Eve, Abraham and Sarah, Jacob and Esau. Because this pattern is so pervasive, commentators pay special attention to the verses in which the pattern is distorted or suppressed. Let us notice, then, the dialogue between Cain and Abel (*Genesis* 4:8): *Cain said to his brother Abel....* Here, we expect to see a set of quotation marks followed by Cain's statement. Instead, the text jars us: *And it came to pass, when they were in the field, that Cain rose up against Abel his brother and killed him.* What happened to the dialogue? Where is Cain's statement? Where is Abel's reply?

Andre Neher, the French Jewish philosopher, suggests that the silence between the brothers at this crucial moment "caused" the murder. Because the brothers were incapable of speaking together, of explaining their predicament, sharing their anguish, "they invented something else, death."[10] Here, the absence of speech, the "exile of the word," as Neher calls it, led to fratricide. Instead of dialogue, the encounter is a "fratricidal monologue." Applying this insight to contemporary families, we can see that the inability or the refusal to communicate, when words are blocked because of indifference, rage, fear, or any other highly-charged emotions, may have dreadful consequences.

According to one interpretation, the story of the fratricide originates in a dream. Eve dreamed that she saw Cain drinking Abel's blood, ignoring his brother's anguished cries. When she told Adam of her dream, he said, "We must separate our sons." That is why Cain became a farmer and Abel a shepherd, each living in his own hut.[11] This reading sets the parameters for the opposing natures of the brothers and the rivalry that tore them apart. It also leads us to wonder about the role of the parents. If Eve had a premonition of her son's murder, why did she not try to prevent it?

Elie Wiesel examines various interpretations of the parents' role in the dispute between the brothers. He notes that Adam and Eve are conspicuously absent from this part of the narrative. There is only one central triangle: Abel, Cain and God. Neither of the parents seems to make an effort to avert the tragedy, which would be a natural reaction when two sons are engaged in a bitter dispute. How should we interpret their apparent failure to intervene? Can it be seen as a communication gap between the two generations? Is their silence another example of the "exile of the word," as Neher calls it?

Wiesel suggests that the parents' muteness may be "the first and probably the most fatal pedagogic failure in history."[12] The scene compels him to ask a barrage of anguished questions. His tone carries a hint of rebuke: where were the parents when their sons needed them? Were they too busy, too absorbed in their own affairs? Could they not have remonstrated with one son and appeased the other? Could they not have acted as a buffer to mitigate the anger? Wiesel's questions help us to see parallels between this story and similar situations in contemporary families. We can speculate that the parents' detachment reflected their unconscious wish for one son to triumph over the other. Or, they may have felt unmoved by the brothers' conflict, or powerless to deflect their hostility. Did they choose to stay out of the dispute, assuming that the brothers would settle it on their own terms? The same dilemma is repeated in the present day when parents cannot decide whether or not to intervene in a conflict between their children.

Let us consider the sequence that led to the murder. Each brother brought an offering to God. Cain gave the fruit of the ground and Abel offered the first lamb of his flock. God favored Abel's offering and had no regard for Cain's. Why? The text specifies that Abel's offering was the *first* lamb, implying that he selected the best of his flock. Cain brought merely the fruit. According to this interpretation, the gift of one brother was perceived as more valuable, more prestigious than the gift of the other.[13] One could object that it looks like a set-up, imposed by God on these two unsuspecting brothers. Cain resents God's preference for Abel's gift, one angry word leads to another, one insult heaps on another, and the drama is set in motion. Violence bursts forth. Cain's rage is seen as a reaction to the ultimate humiliation of failing to gain God's favor. But why did he choose violence instead of words? The scene may remind us of families we know, when rivalry between siblings culminates in rejection and alienation rather than constructive dialogue and compromise.

How can we understand the provocation for murder in this story? What elements contributed to the poisonous atmosphere? At least three possible motives have been suggested: property, ideology, and rivalry over a woman.[14] The first scenario would be a dispute over material possessions. The brothers said: "Come let us divide the world." Cain took the land and Abel took the movables. Cain claimed: "The land on which you are standing is mine! Get off!" Abel reacted: "The clothing you are wearing is mine! Take it off!" Each brother had a conflicting claim, a different perception of what was meant by the lawful division of property.

The second motive may be traced to religious belief or ideology. Each of the brothers claimed portions of the land and insisted that *his* land would contain the most holy places. Cain was certain that his share would include the site of the Holy Mount where the sacrifice of Isaac would later occur and where Solomon would build the Temple. This version implies that Cain assumed superior status because of his ideology.

The third possible motive is rivalry over a woman. One interpretation suggests that the brothers were contending for Eve, a variation on the classical Oedipal theme of a son lusting for his mother. Another version is based on the myth that each brother had a twin sister. Their father had decided that Cain should marry Abel's twin, but Cain wanted his own twin, who was more beautiful. Each of these motives – property and possessions, religious ideology, and rivalry – can be seen to operate in present-day families as provocations for conflict.

How do we envision the two brothers? Wiesel has painted a word portrait, suggesting that Cain is demanding, stubborn, arrogant, temperamental.[15] He needs to win. If he fails, he becomes resentful, hating the world and despising his own vulnerability. Abel is more likable: he is the earnest shepherd, kind, gentle, a dreamer, an innocent victim. But these are stereotypes, merely the outer shell. What lies beneath the surface? We can speculate that Cain had some redeeming qualities. Perhaps he longed for reassurance from his brother. He may have needed to feel that someone would listen to him and empathize with his feelings of inadequacy. But instead, what did Abel do? He remained aloof. He looked away and did not respond. Was he guilty of the sin of indifference?

Some commentators propose that the story describes a predictable sequence, one that may be familiar to us. The two brothers fought and Abel prevailed. When Cain saw that his brother could overpower him, he wept and begged for mercy, feigning weakness. He evoked his brother's sympathy by guile: "What will our parents do if you kill me?" Abel released him and Cain took advantage of the momentary lapse. He attacked Abel and murdered him.[16] The drama played out by Cain and Abel could be transposed to a contemporary setting. Imagine a family with two brothers who are competing for high stakes: a promotion to head the family business or a lawsuit contesting the provisions of their parent's will. One brother feigns weakness, pretends to defer, puts the other off-guard, makes false promises, and eventually gains the upper hand. These are variations on a biblical theme, replicated in our own time.

On the surface, the conclusion of this story seems self-evident. Cain committed murder and was punished. We feel sympathy for the victim and outrage toward the murderer. But Cain did not receive the death penalty; his only punishment was banishment. What would that imply? Was God showing a modicum of mercy to the guilty brother? Some interpretations consider the possibility that this is not a simple question of guilt versus innocence. When his offering was rejected, Cain "burned with anger." This seems like a natural reaction. An older brother is likely to be upset when his younger brother is favored. But why could they not resolve the conflict peacefully? Each of the brothers had his unique characteristics, his own special skills and limitations. Why did Cain need to compete with his brother for the same recognition? When we observe contemporary families in the light of this narrative, we see that competition between brothers can lead to destructive outcomes or to productive growth. If the conflict escalates and anger takes a stranglehold, the family may explode into fragments. Or, if a dispute is understood from an enlightened perspective, it may stimulate a burst of new insights. Brothers can struggle for power or they can learn to share power. Parents can incite rivalry between siblings or encourage them to appreciate their differences. The biblical commentaries help us to consider the profound implications of these contrasting scenarios.

In the aftermath of the murder, God questioned Cain: "*Where is Abel, thy brother?*" He replied, "*I do not know. Am I my brother's keeper?*"[17] How can we understand the meaning of this odd dialogue? Why did God need to ask? Why the petulant reply? If Cain's response had expressed remorse, he might have averted the terrible punishment. On the contrary, he denied his guilt and attempted to project the blame onto someone else, onto God. The sources attribute various excuses to Cain: "Was I to blame? You created me with such base instincts, I had to do it." Or, "You gave me cause to envy him."[18] But in Cain's case, none of the excuses were valid. When we examine conflicts in today's families, we see similar patterns of blame, projection of guilt, and refusal to accept responsibility. In each situation, these reactions have different meanings and lead to different conclusions.

Cain's punishment is perpetual exile; he is banished in the most profound sense. First, he is driven away from the presence of the Lord, the ultimate cutoff.[19] Then, God inflicts additional punishments on Cain. This overload of suffering can be seen as the "worst-case scenario" for the condition of the estranged person. An early commentary depicts seven afflictions.[20] The interpretations in italics are mine.

1. "A horn sprouted from his brow, or a letter was tattooed on his arm signifying guilt."
   *He carries a sign that is visible to everyone, announcing his alienated condition.*

2. "The cry of fratricide called out to him from the hills."
   *He hears a constant, unremitting accusation of wrongdoing.*

3. He is tormented by "palsy, shaking."
   *He has the sensation of unsteadiness; he never feels rooted or solid.*

4. "A constant feeling of hunger."
   *He is never fulfilled or satisfied.*

5. "Disappointment of every wish."
   *Each of his aspirations fizzles out; no effort succeeds; his hopes are repeatedly dashed.*

6. "A perpetual lack of sleep."
*For him, there is no real rest, no sense of closure, no sensation of awakening fresh and renewed.*

7. "The edict that no man can befriend or kill him."
*He is forever alone; he cannot form meaningful relationships or viable commitments; he is in a constant state of alienation from himself and from his surroundings.*

In the worst case, a person who is alienated from his family can never feel fully alive. Without relief or escape from the dilemma, he is a prisoner, condemned for life to be a severed branch on the family tree.

Despite all his troubles, Cain eventually marries and his progeny multiply. According to one interpretation, he was eventually murdered by one of his descendants, thus perpetuating the homicidal pattern. Other legends connect him to Noah and thus to all future generations.[21] We may wonder if the legacy he bequeathed to posterity includes the potential for fratricide. Did Cain provide the seed for the murderous tendencies that must continually be tamed and diverted if the human race is to survive? Perhaps the family conflicts that erupt in every time and place reverberate with echoes of the awesome struggle between the world's first brothers.

## 2. Ishmael and Isaac

The enmity between the two sons of the Patriarch Abraham flares up on the pages of *Genesis* and continues to smolder throughout the ages. To this day, it remains a source of bitter estrangement between two peoples, the descendants of Isaac and those of Ishmael, Jews and Arabs. The narrative presents a family constellation consisting of five persons who form two interlocking triangles: Abraham, his wife Sarah, who is barren, and Hagar, a servant or concubine who gives birth to Ishmael, Abraham's first-born son. Finally, Isaac is born to Sarah and Abraham in their old age. Abraham stands at the apex of both of the triangles: one with Hagar and Ishmael, the other with Sarah and Isaac.

In *Genesis*, Chapter 21, Sarah sends Hagar and Ishmael into the wilderness. To understand the implications of this sequence, we need to examine the verses that precede it. In three separate episodes, God promises offspring to Abraham. But he and Sarah grow old and the promise of a son is not fulfilled. So Sarah takes the initiative: she gives her husband a "handmaid" to bear a child for her. Thus, Sarah introduces a rival into her household, making her vulnerable to the natural feelings of jealousy and inadequacy. Hagar conceives Ishmael, and when she learns that she is carrying Abraham's child, she taunts Sarah.[22] The commentators note: Hagar thinks that she must be more righteous than Sarah, since she, Hagar, has conceived a child while Sarah has not. Hagar's mockery has a poisonous sting to it.[23] The effect of this insult on Sarah is predictable: she is enraged, determined to get rid of this arrogant servant and banish the child she will bear.

Some commentators criticize Sarah for her harsh treatment of Hagar.[24] They point out that Sarah's cruelty has dreadful consequences: Hagar's son survives as a wild, lawless man whose descendants will bring great suffering to the progeny of Sarah and Abraham. This prediction has been realized: Arabs and Jews, the nations that emanated from Ishmael and Isaac, are locked in a perpetual war.

What are the dynamics in this convoluted family system? By casting out Hagar and her son, Sarah exhibits not only an inflexible will but also a lucid vision of reality that is hidden from Abraham's more tangled emotions. Many contrasting interpretations have attempted to elucidate this painful sequence in the life of Abraham's family.[25] Zornberg suggests that Sarah's vision is like a laser beam that "disentangles complexity and cuts to the quick." The request to banish Hagar distresses Abraham greatly, but God reinforces Sarah's decision. He tells Abraham to accept Sarah's perception of the situation and acquiesce to her wishes. What Sarah sees is that these two brothers, Ishmael and Isaac, cannot possibly coexist. Although they seem to be playing together, "there is murder in the wind."[26]

One *midrash*, cited by Zornberg, interprets the interaction between the brothers as a kind of game, with Ishmael shooting arrows at Isaac and then claiming, "but I'm only playing." Ishmael's injured innocence does not fool Sarah. She understands that this is a mortal struggle and Ishmael is deadly serious. She must separate them before the inevitable calamity occurs. Sarah anticipates a recapitulation of the conflict between Cain and Abel. She fears that their rivalry and rage will overwhelm them, culminating in fratricide.

Commentators from different traditions focus on Abraham's response and imagine contrasting scenarios. In one version, Abraham regrets having banished Hagar and Ishmael. Time passes; Ishmael has a family of his own and Abraham goes to visit him. After a sequence of contacts between them, Ishmael gathers up his household, goes to Abraham, and prospers there.[27] This version of the story reflects the commentator's vision of the integrity of the family. If we transpose this sequence to a present-day family, we can imagine the mixed emotions of a father setting out to reconcile with his estranged son. How would he prepare for the journey, and what sort of effort would be effective for the task of repairing a fragmented family?

According to the original text in *Genesis*, Ishmael and Isaac meet only once after the banishment, when they come to bury their father in the Cave of Machpelah in Hebron.[28] A Muslim version relates that Ishmael and his father were reunited in Mecca, where together they constructed the *Ka'aba*, the stone monolith that stands in the center of the city and serves as the focus for the *Hajj*, the Muslims' annual pilgrimage.[29] Different religious traditions find their own ways to achieve a vestige of closure in this ancient story of rivalry and alienation in Abraham's family.

The story of Isaac and Ishmael contains no face-to-face confrontation between the brothers, no battle for power or possessions, no accusations or vituperations. We can imagine that they hardly knew each other. The struggle is played out by the parent generation: one father, two mothers. God determines the moves. The task of Abraham and Sarah is to preserve the essential beliefs and protect the legacy. In this family with intersecting triangles, the sons bear the burden; they become the vehicles for carrying out the parental agenda. Their story can help us to be aware of the triangular patterns in our own families. When the stakes are high, sons and daughters may become the central figures in their parents' determination to preserve the values that are most important to them.

In the end, Sarah prevails and Isaac is acknowledged as the heir. He is the son who inherits the birthright and transmits it to *his* son. But this is not a simple matter of win or lose. Isaac subsequently survives the ultimate trauma of the *Akedah*, (the binding of Isaac, *Genesis*: Chapter 22) and he lives to see his own sons embroiled in a bitter conflict. The family prevails and prospers, but the tensions are handed down to the next generation where they erupt with renewed vigor in a different form.

The struggles of these biblical families are relevant to our own lives. We can recognize our own contentious relationships mirrored on the pages of Scripture. One might ask, have I demeaned one son in favor of another? Will my estranged children come together only to bury me? What could I have done to heal the rift between them? The texts prod us to ask profound questions that have no definitive answers. We will continue to search.

### 3. Jacob and Esau

In the generation after Abraham, the main protagonists are Isaac, his wife Rebecca, and their twin sons, Jacob and Esau. The story unfolds in an aura of mounting tensions. Two brothers struggle in the womb, an ominous presentiment of their subsequent rivalry.[30] Here is a condensed sketch of this family drama: Isaac is attached to his firstborn son, Esau; Rebecca favors Jacob. It seems that Isaac does not see the evil aspects of Esau's personality. The father's apparent lack of awareness, symbolized by his blindness, allows him to ignore the signs of weakness in his favored son. Nor does he perceive the tension between Jacob and Esau and the inevitable rivalry between them. The drama intensifies when Rebecca convinces Jacob to trick his father into giving him the birthright that is due to Esau. Jacob impersonates his brother and succeeds in deceiving Isaac. Esau reacts to the discovery of his brother's deception *with a loud and bitter cry.* He threatens to kill Jacob, who escapes from his brother's wrath by fleeing to a distant land. After more than twenty years of separation and a series of extraordinary adventures, Jacob sets out on a journey to return to his homeland. On the way, he sees his estranged brother approaching. Jacob's preparations for the meeting, his anticipation of Esau's anger, and their subsequent encounter provide the ingredients for many different interpretations of the meanings of estrangement and its aftermath.

Let us consider particular details of this story. First, what is the nature of the relationship between the two brothers? And what is the significance of the twin birth? Jacob and Esau occupied one womb and, during the fetal period, developed side by side. When did they diverge and become two distinct and opposing personalities? At what point did they become enemies?

The brothers are twins, a condition that emphasizes their fundamental connection. Twins are siblings for whom one significant distinction, a difference in age, is missing. These twins share not only age but gender, complicating the necessary task of forming separate identities. Esau, who emerged before his brother, is described in vivid terms: he *came forth ruddy all over like a hairy mantle.*[31] Later, when Rebecca encourages Jacob to obtain his father's blessing in place of Esau, Jacob hesitates, pointing out the obvious difference between them: *Esau my brother is a hairy man and I am a smooth man....* What is the significance of "hair" in this context? The commentators note that hair represents impurity, a lodging place for dirt, something messy and out of place. It is an indication of the differences between the brothers, the visible manifestation of their opposing natures. Throughout the narrative, the image of hair also appears as a symbol of their conflict. (It's no coincidence that the most popular rock musical of the 1960s was called "Hair." The social context was the hippy culture, with its disheveled, wild, hairy rebels. Hair has long been a symbol of the generation gap. For children who use hair as a wedge between themselves and their parents, it becomes a sign of resistance and individuation.) In the descriptions of Jacob and Esau, hair is the tangible sign of their conflict. Recalling the first description of Esau and his "hairy mantle," we can suggest that the roots of their enmity were always there, from the beginning.

Other clues confirm the radical differences between these two brothers. As the boys grew, Esau became a cunning hunter, a man of the field, while Jacob was a quiet, simple man who dwelled in tents. Esau antagonized his parents when he took two wives who were *a source of bitterness to Isaac and Rebecca.*[32] This rebellious act was not enough to alienate his father, who continued to favor him until the climax, the deception, and even beyond.

The deception scene unfolds in a steady buildup of tension. When Jacob assumes his disguise and goes in to his father, he is impersonating Esau. In a sense, he *incorporates* Esau. During this strange episode, one son becomes a combination of the two. Jacob takes on his brother's characteristics, his voice, his hair, his smell. He lies to his father, claiming: *I am Esau, your firstborn.*[33] The deception becomes a transformative moment for Jacob, a crossing of the threshold. As he assumes the persona of Esau, Jacob initiates a fundamental change in himself. Zornberg suggests that "good and evil are intermingled in him." By pretending to be another person, he can imagine a different self; he can expand his range of possibilities. It seems that Jacob can achieve a separate identity only by first becoming Esau, by putting himself in Esau's skin, and then breaking away from him. He is born again as a separate being, not clinging to Esau's heel, but severed from him, once and for all. "The Jacob who leaves his father's presence knows himself as he has seen himself mirrored in his father's blind eyes." As he goes out, he is truly born to selfhood.[34]

Similar patterns are replicated in present-day families, when a traumatic event or an unexpected discovery can be a decisive turning point in the formation of one's separate identity. The process of differentiating from a sibling and becoming a distinct self can occur as a sudden transformation or it can unfold gradually, with many detours, growth spurts, and regressions. The resulting changes are likely to ignite hostility if some members of the family cannot understand or accept the changed person. The story of Jacob's deception and its aftermath may help us to consider the ramifications of this vital process.

What is the role of Jacob's mother in this story? How does she convince him to trick Isaac into giving him the blessing that Esau claimed? One interpretation suggests that Rebecca was "an expert in such matters."[35] She knew that Esau had a dark side, qualities that reminded her of her brother, Laban. She recognized aspects of her own family in Esau and she knew his weak points. Perhaps she was the archetypal Jewish mother, struggling for the survival of her children in a hard, cruel world. She asks Jacob: *Why should I be bereaved of both of you in one day?*[36] In other words, she implies that both of her sons would be destroyed if he does not agree to her plan. One son would murder his brother; she would despise the surviving son and banish him for his crime.[37] Rebecca, Isaac, and their two sons are each pulling in opposite directions. Rebecca has always favored Jacob and now sees an opportunity to solidify his position as heir and successor. She has prophetic powers. She knows that if she does not intervene, one of her sons will murder the other. To prevent this dreadful outcome, she persuades Jacob to steal the birthright. Jacob agrees to the deception, receives his father's blessing, and sets in motion a sequence of escalating tensions and enduring conflict.

The story highlights the role of the mother in family conflicts. Is she a meddler, imposing her own agenda on her children and husband? Or is she the wise, empathic nurturer of her family? Rabbi Adin Steinsaltz paints a vivid portrait of Rebecca as "a woman of great understanding… who was capable of moving anyone who stood in her way." Yet "there is nothing domineering or destructive in her decisiveness; she did what she felt she had to do and then retired to her place backstage."[38] In our own time, the mother in some estranged families appears to resemble this altruistic image of Rebecca. In others, she manipulates the players and adds fuel to the fire of animosity. The various interpretations of Rebecca's role illustrate these contrasting possibilities.

Fleeing the wrath of Esau, Jacob goes into exile for many years. He fathers twelve sons with four different women. Accompanied by his entire household, he sets out on a journey to return to his homeland. On the way, he travels through the territory of his estranged brother. How does Jacob prepare for the anticipated meeting? He sends messengers (some say they are angels), in-structing them to tell Esau his story, to relate where he has been all these years and how he has prospered. They also convey his desire for peace and friendship. When the messengers return, they bring no greeting from Esau, no welcome or reassurance. Jacob receives only the ominous report that *"he is coming to meet you with four hundred men."* The implication is that Esau is still carry-ing a grudge and waiting for the opportunity to take his revenge, to settle the score between them. Jacob is afraid for his safety and worried that he might have to kill his brother to protect himself and his family. He prays for guidance and deliverance. Then, he sends a sizable gift to Esau, many flocks. He takes special pains to balance the flocks between males and females, as a gesture of honor to Esau. When they finally come face to face, their dialogue is marked by Jacob's expressions of humility and appeasement: *"Let me find favor in the sight of my lord."*[39]

What does Jacob's behavior teach us about preparing to meet an estranged sibling? Let us first consider the role of the mes-sengers. Perhaps they are angels, or persons who serve as angels. Jacob does not go directly to Esau; he sends "emissaries." Why? Possibly to stake out the territory, to evaluate Esau's readiness to "bury the hatchet." What are they instructed to do? They tell his story; they fill in the gaps. They let Esau know that Jacob has prospered during the long exile. In a sense, they are "introduc-ing" him to Esau as a gracious person with good intentions. He does not need favors from his brother. In present-day families, an emissary may be able to defuse the tension and serve as a bridge between the protagonists. A neutral friend or relative can deliver a message, transform the original dyad into a triangle, and hopefully, prepare the way for a constructive meeting.

What is the meaning of a gift offered at such a moment? Is it a sign of Jacob's prosperity, an effort to impress his brother? Is it an expression of appeasement, a peace offering? Jacob uses the word *bracha* (blessing) instead of *mincha* (offering) when he presents the gifts to Esau. Perhaps he is offering a substitute for the blessing he had stolen long ago, a kind of restitution. Some commentators suggest that Jacob is debasing himself, apologizing for the deception.[40] The text gives credence to the interpretation of Jacob's apologetic stance: he calls Esau *my lord* no less than eight times during their meeting. Why does Jacob humble himself before his brother? Does this scene recapitulate the scene between Cain and Abel, when Cain feigns weakness in order to seize the upper hand? Various explanations are plausible, but the actual motives for Jacob's behavior remain hidden. We can imagine that his response is an expression of the "archetypal pattern" of the Jewish people, who bend and survive. Or, it could be a reflection of Jacob's confidence in himself as the true inheritor, as the man who was chosen by God to transmit the heritage to future generations. He can afford to be humble, for he knows the Divine source of his strength. Each of these varied interpretations provides a different model for those who seek to understand the tensions that emerge in a fragmented family.

We have spoken of Jacob's role in this scene, but what about Esau? His approach to Jacob is recounted in extravagant terms: *...And Esau ran to meet him, and embraced him, and fell on his neck and kissed him and they wept...*[41] Many contrasting explanations are given for this scene. One suggests that the kiss of Esau is not sincere. He intends to carry out his earlier threat to kill Jacob and he tries to bite him. The phrase "they wept" means that Jacob weeps from the pain of the bite, and Esau from the pain in his teeth.[42] Another view suggests the possibility of a radical change in Esau. Perhaps he sincerely wants to forgive and reassure his brother. He is moved by Jacob's gifts, by his humility. Esau's tears may be a sign of genuine affection.

Benno Jacob[43] examined all the biblical texts that speak of meeting and weeping: Jacob and Rachel, Joseph and Benjamin, Joseph and Jacob, Moses and Aaron, and focused on Jacob and Esau. He noted that none of the other encounters was accompanied by such an effusive display of emotion: running, embracing, falling, kissing, weeping. Jacob does not "buy into" this apparent maneuver. Suspicious of Esau's intentions, he does not trust his sincerity and he refuses to go with him. Leibowitz refers to a much older commentary on this passage. Ramban (Nachmanides) suggests that Jacob's refusal is an expression of his strength. He will not become absorbed or enmeshed in the power of Esau. He does not succumb to his blandishments, nor is he impressed by the exaggerated displays of emotion. Jacob is able to face his estranged brother without losing himself in the process. Unlike the earlier scene with his father, now Jacob does not need to disguise himself. He continues on his separate way, maintaining his integrity and his independence. For these estranged brothers, the conflict is not resolved, but they are able to acknowledge their differences and move on. In this family as in many others, suspension of hostilities may be the most realistic outcome.

The brothers meet only once again, to bury Isaac.[44] This last meeting is not seen as a reconciliation; rather, it is a task performed by two separate persons to honor the memory of their father.

Profound lessons can be learned from these texts. The pattern of loyalties and grudges that emerges in the biblical family is reenacted in the present day, in the lives of actual families. A mother favors one son over another; the scorned son competes for recognition. A father gives up the struggle to determine the future of the family, creating a vacuum that others rush in to fill. The tensions that are generated in the midst of such turmoil affect all members of the family. They may be handed down to future generations, a pain-filled legacy. Or, by studying the wisdom of the ages, we may gain the insights that can resolve a stubborn deadlock.

## 4. Joseph

A turbulent family atmosphere holds the potential for bitter conflicts and estrangements as well as for exceptional creativity and growth. The story of Joseph depicts a family system in which two major estrangements erupt and resolve. From studying the biblical text and selected *midrashim*, we can gain deeper understanding of the elements that contribute to family conflict and its resolution. Thomas Mann, in the Foreword to his magnum opus, *Joseph and His Brothers*, introduces the narrative: "…the primitive occurrences of human life, of love and hate, blessing and curse, fraternal strife and paternal grief, pride and penance, fall and rise, a humorous song of mankind…"[45]

Joseph, the eleventh of Jacob's twelve sons, is the first born to Rachel, the beloved wife.[46] The family constellation is complex: four women who give birth to the twelve sons. From the text, we see how Joseph provokes his brothers' jealousy by his arrogant claims. He dreams that his brothers will bow down to him, and then he taunts them with the dream. When he brings tales to his father, he acts as a kind of "spy" in the family. We have the impression of a clever but naive boy who puts people off balance with his brash, precocious behavior. Joseph is favored by his father, who seems not to notice the tension and rivalry between the brothers. Jacob gives Joseph a special coat, the outward symbol of his favor, and sends him to find the brothers, who are tending sheep in a distant place. The plot thickens when the brothers see him approaching. In a burst of rage, they determine to get rid of this upstart. The possibility of fratricide hovers over the scene, but the brothers cannot agree on the method to carry out the crime. They plan to kill him and throw him into a pit, and then report that he was killed by a beast. Reuven, the oldest brother, urges them to abandon Joseph but not to murder him. Perhaps he intends to return later and rescue him. Judah intervenes with an alternative suggestion. Judah is a son of Leah, who was the sister and rival of Joseph's mother Rachel, a further complication in this convoluted family dynamic. Seeing a caravan approaching, Judah convinces his brothers to leave Joseph in the pit and sell him to the Ishmaelites, their family's enemy. There is the implicit assumption that these wild men will use and abuse Joseph at their whim, thus serving as the brothers' surrogates and punishing Joseph for his misdeeds. Perhaps they imagine that without Joseph, the explosive atmosphere in the family will be cooled. The brothers return to their father, bringing a piece of contrived evidence, the bloodied coat. When Jacob sees the coat, he seems to go along with the pretense; he assumes that his beloved son was indeed devoured by an evil beast. But is he really deceived? Does he wonder about the brothers' involvement in the disappearance of his son? Is he aware that his preference for Joseph has embittered them? Does he sense that Joseph was torn apart by their hatred?

When Reuven returns to the pit and finds nothing, he cries: *"the child is not, and where does that leave me?"*[47] We can speculate that in abandoning Joseph, the brothers also got rid of an essential part of themselves. Reuven's cry may reflect his own sense of desolation, emptiness. In a parallel way, the text also leaves Joseph as an absence, a vacancy. Zornberg calls it the "pit of oblivion."[48] It is as if he has been forgotten by the world. There is no explicit description of his reaction to being abandoned, no mention of his agony, his terror and sense of helplessness. The *midrashic* interpretations help us to fill in the gaps. Some commentators suggest that Joseph's cries are heard only much later. Why the long delay? His cries are not recorded because no one heard them. Many years after this scene, during the confrontation between the brothers, they could finally acknowledge his anguish. At the moment of reconciliation, Joseph can hear himself cry for the first time.[49]

The Joseph narrative contains two profound estrangements. One is between Joseph and his father, which lasts for more than twenty years. The other is between Joseph and his brothers. Each of these episodes provides valuable insights for understanding particular aspects of alienation in families. Here, we will consider the drama of Joseph and his father. The process of reconciliation between the brothers will be discussed in a later chapter.

In the original text, we learn how Joseph was betrayed by his brothers, sold into slavery, and eventually achieved great power in Egypt. During the period of his abandonment, denigration, imprisonment, and subsequent rise to power, Joseph made no attempt to contact his father, to reassure Jacob that he was alive, or to relieve him of his incessant grief. There is no reason to suspect that Joseph was angry with his father, and no rationale is given for the long silence between them. We are left to wonder why Joseph, after becoming viceroy to the king, did not make an effort to inform Jacob that he was alive and well. Why is there no clear motive given for the long separation between father and son? Perhaps it was an inevitable consequence of the buildup of hatred in the family. Or, it could be seen as Jacob's delayed punishment for "stealing" the birthright from his brother Esau. On another level of interpretation, this separation was an expression of Divine will, a necessary component in the sequence of events that brought the Jewish people to Egypt and much later, to their redemption. In many families with a long-lasting cutoff, the "real cause" or the original provocation may have been forgotten. When the rancor dissipates, the protagonists do not need to dredge up old grievances. They can celebrate their renewed connection as a blessing that is reminiscent of the joyous reconciliation between Jacob and Joseph.

How does Jacob learn that his "dead" son is alive? The brothers hesitate to tell him, fearing that the shock will be too much for the old man. How ironic to hear these brothers, who once deceived their father with the story of Joseph's bloodstained coat, now trying to convince him that his son is actually alive. At first, when he learns the news, he is incredulous ("His heart went numb, for he did not believe them."). Only when he sees the provisions Joseph has sent does his spirit come back to life. Zornberg describes some of the *midrashim* that depict this poignant moment.[50] In one version, a young girl, one of his grandchildren, tells Jacob the news. Her strategy is to impart it so that Jacob will "think it" himself, so that he will not faint or die from the shock of it. So she waits until he is praying, and she "sings to him." Her song does not interrupt his prayer or overwhelm him. It intertwines with his thoughts; it becomes a tool for the reintegration of his life. "She has invited Jacob to re-member a world in which despair and hope, discontinuity and continuity, are interlaced in the poetry of his prayers."[51] This *midrash* conveys the delicate balance between joy and agony in the process of reconciliation. When alienation has persisted for many years, great care is needed to protect the fragile beginnings of the task of reconstructing, "re-membering" a damaged relationship.

There is a buildup of tension as Jacob, the aged Patriarch, travels to Egypt with his entire household. As they approach, we can imagine the atmosphere of high expectation mingled with apprehension. The moment of their meeting is one of the most moving scenes in the entire Torah: *Joseph harnessed his chariot and went up to meet Israel (Jacob) in Goshen. He appeared before him, fell on his neck, and he wept on his neck for a good while.*[52] Commentators have speculated on this passage, noting the ambiguity in the wording *"he wept."* Who wept? Some scholars assume it was Joseph who wept with joy, or with relief that his father was still alive. Others suggest it was Jacob who cried in gratitude to find his long lost son whom he had believed to be dead. A different interpretation notes that when Joseph, arrayed in his royal finery, rode toward his father, Jacob did not recognize him. Joseph was struck by the poignancy of the situation and racked with guilt for having been estranged during all those years. It was Joseph who wept in contrition and remorse.[53]

In the biblical text, what is said between father and son at the moment of their meeting? Jacob's first words are *"Now let me die, since I have seen thy face and thou are yet alive."*[54] How does Joseph respond? He does not reply directly to his father. Rather, the text reads: *And Joseph said to his brothers and to his father's house, "I will go up and tell Pharaoh... that my brothers and my father's house have come...."* Joseph's statement appears to evade the peaks of emotion that would naturally occur at such a moment. We find no elation, no apology or explanation, no expression of regret, no detailed narrative to fill in the gaps of their long separation. Jacob does not berate his son or question him. The text only tells us that *Joseph sustained his father, and his brothers, and all his father's household...* The reconciliation between Joseph and his father illustrates that a painful separation may persist for many years and resolve without confrontation, without digging up old resentments or guilt. The protagonists meet, embrace, and move on with their lives.

At the end of his long and full life, Jacob is reunited with his family. He has lived to see his beloved son as the viceroy of Egypt and to embrace Joseph's sons, the promise of continuity. His final legacy is conveyed in the form of blessings, but these are not blessings in the usual sense. The scene is introduced with the decisive phrase: *And Jacob called unto his sons, and said, "Gather yourselves together, that I may tell you that which shall befall you in the end of days."* [55] Many commentators have struggled to understand the meaning of the verses that follow this statement. Although Jacob intended to reveal the future, he seems to change his mind. What we hear is not a series of predictions or prophetic visions of the future of his family at the "end of days." Instead, he confronts them with vivid descriptions of their most essential characteristics, their weaknesses, untamed impulses, vulnerabilities, and unique strengths. His word portraits highlight their vivid differences and the contrasting personalities of these brothers. How can we account for this strange shift in Jacob's intentions?

Words spoken on the deathbed have tremendous significance, so we must pay special attention to these verses and try to understand them. Of the many and varied interpretations, one has special relevance to the topic of estrangement. Zornberg suggests that at the very moment of revelation, the *Shekhinah*, the Presence of God, departs from Jacob. Suddenly, his vision of the future is blocked, shrouded. He is filled with dread. A kind of existential despair envelops him; he is unsure of the meaning of his life. It is a moment of "dialectical tension" between such crucial alternatives as meaninglessness and coherence, blessing and curse. Jacob's spoken legacy to his sons reflects these tensions.[56]

We can imagine the scene, so full of mixed emotions: a frail yet majestic old man at the end of his life, summoning his strength to speak to his sons for the last time. His enormous family is so unlike its immediate predecessors. The text has told us that each of the Patriarchs, Abraham, Isaac, and Jacob himself, had only one brother. Now there are twelve brothers, each with a distinct and separate personality. How could such a heterogeneous family remain connected? What common agendas would bind them, and what awesome forces would tear them apart? As they face their father for the last time, what are they thinking, and what can they say to him?

Zornberg mines ideas from ancient sources and contemporary literature to uncover the deeper levels of meaning in these verses. She points out that Jacob's sons are also concerned about crucial alternatives. Remembering their urge to do away with Joseph and their subsequent fear of his power, they cannot prove to their father that they will preserve the integrity of the family. In response to Jacob's final words, we can imagine they might say: "Listen, father, for we too must speak…with all our diversity, our extreme differences and conflicts, we too are concerned with the question of coherence." It is the father's acknowledgment of his own anxiety and vulnerability that allows his sons to express *their* uncertainties. And their response, "in turn, leads the father into an articulation of blessing and integration."[57] After all the upheavals and dissonance, there is a sense of closure. The dialogue between generations has been completed. In the end, we know that this family will survive. They will resolve estrangements and generate new ones; some of their offspring will preserve the heritage and others will reject it. They will encounter, at different times and places, the blessings as well as the curses. Near the conclusion of the Book of *Genesis*, God's will has been realized. Jacob can die at peace with himself and his family, thus ending one epoch and beginning another in the history of the Jewish people.

How can the interpretations of these profound events be applied to an understanding of family conflict in our own time, in our own lives? On the surface, there is the narrative, the sequence of events. At a deeper level, we see how each of the participants contributed to the escalation of tensions. We may be tempted to blame one and sympathize with the other. But viewed from a wider perspective, the conflict and its resolution may be seen to have redemptive qualities. If rivalry between brothers can be confronted and resolved, it may lead to an enhanced appreciation of family, a new acceptance of disparate points of view. Some of the protagonists will reinforce their individual boundaries and achieve a healthier sense of autonomy. Others may learn to cherish closeness without fear of being smothered. In every family that has reconciled with an estranged member, each person will experience the process in a different way, a way that reflects his or her sense of self and the family's particular structure and emotional dynamics.

## Concluding thoughts on biblical narrative

We have considered the power of biblical texts to provide new insights for our understanding of family conflicts. Various commentaries have served as our sources. The saga of Adam, Eve, and their sons, the narratives of the Patriarch Abraham and his descendants, these ancient legends provide the raw materials for clarifying the inner workings of a family. The values they express, the laws they are struggling to obey, their sufferings and triumphs – all of these are relevant to families today. Elie Wiesel asks, "What is a Jew?" He responds: "A Jew is someone who feels every blow that ever struck his ancestors. He is crushed by their mourning and buoyed by their triumphs. For they were living men and women, not merely symbols or gods."[58] *Panim*, the Hebrew word for "face," is given in the plural form. Each of us has more than one face: your own and Abraham's, my face and Sarah's. Two brothers in the midst of bitter conflict recall the face of Jacob confronting Esau. A favored son who is envied by his siblings mirrors the face of Joseph in the pit. We identify with them in all their adventures, their struggles, estrangements, and reunions. We may not be aware of it, but every one of us, at one time or another, is called upon to play a part in one of these stories. Am I like Rebecca, rejecting one son and favoring another? Are you like Joseph, evoking your brothers' jealousy and suffering the consequences? The legends and stories told in the Bible and interpreted in the commentaries, all of them reflect us and involve us. In Jewish history, the past is unfolding in the present. All events are linked.

### PART TWO: CUTOFF AND BANISHMENT IN JEWISH LAW

Narratives constitute one significant element in the entire constellation of biblical texts. We have seen how the stories of biblical families continue to reverberate in the dynamics of our own families. Let us turn now to a different type of text and explore its relevance to family conflict. Legal statutes specified in the Torah and elaborated in the Oral Law constitute the foundations for an ethical life; they provide the framework for human behavior and relationships. The Hebrew term for this type of text is *halakhah*, derived from the root meaning to go or to walk. These texts have inspired volumes of commentaries on such family-centered issues as the regulations for marriage and divorce, procedures dealing with succession and inheritance, rituals to be performed at life cycle events, and proper behavior on Shabbat and the holidays. Every social group develops methods to enforce the laws that govern the behavior of its members. Similarly, every religious and ethnic community defines its own boundaries and its criteria for belonging. In the body of Jewish law, one extreme means of enforcing sanctions is to invoke the threat of "cutoff" as the ultimate punishment for unacceptable behavior. We will examine specific *halakhic* texts to see how this idea is applied in a religious framework. Then, we will consider how the notion of cutoff may be transposed to the context of family.

The Hebrew root of the verb to "cut off" is *karet*. The term has different shadings of meaning, depending on the context in which it is used. In the Torah, when it is used to signify the threat of banishment or expulsion, it appears more than twenty-five times. The majority of these references are found in the Book of *Leviticus*. The sanction stated most frequently is to be cut off from one's people, from the community of Israel. Although many of these references apply to rituals that seem primitive and archaic to our modern way of thinking, they had a vital purpose for the Jewish people in ancient times. Their intent was to set the Jewish nation apart from the surrounding pagan world and define the precepts of correct ethical behavior. These laws were the means for transforming *Bnai Yisrael*, the children of Israel, into a holy nation, a community that could aspire to holiness and commune with the Divine Presence. Contemporary observant Jews consider these laws to be eternally valid. Their application is not restricted to a particular period of human history or to primitive people who lived long ago and far away. From the Orthodox point of view, they are relevant at all times and places, for everyone who defines him or herself as Jewish. For others who affirm a link to their heritage but do not identify with Orthodox teachings, these laws remain an intrinsic part of their historical legacy.

Following are examples of some of the biblically defined transgressions that are punishable by banishment from the community.

Failure to have a male child circumcised.
>   *...An uncircumcised male child, the flesh of whose foreskin is not circumcised, that soul shall be cut off from his people; he has broken My covenant. (Genesis 17:14)*

Failure to observe the prohibition against eating unleavened bread on Passover.
>   *...Whoever eats leavened bread from the first day until the seventh day (of Passover), that soul shall be cut off from Israel. (Exodus 12:19)*

Doing forbidden work on the Sabbath.
> ...*Whoever does work on Shabbat is cut off from among his people.* (Exodus 31:14)

Not observing the fast on Yom Kippur.
> *"Whoever does any manner of work and does not observe the fast on Yom Kippur shall be cut off from his people."* (Leviticus 23:28–29)

Using the name of God in vain.
> *"Whoever (willfully) blasphemes the Lord...because he despised the word of the Lord and has broken His commandment, he shall be utterly cut off..."* (Numbers 15:30–31)

Each of these infractions refers to a commandment, a basic fact of life that defines the parameters for belonging to the Jewish community. One thread connects them all: these rules of behavior are the defining characteristics of Judaism. Not to observe them, or to choose to ignore them, cuts one off from the center of one's existence, from the values that give meaning to communal life. What is the significance of this punishment? In biblical times, the enforcement of banishment must have been the worst thing that could happen to a person. The threat of cutoff implied eviction from the community and therefore, from all necessary social support and the means for earning a livelihood. To be cut off was tantamount to death, perhaps worse than death itself, since it inflicted the unbearable anguish of personal shame and public disgrace. In the ancient historical context, banishment was the worst possible calamity. For such sinners, there was no recourse, escape, pardon, or recovery.

A parallel concept calling for banishment is found in other sources of ancient and more recent Jewish literature. The term *herem* was used to indicate the status of a person who was punished because of refusal to obey communal authorities. In the period after exile from the Land of Israel, that is, the sixth and fifth centuries BCE, the term referred to various forms of ostracism, including segregation within the community, banishment, or even death. The significance of the punishment is reflected in the solemnity of the ritual, which took place either in the synagogue before the open Ark or while holding the Torah scroll. "A proclamation was made with the sounding of the *Shofar*, while those present held wax candles which were symbolically extinguished after the excommunication was declared."[59] The person was officially banished and several biblical curses were inflicted on him. The proclamation included a public warning not to associate with the guilty person and concluded with a plea for the welfare of the remaining faithful, thus restoring wholeness after the rift.

One term that appears in ancient documents was used exclusively to denote expulsion from the family. The Hebrew word is *kezazah*, a technical term for a ceremony in which a family severs its connection with one of its members (presumably a man) who marries a person beneath his social rank. The Talmud gives a vivid description of the ritual of *kezazah*: "If one of the brothers married a woman unsuitable for him, members of the family come and bring a barrel filled with fruit and break it in the town square, saying, 'O bretheren of the House of Israel, give ear, our brother so-and-so has married an unsuitable woman and we are afraid lest his seed mingle with our seed. Come and take yourselves a sign for the generations (to come) that his seed mingle not with our seed.'"[60] Thus, the act of cutting off a family member was legally sanctioned if it was carried out for the proper reasons.

**Contemporary models**
Although the *kezazah* ritual fell into oblivion many centuries ago, the practice of banishing those who scorned sacred commandments continued to be observed wherever Jews settled. In the year 1906, the rabbis of Aleppo (a city in what is now Syria) declared a *herem* on "certain scoundrels" in their midst. Following is a portion of the edict, a contemporary application of the ancient expulsion decree:

"*...It is well known how serious is the prohibition against Sabbath desecration, and against eating non-kosher meat in a spirit of defiance...*

*He has cut off himself off from the congregation of Israel. He has no religion at all. He is unfit to give witness, to take an oath, or to do anything.... We shall not permit him to marry any of our daughters. Neither shall we accept his sons for our sons-in-law. We shall not perform any wedding for him. We shall not bury him among the graves of proper Israelites....*"

The edict was signed "with abundant love and peace" by more than thirty rabbis and scholars from the community of Aleppo.[61]

Although the legal force of *herem* has lost much of its original sting, the threat of banishment persists in many cultural and religious contexts. Modern Jewish secular literature contains countless versions of the severing of connections from family and community. One example of a man's radical banishment is found in a Russian novel that first appeared in the 1930s. The following episode from *The Family Mashber*[62] represents a direct application of the biblical edict to a contemporary context.

The setting is Russia in the mid-nineteenth century, a period of intense unrest in the Jewish communities of Eastern Europe. The fallout from the *Haskalah* (Enlightenment) movement was fanning the winds of change throughout the Pale of Settlement. Families were caught up in the current; many people were cut off or lost, seduced by new ideas and eager to escape from the rigid confines of religious obligations. The opening chapters of the novel give us vivid depictions of a Jewish village and its inhabitants. We encounter devoutly religious, poverty-stricken families struggling to survive. One prosperous, proud family suddenly faces bankruptcy and disaster. In the midst of the family stories, we meet a man named Mikhl, a poor teacher. From the descriptions of this man, we feel a sense of foreboding. Mikhl is on the brink of a momentous decision, an event that will transform his life and the life of his family. On the eve of the Sabbath, he enters the rabbi's house carrying his *tallit* (prayer shawl), the garment in which pious Jews pray, the garment they wear to be married and to be buried. He pushes his way into the rabbi's presence and states his intention to renounce his Jewish identity. To emphasize his words, he commits a radical, shocking act: he takes the garment from under his arm and puts in down on the table. "I renounce it in life and I renounce it in death. I do not want to be buried in it when I die." Then he leaves the house.

The rabbi and his followers are stunned. It's like a "bolt of lightning on a sunny day." "Gone out of his mind!" cries one. "Evil one!" yells another. His act is "worthy of the Great Ban!" He has forsaken the covenant, turned his back on God.

The tragic events that follow this scene are interpreted by the villagers as punishments from heaven, echoes of ancient forms of banishment. One by one, his students stop coming to study with him. Without money, his family has no food. Winter comes and there is no heat in the house. An epidemic strikes the town and his two sons are among the first to be struck down. There is no money for burial expenses, and no one will take the boys' bodies to their graves. Mikhl's wife, distracted by grief, accuses her husband of murdering his children. The community views his troubles as the deserved outcome of his decision to renounce his Jewish faith.[63]

Mikhl's scandalous act and its consequences are not simply a fictional account of an imaginary happening. In many epochs of our history, a person who refused to obey the commandments and renounced his Jewish identity could suffer the ultimate punishment: isolation and banishment. Remnants of these ancient sanctions adhere to the present day and erupt in family conflicts. We see the pattern when a rebellious daughter is deprived of support, or a beatnik is cut off by his siblings. The ancient rules still apply: to ignore expectations or disregard the family's values may lead to grave consequences. The man who takes revenge on his peevish mother-in-law by refusing to speak to her, the woman who severs all contact with her heartless brother – these families are repeating patterns that have been used for centuries as the punishment for unacceptable behavior.

The themes of family conflict that are depicted in the biblical legends continue to resound across the generations and reverberate in our own families. We will explore the consequences of favoring one child over another, failing to acknowledge a gift, provoking enmity between siblings, and sustaining grudges in the family's sticky web. We will hear echoes of *herem* and *kezazah* in the strident voices of family members who renounce and banish their own relatives. Each of us carries the legacy of the original patriarchal family. Forever we repeat patterns that are familiar and obvious, remote and unknowable. In the lives of families, manifold links connect past and present. The ancient themes will continue to resonate in the future.

# CHAPTER FOUR

# Images of Family Conflict in Secular Literature

## Prelude

Stories of family conflict appear in virtually all forms of literature – in novels, plays, poems, diaries, biographies and autobiographies, in fiction and non-fiction. The topic has inspired writers to recollect, imagine, and elaborate on an endless variety of plots. Through these narratives we, the readers, are able to enter the inner space of other families, families that may be very different, and sometimes remarkably similar, to our own. We see how the disputes originate and we can follow the sequences as they resolve or persist. We come to know the protagonists and how they are perceived by others in the family. As we become acquainted with their foibles and their passions, we discover that certain personality types are likely to aggravate existing tensions or stir up new hostilities. The wicked stepmother, the scapegoat, the prodigal, and the eccentric: these are only a few of the characters who take on the role of villain or victim in many novels and memoirs. The portraits are vivid representations of real men and women. The stepmother mirrors the woman who is habitually critical and carping; she meddles and needles to get her own way. The scapegoat is the passive, deviant person who absorbs the anxieties and animosities of others. The prodigal is the separatist who repudiates the norms, breaks away from the family, and eventually returns. The eccentric is the unpredictable, erratic relative who keeps the family off balance, like a volcano giving off smoke and fumes. Many of these stories reflect familiar themes; the protagonists display characteristics and behaviors we may see in our own families, perhaps even in ourselves.

Part One consists of a sampling of narratives from a wide spectrum of literary works. They represent different periods, cultures, writing styles, and literary genres. Although they are considered to be fiction, that is, imaginary versions of people and situations, virtually all of them were influenced by the authors' own lives. We meet people who are contending for power, love, possessions, recognition, individuality, or simply longing to be accepted by their most significant others, the family. The vividness of their struggle is enhanced by our awareness that the author is writing about aspects of his or her own experience.

Part Two delineates themes of estrangement as they appear in two contrasting literary contexts: one is a turbulent family situation depicted by more than one biographer; the other is an autobiography by a rejected son. These narratives are explicitly non-fiction. They portray real families and actual people.

In presenting these stories, I have tried to preserve each author's style and emphasis, but the process of retelling invariably implies the inclusion of my own point of view. I have selected stories to highlight particular themes and roles in the process of family conflict. The first example describes the tensions that erupt when the younger generation rejects parental values and cuts off from the roots of the family.

PART ONE: FICTION AND DRAMA

## 1. Generation gap and the erosion of family values –
## Sholem Aleichem: *Tevye the Dairyman*

The author known as Sholem Aleichem is most famous for preserving the flavor and atmosphere of Jewish communities in Eastern Europe in the late nineteenth century. His stories resonate with the warmth and humor of family life in the *shtetl*. But they also confront more ominous realities: the splintering and eventual deterioration of those communities in the wake of the Jewish Enlightenment. The fictional travails of Tevye the Dairyman, originally written in Yiddish, translated into English, and later converted into the musical drama *Fiddler on the Roof*, portray various patterns of generational conflict in the life of one Jewish family.[1] The author introduces us to Tevye's seven daughters, or six, or five; the actual number is not clear. Four of the daughters serve as the focus of the upheavals in these stories. Each daughter's choices represent a crucial issue in the breaking away and eventual estrangement of the younger generation from their parents in the *shtetl* culture. While the generational conflict is at the core of these stories, the author uses Tevye's family tragedy to highlight the tremendous political and societal unrest that characterized that period in Jewish history. The yearning for a better life and the first taste of emancipation in many Jewish communities fueled the fires of ambition in countless young people. The resulting battles with their traditional parents and the subsequent alienation of one generation from the other became the predominant reality in the lives of Eastern European Jewish families.

Tzeitel, the first daughter to reach marriageable age, refuses to accept her father's choice of husband and marries a man she herself has chosen. This is a radical break from tradition. Tevye talks to himself:

> "…Well, go argue with today's children!… You can slave for them, you can knock your head against the wall, – they still think they know better than you do…"

Hodl, the second daughter, is "too well-educated." She can write and read Russian as well as Yiddish. She, too, chooses her own mate, a Jewish revolutionary who has passionately embraced the new politics. He is exiled to Siberia. She goes to join him. Tevye sighs, "She's lost and gone forever…"[2]

Chava is the daughter who "marries out." When she chooses a

local, non-Jewish mate, she is bitterly denounced and disowned by her parents. She tries to persuade her father to understand her decision: "But why did God give us brains if we're not supposed to use them?" Tevye replies, "You know, we Jews have an old saying that when a hen begins to crow like a rooster, off to the slaughterer she goes..." Tevye is desperately anxious to prevent the wedding, but the priest performs the ceremony and Chava has taken the drastic step of crossing the religious boundary. Tevye trudges wearily home to his wife: "Get up, woman! Take off your shoes and let's prepare for the seven days of mourning." He tells her to forget about Chava; they will never see her again.

Chava has moved out of Tevye's frame of reference. She has rejected the dependable, familiar religious sphere of her parents and substituted a foreign orbit in which all values and priorities will be radically transformed. In a traditional Jewish *shtetl* family, this kind of rebellion was seen as catastrophic, an incomprehensible break with tradition. To Tevye, the traditional father, none of his daughters' motives makes sense. In many families like his, the rifts were never repaired.

The ultimate cutoff, more final and tragic than any of the others is from Shprintze. She is the daughter who falls in love with a young Jewish "millionaire." Ahronchik, or "Arnold," as Shprintze calls him, has come with his mother to a nearby town for a summer holiday. He meets Tevye's beautiful daughter and sweeps her off her poor feet. As soon as he proposes marriage, his mother whisks him away, never to be seen by Shprintze again. She is simply not in his class, not rich enough or important enough. In that social context, it would have been unthinkable for the daughter of a poor cheese monger to marry into a rich, honorable family like Ahronchik's. Utterly defeated by the weight of poverty and the reality of impenetrable class boundaries, Tevye is powerless to help his daughter. Shprintze, discarded and distraught, has thrown herself into the river and drowned.

Each of Tevye's daughters represents a different aspect of the reality of Jewish life in that time and place. The old traditions were beginning to dissolve. Parental values were no longer automatically accepted by the younger generation. The impact of the Enlightenment had affected virtually every Jewish community – like a pestilence, some would say. But for others, especially the younger generation, it was a breath of fresh air. A schism developed between the core of Jews who retained their traditional identity and those who renounced it and joined the majority culture. This was a period of intense turbulence. The family was at the vortex, the center of its highest concentration.

## 2. The sibling bond, severed:
### George Eliot's *The Mill on the Floss*

Countless authors have written about conflicts between siblings. One of the most poignant descriptions appears in the work of the great British novelist, George Eliot. In the summer of 1869, Eliot wrote a poem with the simple title *Brother and Sister*.[3] At that time, she had been estranged from her own brother Isaac for more than ten years. Her poem expresses the author's wistful recollection of the sibling bond. It opens with these words:

> *"I cannot choose but think upon the time*
> *When our two lives grew like two buds that kiss*
> *At lightest thrill from the bee's swinging chime,*
> *Because the one so near the other is."*

The last verse of the poem alludes to their inevitable separation:

> *"...Till the dire years whose awful name is Change*
> *Had grasped our souls still yearning in divorce,*
> *And pitiless shaped them in two forms that range*
> *Two elements which sever their life's course.*
> *But were another childhood-world my share,*
> *I would be born a little sister there."*

George Eliot was nearly forty years old when she began to create her second major novel, *The Mill on the Floss*. She had struggled through various crises of identity and had already become known as an author. Perhaps her inner conflicts are reflected in the various names she gave herself. Beginning as Mary Anne Evans, the name given to her at birth, she transformed herself to Marian and then to Mrs. Lewes, a public statement of her commitment to George Lewes, the editor of a prominent literary journal. Lewes was unable to obtain a divorce from his wife, but he and George Eliot lived together as man and wife for many years. Their illicit arrangement horrified Isaac Evans, Eliot's only brother, with whom she had sustained a close relationship.[4] In an eloquent letter to Isaac, she tried to evoke his sympathy and begged him to accept her "marriage" to Lewes. The letter was signed "Your affectionate sister, Marian Lewes." It was a valiant effort that proved to be futile. Isaac recoiled from her apparent indifference to his rigid sense of respectability. He forwarded her letter to his "solicitor," who told Marian that she should have obtained her brother's permission to marry. In her response, she admitted that her marriage was not legal, since her husband was not legally divorced from his first wife. This admission became Isaac's justification to banish her from his life. He severed all contact with her. Not satisfied with his own rejection, Isaac exerted pressure on others in the family to break their connection with his sister. Reacting to this cruel rebuff, she assured them that she was not dependent on her family and had no expectation of the slightest favor from them. "With this, she was already distancing herself emotionally from their rejection."[5] Her decision to adopt the name George Eliot, only three years after she became Mrs. Lewes, may have represented a further effort to redefine herself as an independent person with her own separate identity. Perhaps this transformation was a kind of "counter-cutoff," a way to restore her equilibrium after being renounced by her family.

As she began to develop ideas for *The Mill on the Floss*, George Eliot was immersed in thoughts of disaster. Her notes contain references to vivid details of "bridges swept away, houses flooded, fields submerged."[6] In the first long section of the novel, entitled "Boy and Girl," we meet Maggie and Tom Tulliver, the sister and brother whose close attachment resembles the sibling bond between George Eliot and her own brother Isaac. The emergent rupture between Maggie and Tom in some ways parallels the emotional storm that engulfed the author and Isaac. Many situations in the novel have roots in Eliot's own history, but none are more moving than the conflict between the siblings.

In the saga of the Tulliver family, George Eliot uses the terrible force of a storm to dramatize the outcome of Tom's decision to banish Maggie. The blinding rain, the vicious winds, and the culmination of the flood provide the context for the tragic climax in the estrangement of the siblings. Here is the sequence:

Maggie has "sinned" by allowing herself to be lured into a compromising situation with the fiance of her own beloved cousin. They have gone off on a boat ride and are caught in the strong current on the river. When they finally return, their escapade is condemned as scandalous, especially by Maggie's brother. It seems that his sense of righteousness is mortally wounded by his sister's outrageous act. Just as George Eliot's own brother cut her off when her behavior upset his sense of propriety, Tom angrily disowns Maggie when she ignores his values. Maggie is remorseful, wanting desperately to repent and blot out the event. But Tom is steadfast in his refusal to forgive her.

> Maggie entreats Tom: *"I am come back to you – I am come back home, for refuge, to tell you everything."* Tom: *"You will find no home with me…. You have disgraced us all. You have disgraced my father's name. You have been a curse to your best friends. You have been base, deceitful. I wash my hands of you forever… You shall not come under my roof… the sight of you is hateful to me…"*[7]

Driven from her childhood home, cast out by her brother, Maggie seeks shelter with a neighbor. A torrential downpour threatens to flood the banks of the River Floss. The storm gathers momentum and erupts in a relentless deluge of water and wind, inundating the fields, the houses, sweeping away everything in its path. Maggie finds a boat and goes to rescue her brother, but the final catastrophe is an expression of "damage beyond repair." The tragic drowning of Maggie and Tom is the culmination of the cutoff between them. Only in the last moments of their lives are they reconciled.

> *The boat reappeared – but brother and sister had gone down in an embrace never to be parted: living through again in one supreme moment the days when they had clasped their little hands in love, and roamed the daisied fields together.*
>
> *One tomb was erected for two bodies that were found in close embrace... The tomb bore the names of Tom and Maggie Tulliver, and below the names it was written: "In their death they were not divided."*[8]

George Eliot titled the last chapter of *The Mill on the Floss* "The final rescue." We can speculate why she used the word "rescue" to describe the desolate reconciliation between Maggie and Tom. Did she intend to emphasize the notion of recovery from anger and blaming? Rescue from long years of estrangement? The story moves us to wonder about the countless other estrangements, in real life and in literature, that end only with the death of one or both of the protagonists.

Two years after George Lewes died, George Eliot married John Cross, a respectable widower. At that time, she received the first communication from her brother since he had cut her off more than twenty years before. Now he wrote a note of congratulations on her marriage. He spoke of "the present opportunity to break a long silence which has existed between us" and signed the note "Your affectionate brother." It was May in the year 1880. Eliot was sixty years old and one of the three most famous women in England, along with Queen Victoria and Florence Nightingale.[9] Her reply to Isaac was brief, expressing "great joy" to hear from him, and saying "our long silence has never broken the affection for you which began when we were little ones." It seemed that in that letter, she was retrieving earlier memories, echoes of the "Brother and Sister" poem, recalling those indelible images of the two playing together and her admiration, perhaps even worship, of her older brother. A few months later, Eliot became ill and, in December of the same year, she died. Her biography does not refer to any meeting or further communication with her brother. He was among the family mourners at the cemetery, a bleak moment of farewell.

The connection between siblings is one of the most enduring and most vulnerable of all human ties. Brothers and sisters, sharing the same parents and home environment, are exposed to the same values, assumptions, and beliefs. Yet this sibling who is so like me is, ineluctably, "not-me." There is sameness as well as difference, intimacy as well as distance, and neither of these opposite positions can be overcome. This is the paradox, the tension that lies at the heart of the sibling relationship.[10] Despite this paradox, or perhaps because of it, this relationship offers valuable opportunities for individual growth. Within the protected environment of home, where most children can depend on the care and protection of their parents, siblings can experiment with countless roles and behaviors. A sister can battle with her brother, smother him with love, ignore him, threaten, tease and bully him, but he will remain her brother. In most cases, the relationship will withstand all of these onslaughts. In the course of growing up in a family, we can see at first hand the different behaviors and emotions that are expressed by a brother or sister. We can learn to respect our sibling's peculiarities as well as his or her strengths and special skills. Living with a sibling can teach us to value the other person as other, different from oneself, with separate rights and privileges.

The sibling relationship also harbors the potential for vicious animosity. The same paradox, the intertwining of similarity and difference, can provoke fierce rivalry and unrealistic expectations. Bitter battles are waged when siblings compete for their parents' favor, or when one requires the other to conform to his or her values. Contrasted to the opportunities for growth in this relationship is the possibility of fragmentation. Some of the worst-case scenarios emerge when resentment builds up and persists, sparking tensions that reverberate throughout the family. The relationship between Maggie and Tom Tulliver, and between George Eliot and her brother Isaac, provide vivid examples of this pattern.

**3. The role of the scapegoat:**
*Harry Potter and the Sorcerer's Stone*
Scapegoating is an ancient practice of sacrificing people or animals for the well-being of the community. It appears in myths and stories from diverse cultures thousands of years old. As in other basic narratives, the plots describe actual practices and rituals that had crucial significance within a given group. The scapegoat served as a symbolic repository for evil forces. By the act of casting off that repository, the community was cleansed of its sins. In early Judaism, the scapegoat was chosen by the High Priest in Jerusalem for a special ceremony on Yom Kippur, the Day of Atonement. After the priest laid his hands on the goat and confessed the sins of the community, the goat was sent into the wilderness and forced to leap over a cliff to his death. In other cultures, the animal was banished, left to his own fate. This symbolic ritual served as a powerful message to the people that their sins had been forgiven.

In the context of contemporary life, the notion of scapegoat usually refers to a person who is held guilty for something he did not do. He is the innocent victim of another's accusation. Family therapists have noted that the phenomenon of scapegoating appears in many troubled families.[11] Typically, two people attempt to avoid conflict by projecting their problems onto another member of the family. It is a perverse form of a triangular relationship: two people ganging up on the third. The scapegoat is likely to be a person who is weaker or smaller, the easiest target for abuse, blame, and guilt. Often he is a misfit, someone who is different from the rest of the family: it could be a sickly, shy, or mischievous child, or a father who is vulnerable and ineffectual. In some families, a handicapped member is "chosen" as the scapegoat. Because of the extra care he requires or the burdens she places on them, that person may become the target for many of the family's complaints. What is the family dynamic that emerges in this kind of situation? The scapegoated person and the other members of the family maintain a kind of equilibrium that protects them from confronting and resolving the real problems. If the scapegoat does manage to separate herself from the rest of the family, the others will be likely to resort to all sorts of threats and enticements to bring her back into the fold so the status quo can be maintained. Harry Potter, a child who was "different," became a perfect choice for scapegoat in the family of his hostile, prejudiced aunt and uncle.

The adventures of Harry Potter, a series of fantasy books that have become best sellers in the world market, emerge from an atmosphere of acrid hostility in Harry's family. On the first page of the first volume,[12] we learn about the background of the cutoff between Harry's parents and the Dursleys, his wicked aunt and uncle. The Dursleys had everything they wanted, but they also had a secret, and their greatest fear was that somebody would discover it. It would be unbearable if anyone found out about the Potters. Mrs. Dursley was Mrs. Potter's sister, but they had been estranged for several years; in fact, Mrs. Dursley pretended she didn't have a sister, because… What was the awful secret that compelled Mrs. Dursley to reject her own sister? The Potters were "as unDursley-ish as it was possible to be." In other words, they were different, deviant; the Potters were… witches! And what about Harry? His aunt and uncle knew that the Potters had a small son, but they had never even seen him. So it was with a horrified scream that Mrs. Dursley discovered the baby Harry on her doorstep one morning. He had been orphaned by the sudden deaths, actually the murder of his parents, and without warning, he was thrust into the household of his spiteful aunt and uncle. All of Harry's subsequent adventures are played out on the background of this family who hated, feared, abused, and ostracized him.

The descriptions of the Dursleys' outrageous rejection of their nephew, the exaggerated attention they lavish on their own pudgy, spoiled son, and their abhorrence of the deviance, the "otherness" of the Potters provide us with a vivid picture of the explosive force of a cutoff in a certain type of family system. The characterization of Harry is a perfect example of a scapegoat who, thanks to his ingenuity and special talents, manages to extricate himself from the family's sticky web.

### 4. The role of the prodigal

In narratives of fragmented families, the image of "prodigal" refers to a specific pattern of alienation. The stories describe cutoffs between people who are related by birth or choice, people who were originally attached to one another by ties of blood or emotional commitment. According to the classical model, the prodigal's journey consists of four distinct stages: departure from home and family, riotous living in a distant place, reaching a low point, and return. Typically, the hero rebels against his father or someone who represents the father. His rejection of conventional values is seen as a perverse act, a "fall" from some kind of grace rather than a well-intentioned mistake.[13] In the Christian frame of reference, the primary source for the story of the prodigal son appears in the New Testament.[14] Later Christian writings typically depict the prodigal as a sinner who "leaves the fold" and abandons his religious origins. His evil qualities are exaggerated to serve as a warning so others will not be tempted to follow in his path. When he returns, full of remorse and determined to lead a moral life, his repentance is greeted with joy and gladness. Variations on the prodigal theme are depicted in contemporary Christian literature in a wide spectrum of contexts including prayers, poems, hymns, and anecdotal records.[15]

Versions of the prodigal story also appear in secular writings. A person leaves his parents or his spouse; he gives up the familiar routine of everyday life to explore distant places and experiment with different lifestyles. The stories are situated in a variety of socio-economic settings and reflect diverse aspirations. In some versions, a poor boy sets out to make his fortune. Or, the daughter of a rich man decides to abandon the easy life and devote herself to helping the poor. Applying the Freudian theme of the Oedipal conflict to the prodigal's rebellion, one writer suggests that "the son wishes his father were dead, and acts as if he were dead in order to create an independent existence and an autonomous identity for himself."[16]

A depiction of the prodigal appears in Hebrew literature. In a parable recounted in the Talmud, a father is obliged to banish his sons because of their rebellious behavior. The estrangement is unavoidable, the necessary act of a father who must punish those whom he loves. The deed done, the father now sits alone, mourning his loss, while his children wander in exile, bereft of their home and family. In this story, the father figure is a symbolic representation of God and the sons are the Children of Israel. In Rabbinic writings, the story serves as a metaphor for the transformation of Jewish life after the destruction of the Second Temple, to emphasize the depth of God's suffering for the exile He has had to impose on His people.[17]

What of the prodigal who never returns home? In some versions, he continues on his way, his behavior gradually deteriorating to crime, drunkenness, and debauchery. Or, she may try to return and be rebuffed; her repentance may not be accepted. In one variant of the prodigal, a wealthy son returns to his impoverished parents who, envious of his success and enraged at his independence, murder him.

Some of the stories emphasize the joy of the reunion, when the prodigal is forgiven and the family unit is restored. Others, however, end on a sour note. Even though the prodigal returns, the family will be forever scarred by the painful memories of the rupture.

These two roles, the scapegoat and the prodigal, appear with variations in the real life narratives of many fragmented families. In each example, the enactment of the role highlights specific needs in the family and represents a particular position in the dynamics of family life. In the first chapter of this book, we discussed the distinction between a family member who cuts himself off from the others and the one who is cut off or banished from the family. The scapegoat is cut off by the others, degraded, turned away, neglected, or abused. He absorbs the frustrations and hostility of other family members, thus allowing them to behave "as if" everything was normal. But the underlying problems persist; they are not confronted or resolved. In the case of the prodigal, he or she actively cuts off from the family. She moves out of the familiar orbit and goes to seek her fortune or discover her "real" self. Often she leaves anguish and guilt in her wake. If she returns, the family may not be willing to accept her, or they may receive her with mixed emotions. The following section describes a short story in which a prodigal daughter tries to go home, but fails.

## A prodigal's story:
### *Louisa, please come home,* by Shirley Jackson

In response to a story she wrote and published in *The New Yorker* in 1948, Shirley Jackson received thousands of letters from readers, some bewildered, others fascinated, many outraged. Among them was her mother, who wrote: "Dad and I did not care at all for your story… Why don't you write something to cheer people up?"[18] The comment was typical of Mrs. Jackson's attitude toward Shirley, an attitude that had significant impact on the younger woman's life. The story was *The Lottery*, which became one of the most famous short stories of the twentieth century. It aroused more intense reactions that any other similar work, before or since. Apparently, the harrowing narrative reached down to a core of dread that most people manage to repress. Shirley Jackson was capable of exposing raw emotions in her writings. She did it again in a less well-known story, *Louisa, Please Come Home*.[19] The narrative tells of a young woman who leaves home and cuts herself off from everything familiar and known. The conclusion has the jolt of many of Jackson's stories: it is shocking, visceral; it shatters conventional expectations. In this story, we see how a "normal," unexceptional family reacts to the return of a prodigal. A biography of Jackson provides some clues for interpreting this story.[20]

Born nine months and one day after her parents' high-society wedding, Shirley Jackson was not the daughter her mother wanted. A restless, difficult child – brilliant, messy, gawky, and overweight – this is how she is portrayed. During Shirley's adolescence, her mother told her that she was the result of a failed abortion, born too soon after her parents' wedding, an inconvenient happening, a misfit in the family. At times, Shirley was disturbed, depressed, manic, emotionally volatile, a free spirit. But she could also be warm, devoted to her children, a wonderful mother, an adoring wife. All of these descriptions omit the most significant element: she was a splendid storyteller. For Shirley, writing was a passion. It was an essential part of her life.

From early childhood, Shirley was obsessed with books, reading, absorbing ideas, and writing about them. Her parents had no interest in literature. It seemed that Shirley was everything her mother did not want her to be. But despite the tensions in their relationship, a stubborn love persisted between them throughout their lives, along with the anger, pain, hatred, and lack of forgiveness. Her mother's contemptuous reaction to *The Lottery* was typical, reflecting an attitude that characterized the relationship between these two women. In the story of Louisa, the theme of being unacceptable is sounded and then embellished with a twist that turns a homecoming into a nightmare.

Shirley Jackson's mother could boast of an old, distinguished American heritage. Some of her ancestors had fought in the Revolutionary War and helped to design the city of San Francisco. Geraldine Jackson was terribly conscious of where she had come from and where she was going. She longed to be admired for her social position and wealth, two values that Shirley disdained. Extremely vain and determined to project an elegant public image, she was constantly critical of Shirley's unkempt appearance, her unconventional behavior, her school failures, her obsession with writing. Shirley's father supported his wife's ambitions, became wealthy and successful, and provided the proper setting for her parties and social climbing. Shirley grew up as an outsider in her own family. Much later, her own daughters spoke of the "terrible resentment" their mother felt toward her parents, especially her mother. Geraldine had "squashed her," Shirley's older daughter said, "crushed her spirit."[21] One way she punished these superficial, arrogant parents was to flunk out of school again and again. But the most outrageous expression of Shirley's rebellion from her upper class WASP, anti-Semitic family was her marriage to a Jew from Brooklyn. When Shirley married Stanley Hyman, an equally brilliant maverick, her furious parents refused to attend the wedding and threatened to ostracize her. A similar reaction occurred on Stanley's side of the family. His Orthodox father declared his son "dead" for marrying a *shiksa*, (non-Jewish woman) and "sat *shiva*," (traditional mourning ritual), vowing never to see him again.

Shirley's life took many sharp turns and twists, culminating in her early death. I have presented some of the details from her biography as an introduction to her short story, *Louisa, Please Come Home*. Shirley Jackson's literary achievements can by no means be reduced to her own life story. Her novels and short stories are replete with imaginative details and perceptive insights, especially when she describes the forms of evil that can prowl in a person's life. The story of "Louisa" mirrors some of the agony in her own life, but it is also a prime example of her extraordinary literary imagination. It provides us, her readers, with a remarkable variant of an estrangement. The ending is a moment of high drama, a combination of a tug at the heart and a kick in the gut.

As the story begins, Louisa is speaking: "My mother's voice came over the radio; it frightened me badly for a minute. 'Louisa,' she said, 'Please come home. It's been three long, long years since we saw you last; Louisa, I promise you that everything will be all right. We all miss you so. We want you back again. Louisa, please come home.'"

We learn that Louisa left home the day before her sister's wedding. It was the 20th of June, and the date became a kind of milestone for her, almost like a birthday. She speaks in a matter-of-fact tone. "I always knew I was going to run away sooner or later, and I had made plans ahead of time…" There is a broad hint of a strained relationship with her sister Carol. Did Louisa intend to spoil the wedding? Carol would suspect her of stealing some of the wedding gifts. What kind of family is this? Why did Louisa always know she would run away? Perhaps there was no real connection from the beginning.

Paul, the boy next door, had been an accomplice for Louisa's mischievous pranks. At the very moment she left home, Paul appeared, tagged after her and wanted to go along, not knowing of her intention to "run away." To evade him, she jumped on a bus going downtown, bought a round-trip ticket to confuse any subsequent investigation, and off she went. She intended to just "fade into the background" and disappear, carrying the return ticket in her pocket as a kind of "lucky charm."

The narrative provides no transition to the next scene and no explanation of where Louisa went or how she got there. Suddenly she is somewhere else, sipping tea with a "Mrs. Peacock" before she goes off to work. The woman is musing about the girl who disappeared from her "handsome, luxurious home." Together they look at the girl's picture in the newspaper. Louisa asks if the girl looks like her, a teasing, rather risky question, but the woman does not see the resemblance. Louisa is a "non-person" whom no one recognizes. Is the old Louisa fading away, evaporating? Perhaps this hollowness reflects Jackson's feelings about herself. Or, is this the way a person feels when she is severing her connections to everything familiar, cutting off from home?

We are offered the details of the story bit by bit, like crumbs dropped along an icy path. There's a bantering tone in Louisa's narrative. She goes to a movie, has a cup of coffee in the train station. This apparently aimless wandering is part of her "plan" to become someone else. We learn that she is nineteen, has dropped out of college, but no, that wasn't the reason she left home. She had wanted to leave for a long time, so her plans had time to ripen, "till I was sure they were foolproof."

Louisa invents a new persona for herself: she takes a new name, decides to be a "girl from upstate with a nice family and a good background." She settles down in Mrs. Peacock's rooming house and begins to weave the tale of her new self and her imaginary family. As she constructs this new person, there is no looking back, no trace of homesickness. One year after leaving home, she goes downtown, buys a new hat, and comes back just in time to hear her mother's voice on the radio: "Louisa," she was saying, "Please come home." Mrs. Peacock commiserates: "That poor woman... They say she's never given up hope of finding her little girl alive someday." Louisa responds by asking if she likes her new hat, a remark that seems to express her detachment from the emotional intensity of the situation.

Louisa is "free," with no thought of going back. But one day, something happens to change her plans. Paul, the boy from next door, was in the City for a brief visit and he passed her on the street. Impulsively, she called his name. Stunned to see her, he convinces her to go home. She begins to wonder if maybe she really does want to return. She allows him to shepherd her back to her hometown, then into a taxi, to her own street, and to the big old white house. As she walks up to the front door, she cries with relief, shudders with anticipation of the homecoming.

What happens when this prodigal daughter comes home? Is she greeted joyfully? Is she punished for her rebellion, condemned for her independence? Has she changed so much that the family doesn't recognize her?

Louisa's sister stares at her, saying nothing. Her mother looks into her face for several moments, then asks, "What is your name, dear?" Her father speaks gently but treats her as a stranger; he seems to suspect that she is an imposter. Is she deceiving them, pretending to be their long-lost daughter? They test her, asking questions that only a member of the family could answer. She knows the correct answers, but they don't believe her. We learn that she is not the first girl to "return" and claim her family. Others have come, other imposters who also knew the correct answers to their questions. (For the reader, it is a moment filled with horror. What if my own family would not recognize me?)

Louisa's family stands together and looks at her, a stranger in her own home. For one heartbreaking moment, she acknowledges her longing to be connected. "I realized that all I wanted was to stay – I wanted to stay so much that I felt like hanging onto the stair rail and screaming…" But immediately, she is aware that they will never accept her. "Go back home where you belong," her father tells her. "Go back to the people who love you," her mother says.[22]

The prodigal returns, but nothing is the same. Now she understands that she can never go home again. Her family does not know her; perhaps they never did. The reader is left to speculate about the meaning of this story. Did Louisa leave home because her true self was never accepted? Because she was never validated? Did Louisa, like Shirley Jackson, suffer from being "squashed" by her family? Did they need her to be someone else, some other girl who would be more attractive, capable, compliant, more like them? The story ends as it began. Louisa has returned to Mrs. Peacock's rooming house and hears her mother's voice on the radio: "Louisa, please come home…"

In all prodigal stories, the central theme is the quest to discover one's "true" self, outside of the family orbit. Ultimately, the journey leads back to the starting place. The prodigal realizes that his efforts have been in vain. Individuation, the task of carving out a separate identity, does not automatically occur when a person exits the family. Authentic selfhood becomes a reality only when one achieves insight and self-awareness. In Shirley Jackson's story, neither Louisa nor her family has changed. She returns, but her parents do not recognize her; they reject her, again. One story of an actual family with a prodigal son, told here in Chapter Eight, describes a different outcome. Several years after Dan Silver cut himself off from his family, he returned home and was embraced by his parents. He did not express new awareness of his role in the family, nor did he wish to discuss the estrangement, but they accepted him on his own terms. We can study these contrasting outcomes to clarify our own emotional response to persons who have been estranged from us. The stories of Louisa and Dan may help us find constructive solutions when we embark on the task of reconciliation.

### 5. Nihilist in the family: Philip Roth's *American Pastoral*

A nihilist is one who advocates total rejection of established laws and institutions. The term refers to the principles of a Russian revolutionary group, active in the latter half of the 19th century, whose members believed that existing social and political institutions must be destroyed in order to clear the way for a new social order. They employed extreme measures, including terrorism and assassination. The term also connotes a kind of "annihilation of the self," as in an extreme form of mystical experience.

In Philip Roth's novel *American Pastoral*, we are introduced to a "half-Jewish" family in which an estrangement between generations leads to a terrifying climax.[23] The main character is the husband and father, Seymour Irving Levov, a blue-eyed blond Adonis, a rare, fair-complexioned Jew in a sea of dark Jewish faces in Newark. He is a sports hero in his predominantly Jewish high school. They call him "the Swede," and wherever he goes, everyone loves him. He marries a beauty queen, Catholic, wholesome, a stereotype of Americana. She is the beautiful Dawn Dwyer, Miss New Jersey, a music student who was catapulted into the public eye in the Miss America contest. She loses the contest but wins the Swede. They are a "knockout couple." She's a lapsed Catholic; he's an assimilated Jew. Together they go to live on a farm, intending to create an idyllic rural life. Instead, they raise a monster. Their only daughter Merry grows up to despise them and reject everything they stand for. Despite an apparently near-perfect set of parents who adore her, who lavish love, attention, and material comforts on her, she turns into a rebel and a murderer. No one could have predicted her transformation from an affectionate, compliant, bright child to a sullen, fanatical, political terrorist. In the midst of this awesome sequence of events, the "fortification" that was their family falls apart, never to be repaired.

Philip Roth is a second-generation American Jewish novelist who has struggled to come to terms with his own identity. Detailed descriptions of his ambivalence appear in numerous biographies, reviews, and in Roth's own autobiographical writings. Many of the nefarious, warring demons that lurk in the dark corners of his religious odyssey emerge in glaring light on the pages of his literary works. Merry is one of his demons. *American Pastoral* depicts fragments of events that may have haunted some of his own nightmares.

"And what is wrong with their life," Roth asks at the book's conclusion. What led to the demise of this family? Why did this "golden child" trash her own future and her parents' hopes? These are her father's tormented questions, and ours. Early in the novel, Roth anticipates the climax: The Swede wakes in middle age to the horror of self-reflection. Until Merry's disappearance, he had lived a sane, normal life. He had formed himself into a person who "gets rid of the traditional Jewish habits and attitudes, who frees himself of the pre-America insecurities and the old, constraining obsessions so as to live unapologetically as an equal among equals." He had become the embodiment of the Emancipation from the *shtetl*; he had escaped from all the old banishments, segregations, and persecutions. The Swede had made himself into a perfected version of his own father. And grandfather. But his daughter had no intention of following his example. Merry would *not* become a respectable, "perfected" version of her parents, the next-generation, successful Levov. Instead, this daughter would catapult him "*out of the longed-for American pastoral, into everything that is its antithesis and its enemy, into the fury, the violence and the desperation of the counterpastoral – into the indigenous American berserk.*"[24]

The story comes to a terrifying climax with the Swede's frantic search for Merry. He has followed one false lead after another and finally, after months of futile hunting, he finds his daughter. The description is almost too painful to read. A murderer wanted by the police, she has been fleeing from one hideous place to another, raped, starving, obsessed by cultic rituals, barely surviving in a filthy hovel with no toilet, surrounded by garbage, broken glass, bits of discarded furniture, the thudding of traffic overhead, hundreds of trains roaring and shrieking, drunks and vagrants sprawling in dark corners of the alley. It is a terrible scene. Her father barely recognizes his shriveled, stinking daughter. He confronts her, alternating shouts with weeping, questions with threats. There is no way he can understand what has happened to her or how their lives have been wrecked. In this scene, we see evil itself, the antithesis of the Jewish image of *shalom bayit*, peace in the home. We see a home ravaged by this family's emotional chaos.

What is wrong with their life? Perhaps the closeness in the family was too suffocating for Merry. Or maybe her mother, the beauty contest winner, should not have nagged her pudgy daughter to lose weight. If they had moved to the city, perhaps Merry would have had more or different friends. If only… but… perhaps – none of these speculations can account for the ultimate catastrophe. Why does this pampered daughter choose such a violent and ultimately self-destructive way to distance herself from her family? Was she infected by tensions that had lurked in the background of her parents' marriage, cross-currents of their different cultural, historical, and religious traditions? Was her self-destructive behavior a reaction to her parents' compromises and denial? Can we find antecedents for Merry's demise in her own family's history?

We know that the nihilist movement in Russia corresponded to the period of the Jewish Enlightenment, the *Haskalah*, the shift that led thousands of Jews to abandon Orthodoxy and embrace a secular way of life. Merry's ancestors, her Jewish father's grandparents, may well have been part of that movement. Perhaps she was acting out a contemporary version of their struggle, even though she did not know their story. We are left with our own questions about the roots of such a tragedy. The author does not provide us with answers, but his narrative compels us, the readers, to ponder some of the issues he raises. In what ways am I reacting to my own history? How can I achieve a separate identity and continue to be connected to my family of origin? How might such a tragedy be averted?

Roth's message is stated in the final paragraph: "…*the breach has been pounded in their fortification… And now that it was opened it would not be closed again. They'll never recover. Every-*

*thing is against them… all the voices from without, condemning and rejecting their life!*"[25] In this novel, the worst-case scenario of a fragmented family is played out in the harshest terms. For the Levov family, there is no reprieve and no reconciliation. Merry, the nihilist, succeeded in shattering the social and emotional order her parents had upheld. By achieving this most radical form of separation, she destroyed them and annihilated her self.

## 6. The eccentric in the short novel by Thomas Wolfe: *A Portrait of Bascom Hawke*

The works of Thomas Wolfe are enduring portraits of a particular type of American culture between the two World Wars: white, Southern, passionately involved with family matters, quintessentially American. Many of the characters in his writings were based on real people: relatives, colleagues, or friends. In his short novel, *A Portrait of Bascom Hawke*,[26] Wolfe provides a vivid depiction of the two sides in an intensely alienated family. This story was written early in Wolfe's career, when he was down on his luck and without money, before fame descended on him. He dug into his pile of accumulated manuscripts, looking for something that he could fashion into a saleable short story.[27] He found a sketch of his uncle, a piece that he had intended to include in "*Look Homeward, Angel*." It had been revised, and became part of an unfinished story of a young man called David Hawke and his uncle, Bascom. A variation of the character of Bascom appeared later in the epic novel *Of Time and the River*, but the drama of his curdled life is filled out only in the work that bears his name.

Thomas Wolfe's own uncle was an "eccentric" who had studied theology at Harvard, became an agnostic, and had an unhappy marriage. At one time, the uncle had written about his own family: "What an unbalanced, lopsided clan we are…"[28] Wolfe's story of Bascom depicts the atmosphere in that kind of family. The reader is introduced to the "cadaverous and extraordinary figure" of Bascom Hawke, presented to us by his nephew, the narrator. With enormous bony hands, horrible grimaces, horse teeth, sneering and pedantic speech, he howls, thunders, snorts, snuffles. He is clothed in an assortment of odd garments, worn, smelly, and ill-fitting. The mark of his madness is plain, but he had been the scholar in his family, "a man of powerful intelligence and disordered emotions." We learn that like many eccentrics, "his thoughts were usually buried in a world of his own creating," in which he was the central actor. Nothing could shake his powerful egotism. His storms of fury, his wild tirades were aimed at those who had questioned the logic of his universe. But he also could evoke the image of nobility: "the great dignity of his head… that bore an astonishing resemblance to that of Emerson…" At rare moments, he gave the impression of grandeur shrouded in a desperate loneliness.

The novel presents detailed descriptions of Hawke's workplace, his co-workers and their impressions of him. His employer vacillates between mocking him and admiring his intelligence. Fleeting images allow us to imagine the personality of Hawke's wife, a rabbit-like woman who was dazed and seduced by the power of his early passion and then overwhelmed by the unreasoning madness of the "black insanity of jealousy" that poisoned their marriage. Until the final pages, there is scarcely any reference to Bascom as a father. From the descriptions of his unpredictable, often brutal reactions to others, we can imagine that his relationship with his children would have been similarly volatile.

After the children grow up and leave home, Bascom and his wife are alone. Bereft of her children, she comforts herself with excerpts from Wagner's operas, her favorite music. In one especially tense scene, Bascom, in a burst of rage, threatens to destroy her tiny gramophone. She is on the verge of attacking him with a carving knife but she stops, horrified. The next morning, she looks at herself in a mirror and asks, "I wonder if I'm going mad." All of this rich detail provides the background for the moment when, as an old man, he reflects on his life: "I have lived so long. I have seen so much. I could tell you so many things…" He feels exposed; "naked as an infant, his spirit cowered in a dreadful kind of shame…" But his "shame" did not include regret for his uncaring, brutal behavior. The upheavals and violent outbursts that characterize his personality create havoc in his family. Ultimately, he is left with his solitude. Here, we find Hawke's only direct reference to the estrangement that has left him alone and forsaken. He is speaking to his nephew:

> "...with an unmistakable note of bitterness in his voice: 'Have you seen any of my... children recently?'
>
> The question surprised me, because he rarely asked about them: most of the time he seemed to have forgotten their existence... I told him that I had seen one of his daughters the week before.
>
> 'My children – basely and damnably... have deserted me!' he growls with bitter passion. Then, quietly, indifferently, as if stating the fact more truthfully and temperately, he says: 'I never see any of them anymore. They never come to my house and I never go to theirs. I do not care... It makes no difference to me... none whatever!' and he dismisses it with his big-boned hand. In a moment he adds: 'Their mother visits them, I believe... whenever she gets invited....'"[29]

Here again, the tone of contempt is evident, as if he holds his wife guilty of some treachery for visiting her own children. But apathy is also in his voice – he speaks of his wife and children as if they are strangers to him, as if their lives barely touched the edges of his world.

Wolfe provides us with a rare look at the "other face" of a cutoff, a glimpse of these adult sons and daughters and how they perceive their father. From the author's vivid prose, we learn that his children cannot forget him nor can they forgive him. Hawke remains mired in their "bitter memory." They review the "painful annals of their childhood" and recall the frustration and the malevolence of their lives under his roof. "...For them, it sometimes seemed the years were passing like bitter water on one wheel of life: the wheel turned and they got older..."[30]

What are these adult sons and daughters saying about the estrangement from their father? They try to dismiss his warped behavior, but he continues to haunt them, to influence the way they think and feel. The conflict between them has not been confronted or resolved. It still lurks in the "bitter water" of their lives. They mimic his mannerisms; they recall "the painful annals of their childhood." Their anger continues to fester, preventing them from separating from him or achieving real individuality. They are attached to him by barbed hooks. He is a ghostly presence, perpetually embedded in the family. As in many families with unresolved estrangements, the protagonists get older but not wiser. Their growth is forever stunted.

### 7. Brotherly love and hate: Arthur Miller's *The Price*

Arthur Miller, one of the great American playwrights of the twentieth century, won the Pulitzer Prize in 1949 for his drama *Death of a Salesman*. His plays have been performed in virtually every major city in the world and read by millions of people. When he was asked how his work relates to events in his own life, Miller replied, "In a sense, all my plays are autobiographical."[31]

Miller was born in New York City in 1915, one of three children in a middle-class Jewish family. His father had immigrated to the United States from a *shtetl* somewhere in Europe. Miller grew up during the period of the Great Depression. His plays invariably focus on family relationships and the ambivalent attachments to immediate kin. He was especially concerned with the issue of responsibility: who cares for whom, and how. *The Price*, first produced in 1968, depicts the interactions between two brothers as they struggle to understand their prolonged estrangement. The title has multiple meanings. On one level, it refers to the bruised, misshapen legacy of the past; the price is their misery. On another level, the price is the payment for doing what is necessary, for following one's instincts or one's heart. This play provides one of the most vivid portrayals of family conflict in contemporary drama. The protagonists are the brothers, Victor and Walter Franz. The other players are Victor's wife Esther, and Gregory Solomon, the appraiser.

The mood is set as the curtain rises on the first scene, a large room in the attic of a dilapidated house. The old furniture is piled up, draped and covered, as if prepared for a move. Victor enters, dressed in his policeman's uniform. He puts a record on the old phonograph and listens, laughing, to the wild hysteria of the *Laughing Record*. His wife Esther enters. From their dialogue, we learn that Victor has been estranged from his younger brother Walter since their father's death. "The man hasn't called me in sixteen years." But, as Esther reminds him, the cutoff has two sides: "Neither have you called him..." This is the room where Victor had once lived with his father. Now, he is waiting for an appraiser to look at the family's possessions. These fading household objects serve as an apt metaphor for the deteriorating, moldy family relationships that emerge in the course of the drama.

The opening dialogue reveals the ingredients in the conflict between the two brothers: Victor sacrificed his education for his brother's sake by dropping out of school to take care of their aging father, thus enabling Walter to finish medical school. Now a successful surgeon, Walter is divorced, with two sons who are "investigating the guitar." Victor, the struggling cop, has a brilliant son at MIT and an intact marriage. Esther wants her husband to retire, go back to school, and "better" himself. Victor resists her pushing. Now, Esther is nagging Victor to appeal to Walter: "He's your brother, he's influential; he could help..." Victor replies: "I don't need Walter..."

Victor reminisces over the familiar objects: a radio, phonograph, old clothing, a fencing foil and mask, a lap robe, his mother's gowns, her harp, remnants from the good life when the family was together and prosperous. Gregory Solomon, the appraiser enters. An old man with a pronounced Yiddish accent, he looks suspiciously at the piled-up furniture and asks, "What's all this stuff?" Victor explains that his father moved everything up here after the '29 crash. His uncles took over the house and they let Pop keep one floor. Now the building is to be demolished; Victor must dispose of everything.

The family myth slowly unfolds. Victor, the "good" son, had cared for his father by sacrificing his own aspirations. Walter distanced himself from the family and graduated from medical school. During those years, he contributed five dollars a month to his father's care. Victor reminisces bitterly about his favored younger brother: "Whenever Walter would come to visit our Pa, you'd think *God* walked in…"

At that moment, Walter enters, exuding an aura of success, confidence, arrogance. He jauntily asks Victor, "How are you, kid?" – an obvious insult, since he, Walter, is the younger brother. The consummate businessman, Walter quickly takes stock of the situation and offers Mr. Solomon a deal: the appraiser would offer them a high price, Walter would donate everything to the Salvation Army and take the tax deduction, giving his brother half of the "profit." Esther jumps at the idea but Victor hesitates, remembering old hurts, not wanting to be indebted to Walter for anything.

In the ensuing scene, Walter reveals that he had suffered a breakdown, had been "out of commission" for three years. We do not know if this confession is a manipulative tactic or a sincere attempt to be honest. Walter goes on to reveal other aspects of his life, painful episodes that Victor never knew. Walter sees Victor as the *real* success in the family, a policeman who does his job with integrity, a man with a good marriage and a son who is a brilliant student. He, Walter, the successful doctor, has been a failure as a person, a husband, and a father. With a flash of insight, he realizes that he has been pursuing false idols. He speaks of the "terror" of ambition, the fruitless piling up of money, the emptiness of his life. Once the frozen barrier of their long estrangement has begun to dissolve, Walter admits to his brother that his most awful fear had always been to fail like their father had failed. They recall a terrifying moment from the past, the night their father told them he was bankrupt. Their mother was all dressed up for a party. "He made us all sit down; and he told us the money, the good times, everything was gone. And she vomited all over him." Now Victor realizes the significance of that moment. It was his father's humiliation that compelled him to become the caretaker. By holding on, perhaps he could save the family from falling apart. Victor's mission was to stay close; Walter's was to escape.

But sharing insights with his brother proves to be more than Walter can bear. He reverts to his old role as the successful entrepreneur and offers Victor a job as an administrator in his hospital. Esther leaps at the suggestion, seeing it as the promise of a new, better life. Victor is suspicious, hesitant. Walter starts to leave, feeling rejected by the brother he has tried to help. Esther begs him to stay.

Then, the atmosphere becomes charged with tension as the two brothers confront the reality of their estrangement. They recall their father, sitting in that chair, staring into space. The memories tumble out: the conversation in that room when Walter announced that he would finish school "come hell or high water." Victor's question, "Who the hell was supposed to keep our father alive?" Walter's retort, "Who was he? Some exiled royalty? He could go to work, go on welfare..." They uncover some of the misunderstandings, the lies, the secrets that had piled up and formed the wall between them. In a shocking revelation, they discover that their father had been a "calculating liar." He actually had had enough money; Victor could have had a different life, but his father had belittled his ambitions. At that moment, Victor begins to realize that his aging, dependent father had thwarted his chances for a college education in order to keep him close. Apparently, Walter had always been aware that his father and brother were enmeshed, each one needing the other. Backing off from the intensity of their entanglement, he had managed to extricate himself from the sticky web. Now, in the midst of their confrontation, the edifice of the family myth begins to crumble. Their story shatters and the fragments stab them to the heart.

The moment of truth sounds like this. Walter is speaking:

> *"Is it really that something fell apart? Were we really brought up to believe in one another? We were brought up to succeed, weren't we? Why else would he respect me so much and not you?"*

The scene builds with excruciating tension as Walter exposes the raw nerves of the family. It culminates in his revelation that there was no love and no loyalty in their house, only a "straight financial arrangement. That's what was unbearable…" In this dialogue, there is confrontation but no reconciliation. The brothers exhume some of the most painful, searing issues that led to their estrangement, but they do not resolve, forgive, or repair anything. Victor's insights seem to reach to the core of their dispute. He tells Walter: "I am not your enemy… we're brothers." He sees their lives as intertwined, like "two different roads out of the same trap… It's almost as though we're two halves of the same guy." Two halves – one connected, staying on; the other one separated, liberated from the family. Walter sees that Victor has always resented him. "Vengeance," Walter mutters to Esther, "he is sacrificing his life… to prove what a treacherous son of a bitch I am!" Victor responds by refusing his brother's offer of a job. "I can't work with you, Walter. I don't trust you." With this final rejection echoing in his head, Walter picks up one of their mother's dresses, hurls it in his brother's face, and leaves, slamming the door behind him.

In this family the conflict is not resolved. What remains is only a sense of emptiness, desolation, the eternal repetition of old patterns. As the curtain falls, Solomon the appraiser is sitting alone on the stage, listening to the *Laughing Record* on the old phonograph and laughing with tears in his eyes, howling helplessly to the air. We are left with the impression that the estrangement between the brothers, like countless other real families, will continue to embitter their lives.

What are the central issues in Miller's dramatic portrait of these alienated brothers? On the surface, their dispute seems to have originated in competition for their father's favor and his preference for Walter, the younger son. Tensions were exacerbated by the father's ostensible bankruptcy and his two sons' opposite reactions to it. Victor chose to stay, sacrificing his own ambitions to support his father, not knowing that the old man had enough money to get along without him. Was financial security the central issue, or rivalry for the father's favor? Walter reminds Victor that his yearning to be needed had compelled him to stay home and become the caretaker. Walter was the "emancipated" one. He had opted to escape from the family web, to build his life apart from them. Are they really "two halves of the same guy," as Victor says? No, but they are two different ways to be in a family – one who needs to be attached, the other distant and estranged. In this family, neither of the brothers is content with his choice. Both feel that life has cheated them in some fundamental ways. The weight of the past still presses on them. They cannot get beyond the impasse, nor can they ignore it and move on.

Arthur Miller said that in a sense, all of his plays are autobiographical. A recent biography notes the parallels between the plot of *The Price* and events in Miller's own life.[32] Initially wealthy and secure, the Miller family was abruptly reduced to poverty when their father's successful business collapsed during the Great Depression. Isidore Miller had built one of the largest coat manufacturing businesses in the country, but he had invested heavily in the stock market. Suddenly, he was a pauper. The Wall Street crash and its fallout were the formative events in young Arthur's life. Much later, Miller acknowledged that his longing for success was motivated by the bitter memory of financial catastrophe. The dissonance of conflicting emotions toward his father – contempt and admiration, anger and love – would remain with him forever. This ambivalence surfaced time and again in his plays.

The sibling configuration in the Miller family provided an additional source of tension. Arthur Miller was the middle child, sandwiched between his older brother Kermit and his sister Joan. Arthur worked at various jobs, saved every penny, and went to college. He was nineteen when he "fled his ruined father, his devastated mother, and his sacrificial brother," choosing to pursue an education and his own separate life.[33] Kermit had been a finer athlete, a superior student, and a warm-hearted, more likeable fellow. He was also the one who felt obliged to leave college and help support his father. Arthur walked out on the family, saved his earnings but did not share them, became famous, and was a hero in the eyes of his parents. In many ways, *The Price* holds up a mirror to his life.

Is the Franz family Jewish? Does the play intend to portray family conflict through a Jewish lens, or is this family like any other, with universal patterns of rivalry and partiality? Perhaps they are typical of many immigrant families who must carve out a new identity in a strange land.

Arthur Miller's Jewish identity was always a dilemma. The atmosphere of Jewishness pervaded his early life, but he would persistently deny its influence. None of his three wives were Jewish and he distanced himself from any formal religious affiliation. But his grandparents spoke Yiddish, went to synagogue, and observed religious rituals. His friends and neighbors were all Jewish. Although his parents were not observant, they perceived every world event in terms of its impact on Jews. Before he wrote *The Price*, none of his writings dealt explicitly with Jewish themes and the few Jewish characters in his plays were caricatures. Perhaps this play represented a kind of mid-life crisis for Miller. It was written two years after the death of his father, when he suddenly decided to transcribe a much shorter television drama into a full-length play. Working with feverish speed, he completed the work in less than two months. When rehearsals began, tensions were exacerbated. During the initial preparation, the director, a young Belgian refugee, insisted that it should be a Jewish play. The playwright vehemently disagreed.

Miller's biographer, commenting on *The Price*, noted that, "the play's Jewishness was being consistently fudged by the author."[34] If so, why did Miller place Gregory Solomon, the epitome of the "old-world Jew," at center stage? An astute quipster with a touch of the sage, this old man seems to understand the pathos in the Franz family. Perhaps his presence is intended to make us aware of more fundamental issues. With his Yiddish accent and quaint mannerisms, he is a vivid reminder of past times and places. Despite Miller's denial, Solomon may represent previous generations in the playwright's own family, his grandparents or other relatives who remained in the "Old Country." In that traditional patriarchal culture, a Jewish man's prestige was based on his Torah knowledge and his piety. The father had absolute power and his position as head of the family was rarely questioned. He spoke Yiddish, prayed in Hebrew, studied Talmud, eked out a simple living, and expected his sons to follow his example. When Jewish families came to America, everything changed. To become Americanized, men had to succeed in business and support their families. They would also encourage their children to go farther, do better, excel in ways their fathers could never have imagined. In many cases, the demands of the new, foreign culture had catastrophic effects on the family. The old values lost much of their significance. If religious obligations were seen as an obstacle to becoming a good provider, they were abandoned. Without the daily prayers, rituals, and communal religious activities, there was no reliable anchor. The family in *The Price* reflects this sense of isolation. They seem to be encased in a closed room of their own making.

Many authors have described the plight of immigrant families when the father could not cope with the new realities.[35] He would feel impotent, humiliated, disparaged by his wife and children. The tensions that erupted in such situations led to further chaos: rebellion, despair, and in extreme cases, the demise of the family. Perhaps Arthur Miller was aware that the "crash" of a family could have even more disastrous consequences than a financial setback.

A play depends on dialogue to convey its message. In *The Price*, the central issues are expressed in the words spoken by the brothers. This is the playwright's "gift" to us, the audience: we can hear, feel, and see the perspectives from each side of the conflict. We participate in their thoughts and their emotions; we can empathize with the regret and frustration of one, the rage and despair of the other. Arthur Miller provided production notes for the actors: "A fine balance of sympathy should be maintained in the playing of the roles of Victor and Walter... The production must... withhold judgment in favor of presenting both men in all their humanity and from their own viewpoints. Actually, each has merely proved to the other what the other has known but dared not face."[36] It seems that Miller intended to convey the message that each brother's position was understandable, given the circumstances of their lives and the elements in their individual personalities. Perhaps he was also speaking about himself and his own family.

*The Price* is a valuable resource for clarifying many aspects of family process. If playgoers leave the theater with a heightened awareness of the complexities inherent in the sibling bond and a more realistic perception of their own role in the family system, they will have grasped the essential meanings in this drama.

PART TWO: BIOGRAPHY AND AUTOBIOGRAPHY

Literary critics have produced countless volumes on the topic of biography and autobiography. They address questions of subject, context, intention, and outcome. When they discuss the content of autobiography, they ask: How is it possible to write about one's own life when its conclusion is not known? Can a person be both the subject and the object of the same story, the speaker and at the same time, the one who is spoken about? Autobiography is a narrative of one person's experience or a segment of that experience, told in the first person from a unique point of view and colored by the author's own emotional reactions. For many people, the process of writing is a kind of catharsis, an intense therapeutic experience. An effective autobiography will be able to identify crucial issues in the author's life, clarify their significance, and resolve dilemmas. Biography, the "other face" of life stories, is a version of one person's experience, described by someone who has known that person or has studied her life. The themes he chooses to highlight are a reflection of the author's particular interests and areas of expertise. The ramifications of biography have also been explored in many works of literary criticism. Apparently, the role of "eavesdropper," peering into the lives of others, is tantalizing and productive for authors, scholars, and critics, as well as for ordinary readers.

Narratives of an individual life or family provide useful resources for understanding the process of estrangement. In the following section, we shall see how our topic is depicted in two examples of this genre. The first is a biographical account of an actual family in which estrangement and fragmentation culminated in tragedy.

## 1. The saga of Ethel and Julius Rosenberg

"Family time" is a term used to denote the sequence of family-centered events that reflect such crucial decisions as when to begin to work, when to move away from home, and when to marry. These events are always experienced in a particular historical context. "He got married in the midst of the Depression." "She left home just before the end of the war." In every period and place, family time and historical time are intertwined. Political upheavals, economic reversals, and social ferment will affect how an individual family views itself and its surroundings. In a parallel process, the reactions of persons, families, and groups to historical events can modify their outcome. Family time and historical time are reciprocally related; they influence each other.[37]

The saga of the Rosenberg family provides a vivid illustration of the interplay of family time and historical time: that is, how the experience of one family was profoundly affected by the historical events that impinged on its members. The drama was enacted within the context of a toxic political climate and an intensely hostile family environment. It culminated in one of the most highly publicized political trials of the twentieth century. There are many versions of this story, each written by a biographer with a distinct bias, each utilizing diverse sources of information. The story I will tell was derived from sources that focus on the psychological dimension, the personalities of the protagonists, and the escalation of animosity between sister and brother.

Esther Ethel Greenglass was born in 1915 into a unique setting, an environment more chaotic, crowded, poor, and noisy than any other place in America. Hundreds of thousands of people, mostly Jews, were packed into the Lower East Side of Manhattan. Ethel's family, like most of the others, had emigrated from the "Pale of Settlement" in Eastern Europe, where Jewish life revolved around religious observance and family events. Values were determined by religious laws. Daily life consisted of hard work, diligent study, and clearly prescribed rituals. Many of these families had survived the trauma of pogroms in their own and neighboring communities. They had fled for their lives, abandoning property and leaving aged, sickly relatives behind. Now they found themselves in a new environment with manifold and novel opportunities. By 1915, the Jewish community in New York City was already a vibrant, complex society with its own institutions, language, culture, and political affiliations. The immigrants were becoming increasingly Americanized and every aspect of their lives was in flux. This New World ghetto into which Ethel was born presented its newcomers with a rich concoction of choices, from the re-creation of the traditional *shtetl* culture to the stirrings of American radicalism. Many families quickly abandoned the old values. The New World beckoned. For the Greenglass family, this newfound freedom would lead to disaster.

Ethel was a slight, pale girl with a plaintive expression that gave her the appearance of "ethereal woe."[38] Pictures taken during her last weeks in prison show this same plaintive expression. She was the second child and the only girl in the family. Her baby brother David, "little Dovy," was seven years younger. The Greenglass family did not share in the surge of success that some immigrant families were experiencing in the *goldene medina*, the new, golden land. They were bogged down in the misery of their cold-water tenement, caught in a downward spiral of corrosive, grinding poverty. Ethel's childhood was marred not only by a lack of material security, but also by the absence of emotional warmth and encouragement. Her father repaired sewing machines for the garment factories and barely kept his family from starving. He was perceived as a passive, ineffectual "nebbish." Her mother Tessie was an exhausted, embittered woman, disappointed with her life, clinging stubbornly to her Old World values. From pennies she kept in the cupboard, she paid a rabbi to teach religious texts to the boys, but she refused all of Ethel's desperate pleadings for music lessons. "If God wanted you to study music, He would have made it possible." This was the message Ethel heard from her mother again and again. To Tessie, religious training was the only worthwhile learning for her children. Art and music were "sinful" or foolish.

By the time Ethel entered high school, the friction between mother and daughter had intensified. Everything her mother opposed and ridiculed, Ethel pursued. When Tessie scoffed at Ethel's timidity, the girl competed for parts in school plays. Because Tessie could not read or write, Ethel became a prolific reader. Tessie valued religious observance, so Ethel turned away from Judaism. During her adolescent years, Ethel developed a persona that was a direct contradiction of her mother's values and aspirations. "You'll never get ahead," Tessie warned her; "there's no place in life for arty people," yet Ethel was determined to succeed in her pursuit of a better life. Her brother David, seven years younger, was the only one in the family who attended her performances and gave her encouragement. Excessively dominated by his mother, David formed a tacit alliance with Ethel. During their school years, they were closely attached, each dependent on the other for emotional support. At that time, there was no hint of their subsequent estrangement. But it was David who, many years later, would provide the testimony that led to his sister's execution.

At the age of sixteen, Ethel went to work as an office clerk, joined amateur theatrical groups, and entered one talent competition after another, winning small change with her renditions of Yiddish songs. It was during this period that Ethel began to be inflamed with righteous indignation over the pitiful salaries and intolerable working conditions of people she encountered every day. When she was nineteen, she organized a walkout of female workers in her office. Their protest succeeded in shutting down the business. During the next few years, she developed a reputation as a union organizer and activist. Her zeal seemed to be fueled by a powerful inner energy. When she met Julius Rosenberg, an intense young man with similar radical leanings, she had found the man of her dreams.

In the late 1930s, before the United States entered the Second World War, the American Communist Party had reached the acme of its power, claiming more than 100,000 members.[39] Few liberal organizations were without a significant Communist presence. It was the year 1937 in New York City when Julius and Ethel Rosenberg fell in love. Two years later, they married. A few months after their wedding, Julius joined the Party. Ethel had fallen in love not only with a man, but with the excitement of the movement. Before meeting Julius she had been peripherally involved; now, her commitment took on new intensity. Together they would change the world. During the first years of their marriage, both Ethel and Julius were passionately immersed in each other and in their political activities. One of their biographers described the mood of the time: "The flush of radicalism, the emotional high of purposeful activity, the sense of accomplishment and sacrifice for the good of humanity, the work with fine and noble comrades, the love affairs with those sharing a common vision, the expectation that the future was indeed theirs, created a honeymoon effect for most young Communists."[40] At that period and place, the American Communist Party mirrored the larger society, and particularly the Jewish culture from which most of its New York, college-educated members came. The Party values seemed to capture the imagination of these excitable young people, most of them first-generation immigrants who were eager to carve a place for themselves in the American scene. The Jewish yearning for freedom and political equality matched the Communist ideals of power for the working class. Ethel never officially joined the Party, but she attended meetings and served Julius as a "right-hand man" in his work for the "cause." Just as the Talmudic scholar was always male, so was the Marxist. "All the best radicals came out of the Yeshiva."[41] The zeal of the Rosenbergs blinded them to the realities of the "witch-hunt" that was being galvanized all around them. Ten years before she and Julius were arrested for allegedly stealing the secret of the atomic bomb, the FBI had apparently established a file on Ethel Rosenberg. But during the early years of their marriage, they were too immersed in each other and in the movement to recognize the dangers, or to care.

In March of 1943, Ethel gave birth to their first son, Michael. The *brit mila*, the Jewish ritual of circumcision and naming, was held eight days later. Ethel's father Barney was given the honorary role of *sandak*, the person who holds the baby during the ceremony. Also present were Ethel's brother David and his young wife Ruth, who had been married a few months before. At that joyful event in the life of the family, no one could have guessed that it would be David, "little Dovy," who would incriminate Ethel in the crime of treason.

The period immediately following the war was marked by a rising tide of public opposition to the American Communist Party. The U.S.-Soviet alliance that led to the defeat of Nazi Germany had started to erode as soon as the war was over. The Soviet Union's aggressive policies in Eastern Europe and its brutality toward dissident individuals and groups aroused strong emotions among those Americans who were ready to believe the worst about Communism. Just before the 1946 elections, the Republican Party distributed more than half a million copies of an official pamphlet entitled *Communist Infiltration in the U.S.: Its Nature and How to Combat It*. The Democratic Party, counteracting accusations of New Deal liberalism, began to add its voice to the growing anti-Communist furor. The attorney general announced that "Communists are everywhere, in factories, offices, butcher shops, on street corners, in private business – and each carries with him the germs of death for society."[42] The "witch-hunt" was on in full force. Ethel and Julius Rosenberg were to become major targets, some say "victims" of this vehement campaign.

Against the backdrop of mounting political repression and fear, the Rosenberg family was playing out its own escalating storm. Julius was struggling to run his engineering shop. Two of Ethel's brothers, David and Bernie Greenglass, were helping him with the business. Looking for new opportunities, Julius tried to reorganize. He moved the shop into a larger space in a building that housed an Orthodox synagogue and a study hall where he had spent countless hours during his childhood and adolescence. Now an apostate who had transferred his energies to political activism,

Julius promoted his brother-in-law David to a full partner in the business. David was a machinist who had spent almost three years in the United States Army, worked on the atom bomb project, and now had a wife and young son to support. David's collaboration was crucial to the success of the business, but Julius treated him like a younger subordinate, called him "boy," and complained that he was not working hard enough. Perhaps he was envious of David's mechanical skills, or worried that David would outgrow the struggling business and set up a competing enterprise. David grew increasingly resentful of Julius and quarrels between them were a daily occurrence. The overt hostility between Julius and David became so intense that they almost came to blows. The battleground expanded when David's wife Ruth joined in the fray, claiming that Julius was taking unfair advantage of her husband. Ethel agreed with Julius about everything. David had been her favorite brother, but in the conflict between David and her husband, Ethel's allegiance belonged to Julius. He was her "savior," the one who had rescued her from her family. The only occasion when the two families routinely came together was every Friday night, the traditional Sabbath meal at the home of Ethel's parents. We can only imagine the tension and animosity that pervaded those family dinners. Ethel's mother had always sided with her sons whenever there was a conflict between the Greenglass brothers and their sister. At that crucial time in the life of the family, Tessie exacerbated the conflict by openly favoring David and becoming more closely aligned with David's wife Ruth. The sides in the fatal battle were drawn: David, Ruth and Tessie Greenglass against Ethel and Julius Rosenberg.

In September of 1949, David Greenglass walked away from the business, leaving Julius to struggle with a failing enterprise. David demanded reimbursement for the stock he still held and for his initial investment, a loan to the fledgling company. Since there were few assets and no real profits, Julius could not meet David's demands. The Greenglass family sued Julius for the money they claimed he owed to David. Nothing was ever collected, but the accusations and bitterness from this quarrel saturated all of their subsequent encounters. Tessie sided adamantly with David and Ruth against Ethel and Julius. The Rosenbergs, preoccupied with caring for their two young sons and engrossed in their political activities, tried to ignore the family battles. They were totally unprepared for the "bombshell" that fell on them on July 17, 1950, when Julius was arrested on charges of spying for the Soviet Union. Ten men "swarmed into the apartment, opening closets, looking through bookshelves, examining furniture."[43] One month later, Ethel was arrested. This was the beginning of the end for Ethel and Julius Rosenberg. Their two sons were then three and seven years old.

Documents reporting the details of the Rosenberg case fill many volumes. Here is a brief sketch of the main events. This chronology illustrates how the historical process and the family dynamics converged to produce the final outcome.

MARCH, 1943. David Greenglass was drafted into the U.S. Army. He trained as a machinist at various bases in California, Mississippi, and eventually, Oak Ridge Tennessee.

AUGUST 1944. David was transferred to Los Alamos to work on a "top secret" project. Later in the same year, he allegedly began to collect atomic secrets to pass on to Russian espionage agents. His brother-in-law, Julius Rosenberg, was said to be the middleman in the spy ring.

AUGUST, 1949. In a remote desert in Russia, the Soviets tested an atomic weapon that bore a striking resemblance to the bomb the United States had dropped on Nagasaki. The following month, David Greenglass left his brother-in-law's business, accusing Julius of refusing to settle a debt and exacerbating the feud between them.

FEBRUARY, 1950. David Greenglass was questioned by the FBI about persons he might have known while he was stationed at Los Alamos. Later in the same month, Senator Joseph McCarthy addressed an audience in Wheeling. West Virginia. In his infamous "I have here in my hand" speech, he claimed to have a list of 205 Communist party members who were still working for the United States government. Anti-Communist furor was at an all-time high.

JUNE 15, 1950. David Greenglass signed a confession stating that he had been an accomplice in a conspiracy to provide strategic information on the atomic bomb to contacts in the Soviet Union. In subsequent testimony, David implicated his sister Ethel and her husband Julius in various episodes of espionage. One month later, Julius was arrested on charges of having recruited David into a Soviet spy ring.

AUGUST, 1950. Ethel Rosenberg was arrested on the charge of conspiracy to commit espionage with her husband and her brother. With both of their parents in jail, the Rosenbergs' two young sons moved in with their grandmother Tessie. In November of the same year, Michael and Robert were virtually abandoned by their grandmother. No one else in the family was willing to care for them, so they were placed at the Hebrew Childrens' Home, a shelter in the Bronx.

APRIL 6, 1951. David Greenglass was sentenced to fifteen years in prison. The reduced term was a reward for his testimony against his sister and brother-in-law.

MARCH 1953. The trial of Julius and Ethel Rosenberg opened. A headline on the front page of the *New York Times* reported: "Brother says Sister was Spy, Stole Bomb Secret." After two weeks of testimony, the jury returned a verdict of guilty. Later in that same month, Tessie Greenglass visited her daughter in prison for the last time. She tried to persuade Ethel to confess her crime, but Ethel steadfastly maintained her innocence. Ethel called her mother a "witch," and a screaming fight broke out between the two women. Their last meeting ended in bitter fury.[44]

JUNE, 1953. The Supreme Court refused a stay of execution for the Rosenbergs. Ethel prepared a petition for clemency, stating that the case against them "stands or falls" on the testimony of her brother David and his wife. President Eisenhower rejected Ethel's plea.

ON JUNE 19TH, 1953. Ethel and Julius Rosenberg were executed. Tessie Greenglass did not attend her daughter's funeral, claiming that Ethel did not love her or any other member of the family.

During their two years in prison, Julius and Ethel exchanged letters almost every day. Many contain ardent declarations of love for each other and for their sons.[45] The letters recall details of the family conflicts that had simmered over a period of many years. References to the eruptions of hatred, accusations of exploitation, conflicting loyalties, and sibling rivalry are interspersed with reports of the political turmoil and societal upheavals that were swirling around the family. In the face of all the virulent propaganda and the evidence against them, Julius and Ethel repeatedly proclaimed their innocence. Neither of them ever admitted any crime or wrongdoing.

Two concurrent phenomena determined the fate of Julius and Ethel Rosenberg. One was the paranoia that had taken hold of the American public, fueled by the pervasive hatred and fear of everything pertaining to the Soviet Union. The mere suggestion of spying for that terrible enemy was enough to evoke outrage. The other was the tension and bitterness that riddled the Greenglass family during this same period. The hostility seethed and bubbled like a cauldron, culminating in David's testimony, the trial, and the execution of Ethel and Julius Rosenberg. In this real-life drama, the interplay of historical time and family time came to a crushing finale. There was no resolution and no semblance of closure for the family. Fifty years later, David Greenglass finally admitted the lies in his testimony that led to his sister's execution. At last, the few survivors could feel that a modicum of truth had emerged.

In 2001, a journalist named Sam Roberts published a book about the Rosenberg case. Entitled *The Brother*, it chronicles Roberts' efforts to discover the missing pieces in this convoluted story.[46] For the first time, the public was made aware of the sequence of events from the perspective of Ethel's brother. After serving his term, David Greenglass was released from prison. He changed his name and vanished. With the dogged determination of a curious journalist, Roberts spent more than fifteen years searching for him. Eventually he was able to persuade Greenglass to speak about the circumstances that led to Ethel's execution. The result is *The Brother*, an reconstruction of their conversations, supplemented by information gleaned from a variety of other sources including biographies, reviews, newspaper articles, television documentaries, and websites. One condition of their agreement was that Greenglass could not veto anything Roberts wrote. His wife and children did not know that he had agreed to be interviewed until after the book was published. His reasons for finally admitting the past are not clear. Perhaps he was motivated by a lucrative offer that would provide financial security for his family. Perhaps it was his awareness of wrongdoing that finally bobbed to the surface. We do not know.

In its five hundred pages, *The Brother* reports in excruciating detail the intrigues, coded letters, contrived messages, clandestine meetings, secret bank accounts, the subterfuge, and dirty tricks. Greenglass divulged to Roberts an intricate network of people and their devious maneuvers: stealing, smuggling, sneaking, lying, hiding. All of this intense activity was percolating simultaneously on two levels, one reflecting the political aims of the participants and the other, the bitter conflict between the Rosenberg and Greenglass families. Crucial questions spouted at the center of the turmoil: what happened to the small piece of plutonium that David had kept in a lead box? Did he really steal the detonator cap and give it to Julius? Who was leaking classified information to the Russians? In constructing their original case, the FBI had desperately sought answers to these questions. Although many of the answers remain contradictory and unclear, David's disclosures provided a new version of the facts in the case.

The "truth" of this sordid tale is contained somewhere in the fragments of history, scattered through the diverse recollections of the protagonists, onlookers, and commentators. We do know that the entire drama was an elaborate contrapuntal sequence in which historical time and family time were intertwined. Atomic secrets were being conveyed to Soviet agents, but there was not sufficient evidence to arrest David Greenglass. Without his confession, there was no case. The FBI's strategy was to convince David to cooperate, to help the government prove its case against someone else. And that is exactly what happened. David's wife Ruth saw this "cooperation" as a way to save David and herself. She was convinced that Julius had cheated her husband, treated him badly, belittled him. As the government's noose tightened, she saw an opportunity for revenge. When the case came to court, it would be "either them or us."[47] She decided that it would be them, Julius and Ethel. In reporting his version to Roberts, David justified his actions: "You grow away from siblings. Believe me, you do. There's no way you can help yourself."[48] In fact, David had made a conscious decision to sacrifice his sister's life in order to preserve his own. In Ethel Rosenberg's last plea for clemency, she expressed her awareness of her brother's role. Until the publication of Roberts' book fifty years later, David's part in the drama had not been known by any other person.

In telling the story of this tormented family, I do not intend to uphold the guilt or the innocence of Ethel and Julius. There are many convincing arguments on both sides. The point I wish to emphasize is the family process and how it became tangled with the political upheavals during that turbulent period of American history. This is a story of siblings who became mortal enemies. A close, perhaps pathologically enmeshed sibling attachment was transposed into fierce hatred, even unto death. Their conflict spilled over to the public arena, where suspicions of political intrigue and fears of attack were intensifying. The Greenglass-Rosenberg family was in the eye of the whirlwind.

When I studied the saga of this family, two sources proved to be especially helpful: the empathic biography of Ethel Rosenberg by Ilene Philipson, and Sam Roberts' detailed exposure of the role of Ethel's brother. These two narratives provide in-depth explorations of their individual personalities, their roles in the family system, and the sequence of the transformation from enmeshed siblings to adversaries. Ethel Rosenberg was passionately committed to her husband and to his political ideology. Her brother

David believed he had been demeaned and cheated by Julius. Their mother Tessie, acting as a catalyst in the dispute, sided with David and his wife against Ethel and Julius. These five people were the main protagonists in a family war that culminated in tragedy. Fifty years later, David Greenglass admitted that he had lied in court. His main goal had been to protect his wife and children and confuse the FBI by deflecting their suspicions to his sister. When he was asked, "How do you want history to remember you," he replied, "I don't care." But we, the readers, do care. We care enough to wonder and study and try to understand how a family can become mired in such murderous rage, how the grim finale could have been prevented, and most important, what we can learn from their story.

We can learn that close attachments between siblings may have dire consequences when expectations are not met and vulnerabilities are exploited. In this family, the pattern of relationships veered off course and became self-destructive when David turned against Julius and Tessie Greenglass sided with her son against her daughter. The power struggle within the family was transposed to a larger struggle in the context of historical events, leading to deceptions, complicity, and finally, to death. When we examine the roles that were taken up by the major protagonists, we can see how each person fit into the whole and contributed to the outcome. As in every family system, the behavior of each member influenced all of the others. By studying the complex interactions in this family saga, we may become aware of the potentially lethal ingredients in our own family conflicts. Their story may inspire us to seek healthier, more constructive solutions.

### 2. Death without reconciliation: Aram Saroyan's *Last Rites*

The last example in this chapter is autobiographical, the narrative of a son who was rejected by his father. Aram Saroyan describes how, through the act of writing, he was able to confront and understand an intensely painful relationship.

In the spring of 1981, the author of *The Human Comedy* and *The Time of Your Life* was approaching the end of his life. William

Saroyan, a writer who was well known to American readers and audiences in the mid-twentieth century, was dying of cancer. His illness was a fact he had steadfastly withheld from his son and daughter. *Last Rites,* a detailed journal that became a book, is the son's story of his father's death. In a remarkable understatement, Aram says: "We are not an ordinary family."[49]

American Armenians loved William Saroyan. He gave them a sense of pride and recognition at a time when their own ethnic identity had suffered grievous blows. More than a million of their people had been the victims of genocide, the culmination of religious and political strife initiated by Turkey in the period before the First World War. For the survivors who immigrated to America, Saroyan was the spokesman, their champion at a time of great uncertainty and upheaval. He was called an "Armenian national treasure," perhaps because he wrote reassuring stories about a world peopled with normal families and lovable children. One of his biographers noted: "Saroyan's work is full of children; they make an appearance in virtually every major book and are among his best-drawn characters. He deeply loved the world of childhood."[50] In the eyes of his adoring public, he was a hero and a role model. But when he was at home, Saroyan was quite a different person. With his wife and children, he generated constant chaos and scarcely any expression of love. According to his son, he remained twisted and sadistic all his life. "He initiated and carried out a long… psychological war against us, so that we went numb with disbelief and sorrow and deep, deep, murderous anger."[51]

Aram Saroyan, the only son of the famous writer, had been estranged from his father for several years when his sister Lucy told him that Pop was dying of cancer. William was then seventy-two years old, a proud, angry, insular man. Before the estrangement, he would visit his son and grandchildren twice a year for one or two hours. Lucy had remained in touch with him through intermittent letters, but she never received a response. When she learned of his illness, Lucy, then in her mid-thirties, drove up to Fresno from her home in Los Angeles with a basket of food and every good wish in her heart. As soon as she appeared, he screamed at her and ordered her out of his house. When he found out that Aram knew about his illness, he told Lucy that her brother should not come, write, or phone. "Tell him he'll kill me if he does."[52]

The news of his father's impending death struck Aram with a compelling sense of urgency. Alienated all of his life, he was determined to examine their troubled relationship while the old man was still alive. He wrote, "This final episode of his life will very likely be an important one for me to go through with him, one from which I will learn." His insight bore fruit; he did learn a great deal, as his book attests.

The son speaks of his father: "How well I know the black poisons of his soul. I have known them since the beginning of my life... There is no way... to reverse this tide of hate and brutal, hysterical anger... He wanted me to die, to be a disgrace and a failure, to be a blot on his good name..."[53] Aram was a non-person in his father's eyes, relentlessly burdened by the constant undermining of his selfhood. But the son did not acquiesce to his father's dire predictions. He went through a hippy phase (during which he named his two daughters Strawberry and Cream) and emerged as a responsible adult who became a fine writer. The act of writing became his salvation, the means through which he was able to clarify his perceptions of his father but not to admire or love him.

How can we understand the dynamics in this intensely hostile family environment? The man's biography may give us a clue. William Saroyan's own father died before he was three years old. William was the youngest of four children and the only one to be born in the United States. After his father's death, he was placed in an orphanage where he stayed for five years, until his mother was able to retrieve him. At the age of eight, he was a "nascent genius." By the time he was a young man, he had composed his first "masterpiece" and within a few years, he had embarked on a meteoric career as an author, playwright, and man-about-town. When he was thirty-five, he met a 17-year-old Jewish debutante and fell in love. They married, had a son and a daughter, and divorced twice within ten years.[54] Apparently, he never developed a close connection to either of his children.

Struggling to understand his father's rage and to make sense of his eccentric behavior, Aram speculates that William could not bear to be obligated to anyone. After losing his own father in early childhood, he had repressed his own emotional needs. Perhaps he feared that his sudden fame was unreal, that the balloon would burst and leave him bereft. So he adopted a pattern of severing connections with people before they could cut off from him. In his autobiography, Aram hardly mentions his mother, except to note his father's ambivalence and later, his virulent rejection of her. After the first burst of infatuation, William had turned against her, expressing bitter hatred for Jews. He was amazed that he could have debased himself by marrying a Jewish woman. Aram, an impressionable teenager, was forced to listen to his father's tirades, depicting his mother as a cunning, duplicitous monster. Each of her characteristics was exaggerated by William to the status of crimes, forever to be used against her and her children. We can only wonder how they managed to survive in that toxic atmosphere.

The story of Aram's struggle to connect with his father is built on this chaotic family background. Using William's last illness as an opportunity to explore his own feelings and relationships, Aram wrote: "If I can understand him, and myself in relation to him, I can spare myself the anger and resentment that is so much a part of what is between us."[55] Despite the accumulation of humiliation and disappointment, he still longed for a connection. But he sadly acknowledged that he never had a "real" father.

A person who has been repeatedly rejected feels helpless, adrift. He needs to find a way to counteract the rejection, to do something that will transform his passive stance into activity. The natural response is to avoid further conflict, back off and widen the distance. Aram Saroyan's memoir provides us with a vivid example of this process. He describes how, long before his father's illness, he decided to give up the futile effort and channel his energies to build a separate life of his own. For more than four years, there was only a heavy silence between them. But now, as the old man lay dying, Aram's need to protect himself had lost its potency. At this crucial moment, the son determined to find his own voice by writing the story. "The only way I can hold my own now is by writing it down day by day, until the terrible game is over at last."[56]

Aram describes an especially poignant scene. He summons his courage to reopen the contact with his father. Taking his daughter Cream with him, they go to visit the old man in the hospital. Perhaps the child will "soften" him a bit, he hopes. Will he be willing to see them? Aram goes through a series of mental exercises to prepare for any eventuality: he may be kicked out, insulted, threatened, ignored. Reading his descriptions of this painful episode, one can only feel compassion for a son who is so worried that his dying father will reject him again. Aram filled many pages with the microscopic details of the visit. Every gesture, remark, and facial expression is reported, like a sequence of film clips that record each nuance. At one point, the doctor appears at the door, backs away when he sees the visitors, but the old man waves him into the room. "This is my son," he explains. One wonders if this is the first time Aram ever heard his father say these words, "my son." The scene reaches a climax when Aram bends over the bed to kiss his father and receives a spontaneous embrace. The dying man says: "It's the most beautiful time of my life… and death." "For me too, Pop."

Aram tells of the final meeting with his father. He returned to the hospital with both of his daughters. Saroyan seemed genuinely glad to see his grandchildren. He called them by name and in his own inimitable way, he "blessed" them. One he called "beautiful," another was a "ball of energy." His son was a "good boy." Aram left the hospital feeling encouraged by these signs of softening. The old man, as he lay dying, had actually acknowledged his grandchildren. Perhaps he had a change of heart. Could he allow himself to reach out to his family before the final letting-go? Building on this new hope, Aram asked for his father's permission to use one of his empty houses as a base for the hospital visits. Aram and his family lived several hundred miles away, and having a place to stay would ease the strain of the long drive. The old man seemed to agree: "I'd love it, we could all be together."[57] But the pattern had not really changed. The following day, Aram received his father's final answer, conveyed by a cousin. William refused to give his son permission to use the house. Apparently, the terms of his will stated that the house should remain sealed. If this decision was part of a legal agreement, Aram was not told of it. For him, not getting the key was an additional obstruction erected by his father, symbolic perhaps, but vivid and real for the son. So, the change had been an illusion, a passing moment with no real substance. We cannot know if the father had actually felt a particle of affection, a moment of regret. For Aram, the hope for a reconciliation crumbled. The old man's apparent "softening" was only more of the same old stuff, "emotional grandstanding," as his son called it. Even in the last moments of his life, he refused to acknowledge the reality of their relationship. At the end, Aram grew tired of his frustrated efforts to connect. "Let him go his way alone now, as he has always essentially preferred it."[58]

The rejection of his children did not end with Saroyan's death. Aram had suspected that the old man would deprive them of any inheritance. In fact, the will reflected the same manipulative pattern Saroyan had followed during his life. He left small, insignificant trust funds for his son, daughter, and grandchildren, to be used only for a dire emergency. This gesture served as an effective legal obstacle to contesting the will. All of his personal possessions, properties, copyrights, and future royalties were bequeathed to the foundation that enshrined his name. "In effect, he left his estate to himself. He took it with him."[59]

What is the last word in this story? There is no defeat and no victory, only a sense of sadness. Aram's request to his dying father was denied: he was not to be given a key to the house. The key can serve as a metaphor for the cloud of ambiguity that hovered over this relationship. Aram never had a "key" to his father's rejection. It would remain a mystery, a locked door. For the readers of *Last*

*Rites*, it seems that the act of writing the story served as a means of healing for the son. Aram could cherish the memory of those fleeting moments when his father had been able to validate him, when he could express a modicum of affection for his grandchildren. And finally, the son could let go; he could give up the futile struggle and move on with his own life.

In 1948, when Aram was four years old, his father's play *The Time of Your Life* was produced in a movie version. James Agee wrote a review of the film, calling the author a "very gifted schmaltz artist" whose "strength and weakness are inextricably combined." At his best, Agee said, he is "wonderfully sweet-natured, witty and beguiling." At his worst, he tells "damnably silly lies in the teeth of the truth."[60] Many years later, when their father was dying, Aram and his sister returned to this review with new insight. They realized that their father was indeed a mass of contradictions. He was a hero to his adoring public, but with his family, he was a bully. They never knew how he would react or what they could do to be accepted by him. Aram uses a vivid image to describe their predicament: they were continually darting back and forth between a brick wall and a chasm, like frightened deer in the glare of the headlights. By telling his story in *Last Rites*, Aram the son was finally able to extricate himself from the morass of his father's rejection. His real inheritance was the awareness of the contradictions between William Saroyan the public figure and the other Saroyan, his father. Once he had clarified this reality, he could free himself from the destructive elements in his past and build a separate life of his own.

### Concluding thoughts: writing family stories

In preparing to write his memoir, Aram Saroyan said: "The only way I can hold my own now is by writing it down day by day..." The act of writing is not reserved for known authors and skilled writers. Anyone can keep a journal, produce a memoir, record daily happenings in a diary. Countless scenes and episodes have been preserved in the texts of family histories and other forms of personal expression.[61] Many of these texts include guidelines for writing autobiographical stories and using them to work through conflicts. The experience of estrangement lends itself to this kind of effort. Being alienated from one's family can create feelings of isolation, defeat, the sense of being adrift with no anchor. Writing can provide an anchor. In the process of documenting one's reactions, memories, frustrations, and hopes, an estranged person can achieve a new level of awareness, as Aram Saroyan has demonstrated. Reading the narratives of others may inspire us to record our own stories, to preserve the flow of experience as we move from one phase to another. Through the medium of writing, you may discover your own voice and learn how it blocks or blends with the voices of others in the counterpoint of family relationships.

Each of the stories presented in this chapter – fictional, biographical, and autobiographical – provides a variation on the theme of family conflict. In reading and re-reading them, I continually discover new ideas and imagine alternate conclusions. The protagonists take on a life of their own as teachers. They demonstrate how estrangements can erupt from diverse provocations and how the tensions can persist, even to the next generation. We have considered such realities as an eccentric parent, a scapegoat, a prodigal, a rebel who became a terrorist, an angry man whose false testimony helped to send his sister to the electric chair, and a father's persistent rejection of his son. As we listen to each of their voices, we can identify with their struggles. We can "play" with the themes in their stories, imagining how the bitterness might have been averted and how their energies could have been used more constructively. Hopefully, these stories will have the power to guide you and me toward better solutions of our own family conflicts.

# CHAPTER FIVE

# My Family – Estrangement and Reconciliation in Retrospect

---

*"...And you shall hallow the fiftieth year, and proclaim liberty throughout the land unto all the inhabitants; it shall be a jubilee unto you; and you shall return every man to his possessions, and you shall return every man to his family..." (Leviticus 25:10)*

---

This book is both a window and a mirror. It is a collection of stories about others, a window that looks into their lives. It is also my own story, a reflection of my own experience. Writing stories of other families, I have been peering into their lives as I sort out fragments in my own. The following pages comprise the "mirror" of this book, a narrative of one long episode in my family's history.

The estrangement in my family persisted for fifty years and influenced my life in significant ways. The pathway toward a resolution was thorny and often tortuous, but the outcome made it all worthwhile. Here are the details of the story and the sequence of steps I took to examine my role in the family, identify the tasks, and move toward reconciliation with the estranged members.

## Prelude to the feud

I was born in 1931, one year after my parents were married. At the time of my birth, my mother was forty-three and my father was fifty-three years old. My father's first wife had died of a brain tumor three years before, leaving him with two adult daughters and a fourteen-year-old son. My mother had not been married previously and I was to be her only child. When my father's son and daughters heard of their father's intention to re-marry, they were shocked and angry. At their first encounters with his new wife-to-be, they perceived her as haughty, critical of them, and possessive of him. A sequence of tense encounters reinforced their opposition to my parents' marriage. They rejected my mother and became increasingly alienated from their father.

When I was born, their anger intensified. Apparently they could not accept the idea that their father could recover from their mother's death and move on to build a new life. The fact that he could have a child with "another woman" was particularly repugnant to them. They attached themselves more closely to the relatives on their mother's side of the family, who joined in the rejection of my parents and me. In retrospect, I can imagine how this process was set off. My mother, unsure of her role in her new family, might have appeared aloof, an outsider. Her awkward efforts to "fit in" may have only succeeded in painting her into the "wicked stepmother" corner. In contrast, my siblings sustained an image of their own mother that placed her solidly in the opposite corner, where only angels and saints could tread. The dichotomy had been erected and the process of estrangement was set in motion.

## Family background

My father was one of eight children. All of them were born in America, in Buffalo, where my grandparents had settled. His mother, my grandmother Rosa, had come to the "new world" from Lithuania when she was about sixteen. I imagine that she called it the *goldene medina*, a Yiddish phrase implying a place of hope for those who were fleeing from the pogroms and persecutions in Europe. She married a young widower with one small child named Sam. Subsequently they had seven children together, three boys and four girls; Sam became the eldest brother in this large brood. My father was one of the youngest. The children were raised in a traditional Jewish home. As they grew, married, and had children of their own, all of them remained in Buffalo. Some continued to live in the same neighborhood and were affiliated with the Conservative synagogue their parents had helped to establish. I remember that my father was in frequent touch with his sisters and brothers and their expanding families. My mother was especially fond of her sisters-in-law. During my childhood, we visited often with the aunts and uncles; I knew and liked many of my cousins. Our families would gather for Jewish holidays and lifecycle events. The warmth and good humor that characterized our interactions with that segment of my father's family stood in vivid contrast to the hostility and rejection I felt from the people on the cut off branch.

The house where we lived during my childhood was the house in which my father had lived with his first wife and children. Many years later, I learned that my mother's presence in "their mother's house" was another source of friction in the already-tense family. For about a year after my birth, my brother Cal lived intermittently with us, but he soon moved to one of his mother's relatives and then to another city, never to return except for rare, brief visits. I will say more about him later. Annie, the younger of my sisters, had already moved to New York. Betty, who was married and had two daughters, continued to live in Buffalo. I would see her occasionally but she would never speak to me and I do not recall that I ever visited her home.

One month after my tenth birthday and a few days before the Japanese attack at Pearl Harbor, my father suffered a "slight stroke" that resulted in paralysis of one hand. His doctor told him it was a "warning" to slow down, but he was a vigorous, energetic man with a vivid memory of the Depression years, and so he ignored the warning and continued to work long hours. Three months later, he had a massive brain hemorrhage and died. My memories of this period are blurred and unreliable, but I suspect that neither of my sisters came to their father's funeral. My brother did come, but only to the cemetery, and I did not see him again for more than twenty-five years. In a remarkably generous act (in Hebrew, it would be called *chessed*, a blend of sensitivity and loving-kindness), my mother buried my father next to his first wife. His son and daughters never acknowledged this gesture. After my father's death, all contact with his first family ceased. Their bitterness was further exacerbated because he left no will and his children incorrectly assumed that they had been deprived of a substantial inheritance. During my childhood and well into my adult life, I had a vague sense of sisters and a brother but no concrete experience of any connection to them. For more than forty years, I felt only bewilderment and resentment toward that entire segment of the family, identified them as the "enemy camp," and never expected to initiate any contact with them.

### "The end is where we start from"
Here, we will do a "fast-forward" to the present day. On my kitchen shelf is a recipe for my sister Annie's "autumn apple cake." In my closet, there is a pair of cozy crocheted slippers, made for me by Annie. A soft, hand-made comforter in stripes of red, white and black is on my bed, a birthday gift from Betty. I have a file full of letters from both of my sisters, as well as a collection of Annie's poems, written during the last ten years of her life. On my computer, there is an active, ongoing exchange of email messages with one of Betty's daughters. How did I get from "there" to "here"? What were the steps in the process of reconciliation?

### Exploring a cutoff: phases in the process
I had been working as a psychologist for several years when I decided to expand my skills and knowledge by studying family systems. I joined a training group based on Bowen Family Systems Theory and embarked on a new sequence of learning. As part of our preparation to qualify as family therapists, each

of us was required to explore the dynamics in our own families. We were advised to examine our family history and concentrate on our own involvement in the system. As my colleagues began to share their stories with the group, we heard about the fallout from family secrets, smoldering feuds, and ancient misunder-standings. Their descriptions of the tangled webs in their own families reinforced our perceptions of the enormous complexity of family process.[1] As I began to wonder about the quagmire I was getting into, my resistance escalated. Why should I submit myself to this ordeal? Why not let these things alone? But one by one, each of us broke out of the impasse and moved ahead. Many of the experiences reported by my colleagues were painful, others were enlightening, a few were traumatic. One woman was greeted by a gun-toting uncle who threatened to shoot anyone from her branch of the family! In comparison, my situation was less risky but almost as challenging.

With the group's encouragement, I began to review the impli-cations of the estrangement and consider how it had influenced my emotional reactions. I decided to pay closer attention to the impulse to cut myself off from unresolved conflicts and to reject people who disagree with me. One member of the group noted that those who see themselves as victims of a cutoff are likely to seek enmeshed, dependent relationships that provide reassurance and comfort. I wondered how the effort to compensate might be operating in my own life. This sequence of questioning led to heightened vigilance and a new sense of awareness of the connec-tions between past events and current patterns of my behavior.

The next step was to review the history of my family and chart its constellation, noting the major events and significant changes. I constructed a "genogram," a diagram that is used by family therapists to depict the generational patterns, the dates of births, deaths, and other nodal events. I noticed that there were many gaps and a few empty branches. Part of my task would be to collect information and fill in some of the blanks. Then, I framed some questions for the next stage of my exploration. The work was now taking on the mood of an archeological expedition, with specific directions and tasks. Having come to this point, I was ready to try out a series of strategies that would culminate in face-to-face contact with the estranged members of my family.

In confronting a cutoff, one can expect to be buffeted by recurring emotional surges: spasms of anxiety, disappointment, frustration, rage, and occasionally, euphoria. With the group's help, I had come to realize that highly charged emotional reactions would be counter-productive. I needed to dampen my usual re-activity with some intellectual curiosity. Working in an academic setting, it was natural for me to turn to a related field of interest. I assumed the role of a researcher and focused on aspects of the literature in anthropology and social evolution. The details of my research are described in a previous publication.[2] During the process of studying lineage and inheritance patterns in other cultures and exploring the implications of "natural selection" for the survival of a prolonged estrangement, some of my emotional intensity was transposed into objective inquiry. I was able to observe the estrangement from a more detached point of view and play with ideas in a different way. By scrambling the pieces of my family puzzle, I conjured up various scenarios and outcomes. I began to ask myself audacious questions. What if my sisters had been brothers? What if my father had been divorced instead of widowed? (Things could have been much worse!) How would I have felt in my sisters' place? Why was my mother so willing to assume the role of wicked stepmother? Did my father ever try to connect the alienated parts of his family?

This torrent of questioning served to break through a shell of rigid assumptions and open up a range of new possibilities. I became more aware of the gaps in my knowledge and the narrowness of my perspective. My curiosity was whetted. Why had I never asked about my father's first wife? Why had I not discussed the estrangement with my mother? After so many years, several of the key players had died. Who was left to connect with, and how would I find the remaining sources of information?

## Small steps to dead ends

These questions led me to the next step. It seemed like the right time to attempt direct contact with someone in the "enemy camp." From a cousin who had maintained intermittent contact with parts of the cut off branch, I was able to obtain the necessary address. I composed a brief letter expressing my interest in knowing about people in the family, especially those I had not heard from in a long time. I mentioned nothing about conflict or problems, only a wish to "be in touch." I sent this letter to my oldest sister's daughter, a forty-five year old woman with a family of her own. I did not receive an answer.

During the next few months, while I waited in vain for a reply to my letter, I reviewed portions of the literature on family dynamics and continued to play with ideas. Then, I attempted a somewhat indirect approach by requesting a meeting with one member of the so-called "enemy camp," a niece of my father's first wife, still living in Buffalo. At first she was reluctant. It was only after I sent her several reassuring messages and spoke with her on the telephone that she finally agreed to meet with me. I had never met her and her suspicions about me were revealed in her first question: "Do you intend to harm anyone in the family?" Since the animosity had begun before my birth, it seemed like an absurd question, but it did give me a clue that the "heat" from the estrangement was still smoldering in the family. I had planned my questions carefully. I was determined to assume the role of curious observer, not casting blame or seeking sympathy but merely wanting to know what she remembered about the family and how she perceived the situation. I was rewarded with a barrage of vituperations. Her recollections were colored with lurid tales about evil deeds and misplaced loyalties. I tried to listen calmly to her melodramatic stories, but her impressions were so different from my own image of the family, it seemed that she must be talking about strangers or aliens. She was giving me clear evidence that even after fifty years, the intensity of the hostility was essentially unchanged. Our conversation ended with her emphatic insistence that my sisters and brother would never be willing to meet with me. I left her house feeling utterly exhausted, but also excited and challenged. Now I was armed with new information. Her warnings had actually intensified my determination to move ahead. The dark hole in my family's past had been opened; the vipers were alive, kicking, and at least partially under my control.

## A different strategy

In the aftermath of my meeting, I returned to the training group to review my progress and plan my next move. The previous strategies had succeeded in defusing some of the emotional intensity and arousing my curiosity about particular events. I actually began to feel like an interested observer, no longer caught in the current but now able to navigate my own course and even ready to try a radically new direction.

During a visit to my hometown, I went to the cemetery where my parents are buried. As usual, I placed flowers on their graves. But in a totally new frame of mind, I also put flowers on the grave of my father's first wife, the mother of my estranged siblings. For me, this act had great symbolic significance, even though no one was there to see it. This small gesture was a gift to the grave of a woman I had never met, a woman whose death had made my birth possible. It was startling to realize that I had begun to use her name, Rivka, for the first time. What changes had occurred that enabled me to do this? I had replaced my habitual pattern of denial and hostility with an awareness that her life and death were real and meaningful for me. My previous self-image as a helpless victim had been transposed into a perception of the larger family system in which I was a separate but equal member. Now I could feel sympathy for the family's situation at the time of her death. I wondered what my sisters could tell me about their mother, and what they remembered about that earlier period in the history of my family.

## Meeting face-to-face: apprehension and actuality

The time was ripe to attempt a direct contact. My colleagues in the training group reassured me that the effort itself would be worthwhile, even if I failed to get a response. Circumstances in my own life, especially my impending marriage, had provided a new measure of support and encouragement. From impressions I had obtained from other family members, I inferred that the younger of my two sisters would be more likely to respond. I learned that she had recently moved to Denver to be near Betty, who had been living there for several years. After a few false starts, I composed the following letter:

> *"Dear Annie,*
>
> *It's been a long time since I've had any news of you or Betty. Recently, I've been thinking about the family and wondering how you are. I'm planning to be married soon, and I guess such important milestones stir up thoughts of family. Last month, Gene (my future husband) and I spent a weekend in Buffalo so he could meet some of the cousins. It was interesting to reminisce about the old days, and to see how various parts of the family have aged and changed. We also visited the cemetery because I wanted him to see my parents' graves. You are all so far away, and you probably don't get back to our hometown very often. I thought you might like to know that I left a plant of yellow mums on your mother's grave.*
>
> *I hope all is well with you and your family..."*

A few weeks later, I received a reply from Annie, expressing her appreciation for my gesture at the cemetery and indicating her willingness to be in touch. After an exchange of letters, she invited me to visit her in Denver. I accepted the invitation.

It was a cold, cloudy day in January, 1983. As the plane began the descent to the Denver airport, my anxiety level escalated. In a matter of minutes, I would come face-to-face with two sisters whom I had not seen for almost fifty years. In the previous decade, they had both been widowed. Annie was then seventy-two; Betty was five years older. During my entire life, I had only the most hostile impressions of them. Now, mixed with my apprehension,

I felt a certain curiosity. After all this time, how would they greet me, and how would I react? I felt unclear about my role. I didn't know what a "sister" was supposed to do. If my husband had not been beside me, I might have been tempted to avoid the meeting and go back home. But there they were, waiting at the gate. The moment had arrived.

The first greetings were hesitant and tense. None of us felt comfortable, and we stood there trying to get our bearings and figure out how to communicate. Annie seemed more at ease and was able to joke a bit; she even gave me a quick hug and a smile. Betty looked rather grim and unbending. On the way out of the airport, she remarked that I resembled my mother. I didn't know if that was a compliment, an insult, or simply an opening gambit.

Applying the advice I had heard from my colleagues in the training group, I was determined not to accuse, not to express anger, recrimination, or blame. Nor would I expose my feelings of sadness, or tell them how unfair their rejection had been. Imagining their reactions, I had vowed not to defend my mother or try to correct their false impressions. Noting this string of "nots," I realize that I had no clear plan of what I *would* say or do.

During our preliminary conversations, I took on the role of "reporter" and carried a "prop," a small notebook that helped to reduce my nervousness and gave me something concrete to do. As a "reporter," I could assume an observer's point of view even though I was obviously a participant in the situation. I began by asking safe, neutral questions about their birth dates, addresses, the names of their children and grandchildren. Eventually I was able to ask more risky questions and respond less anxiously to some of theirs. My husband was going to a nearby city on a work assignment and Annie had invited me to stay with her. I was touched by her offer but I gratefully declined, opting to stay in a motel and have a safe haven to escape to, if necessary.

During the next few days, I spent many hours with Annie and together we visited Betty twice. At first, I felt more comfortable with Annie. She was a warm, out-going person with an occasional "bite" in her manner. In the midst of a conversation about mundane things, she would introduce a sharp barb that threw me off balance. I found myself wondering if this pattern was reserved for me, or if she behaved this way with others as well. It took several visits and considerable time before I could feel comfortable with Annie's style and realize that her barbs were actually her awkward efforts to be humorous. With Betty I was more wary because at that early stage, she was visibly hostile and suspicious of me. I felt as if I needed to "prove" my good intentions to her again and again. It wasn't until much later that I could feel relaxed and even affectionate toward her.

### Reviewing family history, together

Reviewing my notes from those first meetings, I can see how we began to connect by sharing family stories. This "sharing" took the form of them telling and me listening. I learned quickly that they were not interested in hearing about me, and certainly not about my mother, who had died several years before. So I was the one who initiated the inquiries, and they responded with stories. When I asked about Rivka, their mother, I learned that she was born in Galicia and had come to America in the 1890s at the age of fourteen with her younger brother and sister. They remembered that she, (like my father's mother) had called it the *goldene medina*. She was the oldest of seven children in her family. She was a singer who loved music, just as Betty did. This new fact gave me an unexpected sense of kinship with them, through the common bond of music. As they continued to recall these memories of their mother, who had been dead for more than fifty years, I had a new sense of awareness of this woman whom I had never known, whose death had allowed my parents to meet and marry. For the first time, they were speaking about their mother with me. In a sense, they were restoring her position in the family circle, which seemed to grant us a measure of healing.

As we began to feel more relaxed together, Annie and Betty recalled many more anecdotes, some funny, others sad, a few angry. Most of them were simply mundane tales of life in the family. I learned that they had moved to the house on Norwood Avenue in 1918, when they were children, and had lived there until after their mother's death, more than ten years later. They each had a nickname, given by their mother: Annie was "Gypsy," our brother Cal was called the "Savage." They recalled that they were not allowed to wake their father except with a kiss. He used to *daven* (pray) in a corner of the living room, wearing the traditional *tallit* (prayer shawl) and head covering. I have no similar memory of my father and their descriptions gave me a new image of him and his values. Their mother canned vegetables and stored her preserves on shelves in the basement. Now, more than sixty years later, they could still recall the taste of her jam and the arrangement of rooms in the house. At one point in the flood of reminiscences, when we were laughing together about a hilarious episode, Betty looked at me and said, "Now you have sisters!" It was a bitter-sweet moment for me, since at no point did they express any regret for the long estrangement, nor did they ever question their own motives in cutting me out of their lives for those many years. But suddenly, there we were: sisters, at last.

Betty recalled many objects from their childhood home: the chandelier, the tapestries, an ashtray in the shape of a snake, the cloisonné candlesticks on the mantle, their mother's gold-rimmed dishes. While they were waxing nostalgic about these precious things, I was marveling at the power of objects to take on the "persona" of their owner. Because these household articles, so familiar from my childhood, had been their mother's possessions, they had been endowed with infinite significance. Now I realized how much they meant to Annie and Betty and why they had been preserved in their memory for more than fifty years!

Later in the conversation, there was a sudden shift in the mood; the stories turned into accusations. Where was their mother's diamond ring? And the hand towels with embroidered flowers? What happened to all the precious things that really belonged to *them*, especially the gold-rimmed dishes? One after another, the complaints tumbled out. I had no way to disprove their claims. I could only murmur a simple acknowledgment: "You must have felt very sad." I was convinced that my role was not to contradict their perceptions or to defend my mother, but merely to allow them to ventilate those ancient grievances. This sequence of listening and acknowledging their pain seemed to be an essential part of the process of healing. But my reaction to this episode went beyond mere acknowledgment. I sensed that a tangible expression of "putting things right" was necessary in this situation. When I returned home, I sorted out the gold-rimmed dishes that had been left to me by my mother, the same dishes they claimed as "theirs." I selected four sets of each piece, wrapped them carefully, and sent one package to each of my sisters. They were amazed and delighted at this offering. In the process of reconciliation, the reciprocal acts of giving and receiving gifts can take on special significance. The dishes, as a tangible symbol of the settling of old scores, paved the way to a new chapter in the saga of my family.

**Variations on the theme: one family, other fragments**
The process of connecting with my sisters continued during several subsequent visits, in their city and once when Annie came to my home. During these meetings, I learned a great deal about them and about myself. But with my brother Cal, the experience was quite different. Cal was the only son and the youngest of my father's first family. My most enduring memory of him was a scene from fifty years ago, when he appeared briefly at my father's funeral. Who was he, and what role did he play in the estrangement?

At the time of my parents' marriage and during my earliest childhood, Cal was a teenager. While in high school, he and three friends formed a singing quartet. They rehearsed the current popular songs during all their spare hours. For a while, he tried to remain in our home, but apparently the tension between him and my mother was too uncomfortable, and he moved to the home of his mother's sister. My only tangible reminder of that early period is his gift to me of a small white *siddur* (prayerbook). It bears an inscription dated 1927, from his aunt, probably a gift for his *bar mitzvah*. On the same page, written in his boyish hand in pencil and upside down is his greeting to me, dated 1934, when I was three. I do not know why he chose to give me this special gift, but I have always cherished it. A few years later, when his career as a singer began to flourish, he moved to New York and returned home rarely, perhaps once or twice a year. I have a vague recollection of a festive dinner for him at our house, served with much fanfare and pride and the best china. But after my father died, he cut off from us completely. I had no further contact with him for more than twenty years.

Out of the blue, when I was about thirty-five, married to my first husband and the mother of two children, Cal phoned me from his home in New Jersey. With no explanation, he asked if he could visit us. Since I hadn't seen or heard from him in many years, I was surprised and excited, wondering who this "brother" would be. He came to my home and as we talked, he explained that his psychoanalyst had urged him to contact me as a way to learn about himself. We spoke casually about current events, staying on neutral ground and not touching on any topic that could be toxic or controversial. My mother was present at that meeting, quite old and frail by then. She was curious, a bit suspicious, and yet pleased at his efforts to reconnect, but there was no further contact between them. Subsequently, Cal and I arranged to meet, once in New York, on his familiar turf, and once again in my home. As we became acquainted, I felt drawn to this jovial, affectionate man who probably resembled my father in appearance and personality. My fondness for him grew at each of our meetings. He and his wife attended one family celebration, the bar mitzvah of my son. A few years later, I heard from a distant cousin that Cal, then fifty-nine, had died suddenly of a heart attack. No one in his family had notified me of his death. To this day, I have not met either of his adult children.

During my visits with Annie and Betty, we spoke often of Cal. I was surprised to learn that their attempts to remain connected to him had been discouraged by his wife, who did not wish to be related to any part of his family. Neither of my sisters had been present at their brother's funeral, and they were no longer in touch with his son or daughter. During their childhood, Annie had been especially close to him, and now she recalled many anecdotes from that period. It seemed fitting that the three of us could finally express our loss and mourn for him, together. I mentioned that no one in Cal's family had told me of his death. "It's your fault," Annie said, chuckling, apparently recognizing the irony. "We didn't know how to find you!" As far as I know, neither Annie nor Betty had ever tried to locate me. It was reassuring to realize that now we were feeling relaxed enough to joke about our long estrangement.

### Clarifying the salient themes

The process of reconciliation evolved over a period of almost six years. My journal contains descriptions of many conversations with my sisters and other relevant events that occurred during that time. Reviewing my notes, I have tried to tune in to the salient themes and sort out the various motifs. I can identify at least three levels in the process, each with its own emotional components. First, there was the task of clarifying the various versions of the estrangement and sorting out the accusations, distortions, and misunderstandings. Second, the meetings with my sisters allowed me to create a bond with them and hear their account of my family's history. Finally, I achieved new insights about myself and my role in the family.

During my visits with Annie and Betty, I was often overwhelmed by the deluge of grumbling, eruptions of accumulated anger and resentment, all emanating from them and bombarding me. These included snide remarks about my mother and insinuations that my father had married her only because he was so lonely. There were also descriptions of particular events that had exacerbated the hostility between their family and mine, incidents they had repeatedly dredged up to fuel their righteous anger, words spoken in haste, disputes never resolved, possessions not shared. These recriminations were most difficult to hear and the most tempting to contradict. Many times I was on the verge of jumping in with all four feet to defend my mother, correct a false impression, try to evoke a bit of sympathy for me, the innocent child. It took strong determination to resist reacting to these provocations. Instead, I merely nodded, said something neutral ("you must have really been upset about that," or, "I never knew that"), and continued to listen. It seemed to me that they needed to rid themselves of some of this stored-up anger before we could go on to build a more positive connection.

The second level shed light on my sisters' lives and their perceptions of our extended family. Annie and Betty never seemed to weary of talking about the relatives. As long as I was willing to listen, they taught me family history. I learned that their mother had come to America with a younger brother "hiding under her skirts," and that she had subsequently become the matriarch of her family, guiding and supporting all their endeavors. It was for this reason that she was so admired and her early death was mourned so intensely. The "little brother" became the patriarch, and it was his success in business and his questionable financial manipulations that later became the basis for another bitter conflict in the family. Hearing these stories, I was suddenly aware of the contagious quality of estrangements and their tendency to hop from one branch of a family tree to another.

As my sisters reminisced, I learned that their parents had a baby girl who died in infancy, a loss I had never known about. Now I wonder if my father had welcomed me, the child of his later years, as a replacement for that dead infant. In the course of excavating family history, some questions will remain unanswered.

Again and again during our meetings, Annie and Betty extolled their parents' "perfect" marriage. Many of their stories were nostalgic recollections about the house and neighborhood where they grew up and where I was born and raised. They described our grandmother, who lived nearby but whom I never knew because she died when I was an infant. They remembered that she called her son, my father, by his Hebrew name "Shimon," the same name I gave to my son. They believed that our father "lost all his money" in the stock market crash of 1929. One minute he was a "millionaire" and the next, a pauper. But they were certain that when he died more than a decade later, they had been deprived of a large fortune. I did not attempt to correct their impressions, but continued to gather information and fill in the gaps in my perceptions, thus gaining a broader perspective of my family and a better understanding of their feelings. As we grew more comfortable together, they could share confidences with me. Annie told me of her problematic relationship with her only daughter. I was surprised to learn of other estrangements and feuds in the extended family. These new perceptions seemed to strengthen the connections between my sisters and me.

The third level emerged as I gained new insights about myself. I began to realize how many of my attitudes and assumptions had been influenced by the estrangement. In the process of transposing the anger to understanding, my self-image of a "rejected child" faded. One of the rewards of the reconciliation was a new sense of my role as an equal member of the family. Many episodes contributed to this transformation, but one stands out as a particularly vivid example. One of my visits with Annie coincided with the anniversary of our father's death. Annie had never observed it before, but this time, we lit the *Yahrzeit* (death anniversary) candle together and said the appropriate blessings. For me, and I think also for her, it was a very special moment when we could share our separate memories of our father and confirm our relatedness.

Another especially meaningful episode occurred when Annie and I visited Betty at the nursing home. A few weeks before my visit, she had suffered a second stroke. Her speech was muddled and she was very frail. But despite her weakened condition, she roused herself to welcome me. I held her hand, patted her face and hair, wondering if she had been anticipating the end of her life. My hunch was confirmed when she asked me if I thought there was a life after death. I told her that heaven is the place where "you meet all the people you love and you don't have to speak to anyone you don't want to." My response seemed to reassure her. She smiled and murmured, "I'm glad we finally got together." She spoke of her mother and our brother as if she expected to be reunited with them. I showed her my new earrings and she responded: "Wear them in good health" (just as my mother would have said). Before I left, she told me to "have a good trip and be careful." (Again, the same phrase I had often heard from my mother). I bent to kiss her and whispered, "You are a nice lady." I had the impression that my expression of affection really mattered to her. Suddenly, I began to weep, deeply moved by this experience.

## Departures and conclusions

Betty spent the last two years of her life in the nursing home, suffering the effects of a series of strokes. On my last visit, she was toothless and weak. Although her speech was labored, she reminisced about the old house where we had both lived at different times. She remembered the arrangement of the rooms, her mother's sewing machine in one corner, the man who came to deliver ice, and the organ grinder with his monkey. In her mind's eye, she walked with me down the street of her childhood, naming each neighboring family. This flood of memories seemed to comfort her and strengthen the bond between us. I did not see her again, but I will cherish the memory of those last visits with this woman who had become my sister at last.

Less than a year after Betty died, Annie became ill and moved back East to be closer to her son and daughter. Whenever I spoke with her on the phone, she sounded depressed and frustrated, separated from her old friends and becoming increasingly frail. Her descriptions were punctuated with subtle complaints and snickers: "You don't know me very well," "You haven't come to visit me lately; why not?" and "That's about all I have to say." I heard these barbs as confirmation of our new bond. Now she was comfortable enough to express her impatience with me and with her own diminishing strength. Annie died at the age of eighty-six, sitting in her rocking chair with a piece of crocheting in her lap, unfinished.

The process of reconciliation is also unfinished, always incomplete. With all the insights, discoveries, and transformations, there is still more to be learned. In the years following the deaths of my siblings, I have been able to sustain a connection with only one niece, my sister Betty's younger daughter. The others apparently never perceived a connection with me, and I have not felt the need to impose myself on them. In relation to my siblings, I can rejoice that the old hostilities were replaced by a sense of real affection. For me, the writing of this book is a heartfelt reconciliation ritual. By sharing the steps in our journey, I am honoring their memory.

In my file is a stack of letters from Annie. Many of them contain long, detailed descriptions of her activities, friends, the weather, her beloved mountains. They invariably conclude with affectionate greetings and some reference to "isn't it wonderful that we found each other?!" Here is one of her poems, sent to me just before my last visit.

"I scrubbed and I polished
I dusted and swept
I threw out the garbage
that should never have been kept.
The car was spit polished
with Simonize goo
And all 'cause we're waiting
We're waiting for YOU!"

# CHAPTER SIX

# Five Families, Still Estranged After All These Years

---

*"Everything has its season, and there is a time for every-thing under the heaven."* But how do we understand the "season" for estrangement? When is the time to scatter, to hate, and to cut off from one's own family? Will the fragments ever be restored to wholeness? How can the rejected persons sustain the hope that their scars will eventually be healed?

---

## Prelude

The stories in this chapter tell of real families in which estrangement is an ongoing, painful reality. They encompass a wide gamut of emotions: disappointment, frustration, longing and grief, enduring affection and bitter rancor, despair and hope. Similar to the pathos that reverberates in the music of a great symphony or choral masterpiece, these stories speak to us from the depths of human experience. The families are not abnormal or exotic. In some ways, they may resemble your family and mine. The stories were told to me by one member of the immediate family – in most cases, a parent, son, daughter, or sibling. Virtually all of the storytellers have been cut off by a family member. Many of them express bewilderment, sadness, and, it seems to me, a genuine lack of understanding about the sources of the cutoff and their role in it. They feel the anger and rejection; they have tried to find answers. At first, many blamed themselves, asked for forgiveness and were rebuffed. Some now feel "wronged;" they perceive themselves as victims. Heartfelt expressions of hope appear in many of their descriptions. Others seem to be resigned to a condition of permanent alienation. I have observed that many of those who initiate a cutoff are seeking change, independence, and separation. The relatives who are left behind are more eager for attachment and continuity. However, this is not always the case. The provocations are complex and multi-layered. In some situations, a person will cut off from a cold, indifferent, or rejecting family to seek the closeness she has missed. She may try to find a substitute family that can provide the validation or sense of belonging that was lacking in her own family. Or, a person will distance himself from one family member in order to preserve his connection with another. In the stories that follow, you will find many of these themes.

As I collected and interpreted these stories over a period of years, I came to realize that estrangements in families are pervasive and repetitive. It is rare to find a person who cannot recall an episode of alienation in his own family history or in the families of friends or neighbors. A collection of stories about family conflict is like an improvisation with endless variations. There will always be additional stories to tell and different themes to be elaborated.

Reb Nachman of Bratslav said that the function of a story is to wake up those who are sleeping.[1] He was speaking about the power of narratives to rouse us from spiritual lethargy and challenge our indifference to essential truths. But stories have the power to stimulate other levels of awareness as well. Descriptions of fragmented families may provide the incentive to unlock repressed episodes in one's own family history. The storyteller presents the narrative; some readers recognize a pattern and transpose it to their own experience. Others will not grasp the connections. But if you have been "sleeping," some of these voices may serve as a wake-up call. Perhaps you will see yourself mirrored on these pages. In the midst of these stories, you may rediscover your own family.

Each of our stories starts from a certain point and finishes in the present. But these beginnings and endings are not like a race with a starting flag and a finish line; they are more like signposts along the way. All stories are incomplete and ongoing. Studying real families and recording their narratives is similar to the experience of entering a theatre in the middle of the first act and leaving before the final curtain. We see only a piece of the action. Many questions remain unanswered and some important details will inevitably be missing. Where are the "roots" of the conflict? Who were the grandparents of the protagonists, and what patterns from previous generations are being repeated in the current situation? What will happen in the years to come? Family relationships change over time. How will the death of the main characters alter the way family members perceive each other? We should be aware of the ambiguities and unanswered questions as we move ahead.

I have chosen narratives that illustrate particular family constellations and patterns of conflict. Many of these families are Jewish. Religious themes are prominent in some of the narratives, blurred or invisible in others. Each story in this chapter depicts a situation in which a conflict erupted and persisted, without repair or resolution. The families are real and the descriptions of family dynamics are accurate, but all names and some details have been changed to ensure confidentiality.

1. A "CHILDLESS" COUPLE AND THEIR DAUGHTER

THE FAMILY: *Trudy and Steven Aronson and their daughter Margaret; Trudy's sister Diane and her husband, Albert.*

Before the estrangement, the Aronson family appeared to be a model of middle-class solidarity. The subsequent sequence of events leading to alienation from their only daughter has caused profound misery to these stunned parents. Their story was told to me by Steven and supplemented by Diane, Margaret's aunt.

The family consists of the parents and one daughter Margaret, now in her late thirties. Both parents are capable, successful professionals: Steven is a pharmacist; Trudy is a teacher in a local college. Margaret, their only child, was born when both parents were in their mid-thirties. The first and only grandchild, she was welcomed with much joy by the entire family. Her mother's parents were respected leaders in the local Jewish community. Grandfather Morton was a judge. Grandmother Edith, an elegant, aristocratic type of woman, was an active volunteer for various artistic and religious organizations.

Margaret grew up in an upper middle-class milieu, attended a private girls' school and a large university in a mid-Western city. The parents, ostensibly assimilated into the mainstream of urban intellectual society, sent their daughter to a Reform temple but observed few, if any, religious rituals or obligations. According to Steven, Margaret had a normal childhood with an adoring family, grandparents, aunts and uncles, and many friends. She was an exceptionally pretty girl who enjoyed sports and social activities. Her grandparents lived nearby and she visited them frequently as their only cherished grandchild. But unlike her parents, who rarely criticized her or complained about her behavior, Grandmother Edith was outspoken in her views, not hesitating to tell Margaret that she was too fat, her hair was too long, her clothes were tacky. Margaret seemed to pick up on this behavior and at times could be very outspoken and harsh in her appraisals of others.

Trying to make sense of what happened later, her aunt recalls that Margaret was one of the few Jewish students in her school. Although her parents and grandparents frequently socialized with their upper-middle class WASP friends, Margaret felt like an outsider in the school environment. Characteristically a quiet, reticent child, these qualities become more noticeable during her teen years. Her parents attributed her withdrawn behavior to adolescent tensions. At the university, Margaret dated several students. During her junior year, she met a man who was older and not in her crowd. On their third date, he made unwanted advances. When she tried to resist him, he threatened to rape her. After that traumatic experience, Margaret became even more introverted and anxious. She rarely went out, her interest in school and friends diminished; eventually, she sought help from a therapist. Her parents worried about her mood swings and increasing isolation. She left college during her senior year, returned home, and took a job as a clerk in an accounting firm. However, she continued to be periodically depressed and withdrawn. She no longer confided in her mother. Her relationship with her father because increasingly more strained. Margaret would turn suddenly irritable when he tried to speak with her about any personal matter. Aunt Diane, a successful entrepreneur married to a prominent physician, had served as Margaret's role model during her childhood and adolescence. But Diane recalls that she had never been able to penetrate Margaret's armor and their relationship was never "close." At one point, Margaret abruptly refused all further contact with Diane.

Several months after returning home, Margaret moved into a small apartment of her own. Contacts with her parents became less frequent and more awkward. The tension came to a head after a family dinner to celebrate her father's birthday. She had agreed to attend, but made only a brief appearance at the end of the party and left without any explanation. The next day, when her mother phoned to express their disappointment, Margaret burst out with an enraged torrent of accusations. She claimed that they had been terrible parents; they had always tried to control her life. She did not want to see them again. Her mother wept, her father protested. Both parents tried to reason with her, insisting that they loved her and would always love her. Margaret terminated the conversation by hanging up the phone. For several months, Trudy and Steven had no direct contact with her. Despite their repeated efforts to phone, write letters, ask friends to mediate, she did not answer any of their messages. During this period, they heard rumors that their daughter had "come out" as a lesbian and had moved in with her female partner, a woman they had met previously as one of Margaret's friends.

About six months after the birthday episode, Trudy Aronson's speech suddenly became blurred and she was diagnosed with a mild stroke. Steven left a message on Margaret's answering machine, describing Trudy's crisis. Margaret immediately came to the hospital and her presence was reassuring. Trudy felt enormous relief and gratitude that the impasse had been resolved. Margaret promised to visit her parents again the following week. However, a few days later they received a brief note from her, saying only that she would not be seeing them again and warning them not to try to contact her. When Aunt Diane phoned her and mentioned the residual effects of Trudy's stroke, Margaret angrily accused her of "emotional extortion." And when a close friend of the family happened to meet her on the street and asked why she had not seen her parents, Margaret replied: "If they don't know, there's nothing I can say to them."

Nearly a year passed with no word from Margaret. Suddenly, she phoned her parents and arranged to get together for lunch. A brief period of quasi-reconciliation followed, with intermittent meetings and pleasant, impersonal conversations. But suddenly, in the midst of one of those meetings, Margaret grew irritable and spat out: "I can't do this anymore!" thus ending the temporary respite.

Trudy and Steven have become accustomed to a recurring zigzag pattern, often repeated with variations. "Now you see her, now you don't," her father says wanly. Margaret's Uncle Albert, with whom she had been especially close, celebrated his eightieth birthday. Margaret told her parents that she "might come" to the party but did not appear. Nor did she attend his funeral a few months later. Subsequently, she came to another family event for a few minutes and left with the comment, "I'm meeting friends." A few weeks later, she agreed to meet her parents at a restaurant but did not come, a sequence that has since been repeated several times. Once, her father happened to see Margaret in a supermarket. She greeted him guardedly, reached out and shook his hand, and went on her way. A similar meeting with her mother was equally frustrating. Trudy impulsively asked Margaret if she would rather have a handshake or a hug. Margaret replied that a hug would be nice. They embraced awkwardly and spoke for a few minutes. Steven calls these chance meetings "sightings," when they catch a fleeting glimpse of their daughter, only to be rebuffed again.

Recently, during another unplanned encounter with her mother, Margaret denied that she's a lesbian: "I know you think I'm living with a woman, but that's not true." Her parents insist that it makes no difference; they would be happy to accept their daughter on any terms, but there are no terms. Trudy and Steven are frustrated and exhausted from this repetitive ride on an emotional roller coaster. At the present time, more than ten years after the initial estrangement from their only child, there is no contact between Margaret and her parents. She has an unlisted phone number and changes it periodically. No one in the family knows how to reach her.

*The story of Margaret Aronson is similar and also distinctly different from the following narrative of the Berger family. In terms of their economic status, family constellation, and individual personalities, these two families have little in common. However, one theme is predominant in both families: estrangement from an only daughter. At the conclusion of this story, we shall focus on the salient issues and consider what can be learned from observing the patterns of attachment and alienation in these two families.*

## 2. A SINGLE WOMAN AND HER ESTRANGED DAUGHTER

*"You want to see me a lot more than I want to see you, so just live with that!"*

THE FAMILY: *Tamara Berger, her daughter Pesha, and Pesha's father Ken, deceased.*

I first heard about Tamara in a casual conversation with a friend. "If you're interested in estrangements, you should talk to Tamara." I phoned to make an appointment and told her briefly about my interest in family conflict. She agreed to meet with me, gave me directions for finding her apartment. Tamara, formerly from New York, lives near Tel Aviv, in a small town inhabited mainly by new immigrant families and older, retired persons. The location was not easy to find, but after a few wrong turns and dead-ends, I finally arrived at a rather dilapidated building with many entrances, overgrown grass and bushes, laundry hanging from windows, babies in buggies – a typical low-income neighborhood.

When I entered her small, cluttered apartment, I was not prepared for the sight: a tiny, wraith-like woman, thin gray hair in a bun, spindly arms and legs, sitting in a wheelchair. A black cat lay at her feet, purring contentedly. I was immediately struck by the vitality in Tamara's face, despite her obvious disabilities. She welcomed me with such warmth that although I had not met her before, I impulsively bent and kissed her, feeling drawn to this woman. Later I learned that she has suffered from an eating disorder for many years. Because of progressive weakness in her limbs and pervasive fatigue, she uses a wheelchair for household chores. With no preamble, she plunged into her story. I sensed that she really needed a sympathetic ear.

"It was the happiest day of my life when I brought my daughter home from the hospital." With this poignant reminiscence, Tamara began to describe the background of her estrangement from Pesha, her only child. Pesha was born in Israel a few months after Tamara and Ken were married. The couple had met when they were volunteers on a kibbutz. Both had come to Israel in search of adventure. Although neither of them claimed to be motivated by religious commitment or idealistic aspirations, they were yearning for a sense of belonging, a homeland. Pesha was conceived during their courtship and Ken urged her to have an abortion. Tamara was ambivalent about the decision to continue the pregnancy or terminate it. Later, when heated disputes erupted between them, each of them claimed that the other had pushed for an abortion. Three days before their wedding, they went to an abortion clinic, a seedy, awful place. Just before they were admitted, a friend who had accompanied them grabbed Ken by the ear and threatened to punch him if they didn't get out of there, telling them that abortion went against everything sacred in the Jewish tradition. They left the clinic, continued to make plans for the wedding, and waited out the pregnancy.

When the baby was born, she had severely deformed feet, a defect that required frequent and painful manipulations during the first two years of her life. Hearing Tamara describe those early problems, I wondered if Pesha's impairment was an ill omen, signaling that she would always have difficulty keeping her balance. Ken was fifteen years older than Tamara and she was his third wife. The marriage proceeded on shaky ground, with repeated arguments and trial separations. Ken was "lazy," "stingy," not successful at any job and no help at home. At one time, Tamara was holding down three jobs to make ends meet. When Pesha was ten, her parents divorced. Tamara took Pesha to the United States, despite Ken's opposition to the move. For about a year, Tamara tried to create a better life, but none of her efforts seemed to work out and they returned to Israel. Ken responded to their return by becoming angry and intimidating; he demanded visiting rights with Pesha and refused to pay child support. At one point, Ken went to Pesha's school, yanked her out of class, and threatened to attack the teacher who tried to stop him. He took the child to his "pad," later sending her home on a bus alone at night.

During the next five years, Tamara and Pesha moved twice, back and forth between Israel and the States. Tamara claimed that Ken never wrote to Pesha; Ken insisted that Tamara tore up his letters. The battles continued while Pesha struggled through a turbulent adolescence, culminating in a week in jail for selling and using hard drugs. Tamara tried to find a school that could contain her restless daughter, but the girl floundered and failed in each place. In her late adolescence, Pesha became increasingly rebellious, eventually going off to Europe with a girlfriend. By the time she was twenty, she was entirely on her own, living in Israel and continuing to "sow her wild oats." A pattern developed in which mother and daughter would be angry and out of touch for many months, accidentally meet, speak briefly, perhaps go to see a film together, sustain an apparently friendly connection for a few weeks. But then, Pesha would suddenly provoke an argument and break off again. Frequently she would accuse her mother of trying to control her life or focusing on her own interests instead of Pesha's. Their encounters would culminate in Pesha calling her mother "ugly," and Tamara dissolving in tears. Then there would be a period of months or years with no contact. Tamara's letters would be returned unopened, "address unknown." After giving up the futile struggle, Tamara would suddenly receive a note or phone call from her daughter. They would make plans to meet, but Pesha would cancel at the last minute, change the time or place, or just not show up. Tamara's physical disabilities put severe limits on her activities, and the effort to accommodate Pesha's whims took more energy than her mother could summon.

A few years ago, Ken died. Pesha subsequently accused her mother of abandoning him and causing his death. Tamara consulted a therapist about the ongoing problems with her daughter. The therapist interpreted Pesha's behavior as "her father reaching out from the grave to destroy whatever connection remained" between mother and daughter. Tamara feels that she can't do anything right in this relationship: "Pesha blames me for the war in Bosnia, the famine in Ethiopia, for every bad thing…"

Currently, Pesha is in Canada, Tamara lives in Israel. They communicate occasionally by email but Pesha refuses to see her mother or give Tamara her address or phone number. During their most recent exchange, Pesha told her mother "You want to see me a lot more than I want to see you, so just live with that!"

Before I left the meeting with Tamara, she asked me to look at her collection of family photos. With great effort, she lifted several large scrapbooks from the shelf and together we looked at the pasted remnants of her life. There were pictures of a grinning child, a happier Pesha with her proud mother, and other photos of Tamara as a child with her own sisters. When I noticed that she was crying silently, I asked about her sadness. She confided that she has been estranged from her only surviving sister for more than twenty-five years. At the time of our meeting, it seemed unlikely that either of these severed relationships, with her daughter or with her sister, would ever be mended.

**Comments:**

Let us consider these two families, the Aronsons and the Bergers, each with an only child, an unmarried daughter. Steven Aronson asked me if the alienation from his daughter could have been caused by their affluence, their exaggerated praise for her achievements, their closeness. Tamara Berger wondered if her daughter's hostility could be the result of their chaotic life style, the bitter separation from Ken, and the struggle to survive in difficult circumstances. Both sets of parents are understandably searching for an answer, wondering what they have done to cause the estrangement. It is doubtful, however, that any one of these factors could have been the "cause." For both of these families, the element of "only child" may have exacerbated the tensions. As unmarried, childless daughters, Margaret and Pesha represent a potent source of frustration and sense of failure; they symbolize the end of the family. With no other children and no hope of grandchildren, the estrangement from their only daughters is especially painful for these parents.

In some families, the position of only child – especially the only daughter – carries with it a heavy burden: the expectation that she will provide all the gratification, satisfy all the parental needs and eventually, reverse roles and become the caretaker of the parents. Despite all reassurance to the contrary, the burden may be perceived as excessive. In such a situation, the daughter could see the cutoff as a liberating act. On her balance sheet, separation may seem preferable to sustaining the connection. Lacking input from Margaret or Pesha, we cannot know their side of the story or understand their reasons for alienating themselves from their parents. Perhaps they have tried to create connections with surrogate families who provide them with the quality of love and support they could not find at home. An alternative possibility is that each of them has chosen to be a "loner," persistently avoiding all close relationships. For us, these speculations will remain unconfirmed.

In the case of Margaret, it appears that her personality characteristics, her vulnerabilities, the trauma of the threatened date rape and its aftermath, all contributed to the pattern of alienation from her parents. Perhaps by limiting the degree of contact and the frequency of their meetings, Margaret has found a way to take control of the relationship. In the Berger family, the attachment between mother and daughter was marred from the beginning. The volatile marital relationship, Pesha's early deformities, and her mother's tendency to cut off from other significant people in her life – each of these may have contributed to their subsequent problems. The frequent moves between Israel and the States apparently also had a destabilizing effect on the family. All of these factors may have exacerbated the alienation between mother and daughter, but no single element could have created sufficient grounds for a cutoff. Since neither of these young women has indicated her willingness to confront the real issues and work toward reconciliation, it is doubtful that the parents alone will be able to find a satisfactory solution to the impasse. Perhaps by clarifying their own roles in the process and accepting the situation with all of its pain and limitations, they can learn to forgive themselves and thus reach some degree of closure.

In my discussions with the Aronsons and with Tamara, I was struck by the realization that these parents no longer know their own child. They spoke of the "stranger" who "used to be" their daughter and the feeling of unreality that comes over them each time they meet, when they cannot find a coherent way to communicate with her. Their descriptions recalled a drawing I saw several years ago at an exhibit of contemporary art. It was a wall-sized contour map of the United States, with mountains, rivers, and borders sketched in. From a distance, it appeared to be a conventional map. At closer range, something seemed not quite right. Looking more carefully, I could make out the place names of cities and towns: "Murky," "Frail," "Outrage," "Tinytown." Some names were repeated in different locations: "Lost," "Lost," "Faraway," "Faraway." A town called "Dallas" was in the middle of Minnesota. The topography was "wrong" – mountains were not in their proper place; rivers flowed in circles. The entire map, despite its familiar outline, was a different, alien representation. Trying to make sense of it, I felt bewildered and off balance, not sure whether to chuckle or gasp. In retrospect, I see the map as a metaphor for an estranged relationship with a daughter, son, parent or sibling, someone whose features had been so familiar but who now seems like an alien, a stranger. The memory of closeness remains: the sound of her voice, the wry smile, her distinctive gestures. But the other person is no longer the same. When Margaret's parents catch a glimpse of their daughter at a rare "sighting," Margaret is not the person they remember. If Pesha keeps an appointment with her mother, Tamara feels awkward and uneasy, not knowing what to expect. This sense of strangeness is one aspect of the estrangement. The persons who are left behind must learn to live with the new reality.

### 3. THE YANKEE AND THE GREENHORN: CUT OFF BY SILENCE

THE FAMILY: *Stella and Herman Coplon; their daughters Millie and Faye, Faye's husband Abe Freedman, Abe's mother Bessie.*

Stella was born in New York City to Jewish parents who were assimilated and firmly rooted in the American culture. She was raised to appreciate secular values and modern styles. Her clothes came from elegant shops; she always appeared chic and manicured. Her granddaughter Anna, who shared this story with me, describes her as beautiful in her youth, handsome in old age, but "vain, cold, austere." When Stella was in her mid-20s, she married Herman Coplon, a man whose background was similar to hers. Their two daughters, Faye and Millie, were raised in an upper middle-class neighborhood in Manhattan. Their neighbors and friends were from the same social class; most of them were not Jewish. Millie followed the path preferred by her parents: she attended a posh private school and chose a husband whose family resembled her own. Faye was the rebel. When she married Abe Freedman, who came from a traditional Jewish family, Stella was not happy with her daughter's choice. She was embarrassed by the old-fashioned appearance and behavior of his parents, especially his mother, Bessie, who, in her eyes, was a "greenhorn." In vivid contrast to Stella, Bessie had been born in Russia, continued to observe religious rituals in her home, spoke Yiddish, wore quaint, European-style clothes, and struggled to communicate in heavily-accented English. At every family gathering, Stella managed to insult Bessie and make snide remarks about her speech or her dress. She told Faye that she was embarrassed to have a *greenhorn* in the family. Abe bitterly resented Stella's demeaning treatment of his mother and he stopped speaking to Stella. After Bessie died, his anger at Stella persisted.

As Stella aged, her stubbornness and pride became more exaggerated and after Herman's death, she grew even more set in her ways. Near the age of eighty, she became ill and spent several weeks in the hospital. There is a family anecdote, often recalled, of a typical "Stella tale," an episode that occurred in the hospital when Stella yelled for help: "Nurse, nurse, I'm dying! Bring me my curlers!"

At one point in the course of Stella's illness, the doctor told the family to expect her death within six months. He advised Faye to take her mother home and provide care for her. Faye's sister Millie was living abroad and could not assume responsibility for

Stella. The only alternative was to put the old woman in a nursing home, a decision that Faye could not accept. Despite Abe's smoldering anger at his mother-in-law, he reluctantly agreed to take Stella into his own home and pay for her care, but he steadfastly refused to speak to her or have any direct contact with her. So, when she left the hospital, Stella went to live with Faye and Abe, presumably for less than six months, since the doctor had assured them that her death was imminent. However, she stayed for almost twenty years, and lived to the age of one hundred and two! Except for the last few years in an old age home, Stella remained in Faye and Abe's home. At no time during those twenty years did Abe address a single word to Stella. Anna, Faye's daughter, told me how the "vow of silence" affected everyone in the family. Stella would sit in one room, Abe in another, and Faye would go from one to the other, carrying on "separate but equal" conversations aimed at preventing escalation of the tension. They would eat at the same dining room table and ask for the salt or the bread through an intermediary. The tension was palpable; you could almost "taste" it. Various attempts were made to enlist the help of an intermediary who could dilute the hostility. But neither side would back down, apologize, discuss, or try to resolve the problem. Twenty years is a long time to persist in anger and silence. In the Freedman house, it became the status quo. No one who witnessed it would ever forget it.

**Comments:**
The cold war in this family was provoked by Stella's contempt for Bessie, the "greenhorn." Stella resented the presence of an old-world, "odd" person in the family. Each of the three main protagonists, Stella, Bessie, and Abe, had a different view of the "correct" way to behave. For Stella, fitting in was the way. For Bessie, commitment to traditional values was the important thing. And for Abe, taking care of an aging mother-in-law was a "mitzvah," an ethical responsibility. At the same time, he could not accept her with grace. He took her into his home but not into his heart. In this way, he obeyed the commandment that requires a Jewish

person to care for an ill relative, yet he punished her by his silence. The result was an atmosphere filled with tension that could be relieved only by Stella's departure or death.

Andre Neher, the French-Jewish philosopher, discussed the phenomenon of "silence" and analyzed its diverse meanings. He wrote: "Just as there is a time to speak and a time to keep silence…, so there is a manner of speaking and a manner of keeping silence. If silence can be a sign of weakness, distraction, or ignorance, it can also be the expression of knowledge, willpower, or even heroism."[2] Reflecting on these ideas, we can suggest a different interpretation of Abe's silence. Perhaps he was exerting an extreme form of willpower to suppress his feelings of resentment. For him, silence was preferable to angry outbursts or sarcastic remarks. Was he trying to protect his family from the upheavals that occur when rage is exposed, hurled, spit out? Abe's silence may have been a heroic deed rather than a prolonged, wordless tantrum. We do not know.

In Chapter Two, I described the elements that have contributed to the persistence of the Jewish "identity system." Scholars have seen how, in every time and location, Jews invariably lived in an ambivalent situation. They were closely identified with the local, majority culture and, at the same time, they were indelibly connected to Jewish traditions and beliefs. They were at once the "other" and the "same." It seems that this "double tradition" was being played out in the conflict between Stella and Bessie. The Coplon family could serve as a miniature model of the persistent identity system. While Stella had aligned herself with the majority culture and behaved like a typical American "lady," Bessie had remained "the same;" she had retained all the characteristics of a traditional Jewish *bubbe*, an old-fashioned grandma. We can speculate that Bessie's presence was an uncomfortable reminder to Stella of the ambivalent nature of Jewish existence. Perhaps Stella's determination to assimilate was challenged by Bessie's undisguised, old-world mannerisms. Since the major players in this family drama are no longer alive, there is no way to know their motives. Like all family stories, some questions will never be answered. But the Stella/Bessie stories continue to resound in the family's oral history. Hopefully, the preserved memories will serve as useful lessons to future generations.

4. THE SIBLING BOND, SEVERED.

THE FAMILY: *Emma Fineman and her husband Joe; Emma's brother Lenny and his wife, Lona.*

When Emma Gold was born, her five-year old brother greeted her arrival with disgust. "I wanted a brother I could play with! What can I do with a *girl?*"

Emma and her brother Lenny came from a family that had once been traditional, Orthodox, but like many "enlightened" Jewish families from Eastern Europe, had transferred their allegiance to left-wing, liberal politics. Emigrating from Russia to the New World at the beginning of the century, the family settled in Detroit. Emma's parents met at a Socialist youth rally, married in the early 1920s and had two children, Lenny and Emma. Despite Lenny's initial disappointment, he learned to tolerate and even to enjoy having a sister. Emma recalls that she shared a room with her brother until they moved to a larger house when she was ten. She told him her secrets, stood by the sidelines, and cheered when he hit a home run. When she struggled with her math assignments, Lenny was the one who sat patiently and helped her.

When Emma was twelve and Lenny seventeen, their father was rushed to the hospital and died after a brief illness. The shock of the sudden loss was softened for Emma by Lenny's reassuring presence. During the following months, he assumed a protective, fathering role with his sister. He gave her advice about how to relate to boys, tolerated her friends' visits to their house, and provided valuable support during the period of their adjustment to a fatherless household.

When the Second World War broke out. Lenny enlisted in the Air Force and was stationed in California, where he remained for the duration of the war. After he was discharged, he came home and enrolled in a local college to study accounting. During this period, both Emma and Lenny met their eventual spouses. Emma began to date a medical student named Joe Fineman. After a brief courtship, they were married. Lenny had met Lona before the war and now began to date her more frequently. The two couples often went out together. Emma remembers her initial, ambivalent response to Lona. There was something about Lona that put Emma off, a vague sense of disapproval, a certain petulance in Lona's manner. The two young women were dissimilar in many ways: Emma was shy, quiet, and very pretty. Lona was brash and bossy. Emma noticed that when her brother was with Lona, he seemed to suppress his characteristic assertiveness and became passive and dependent, "like putty," Emma recalls. The two couples were married the same year, each attending the other's wedding. For a gift, Emma's mother gave Joe a gold watch. Since Lona already had a watch, her future mother-in-law gave her a silver dresser set, which later became one of the elements of contention in the escalation of animosity between Emma and Lona.

During the early years of their marriage, Emma and Joe made repeated efforts to continue the pattern of "double dating" with Lenny and his wife, but each time they were together, a vague sense of tension filled the air. When they would all be invited to dinner at their mother's house, Emma and Lenny would try to resume their former closeness but invariably, Lona would interrupt their conversation or leave early, claiming a headache. On each of these occasions, there was a perceptible buildup of agitation. After several uncomfortable encounters, Emma phoned Lona and asked to meet her for lunch. Lona refused. Emma tried to open up the problem by suggesting that they " talk about the bad feelings between us." In an effort to placate Lona, Emma acknowledged that maybe she, Emma, was at fault. "I don't know what I did to offend you, but whatever it was, I'm sorry. I hope we can try to improve our relationship…" Lona replied curtly, "I'm not interested." However, she did not hang up, but instead, she confronted Emma with a long list of complaints: Emma had insulted her, Lenny's mother hadn't given her a gold watch for a wedding gift, the dresser set was tarnished, she felt ignored at family gatherings. One final blast: "Lenny's favorite uncle doesn't visit us because we don't have fancy furniture like yours!" Emma refers somewhat wryly to this outburst as the "telephone tirade."

The years passed without any real change in the pattern of communication between the two couples. Intermittently, Lenny would try to resolve the tensions, confide in his sister, and express regret at the distance between them. At one point he seemed to be on the verge of leaving Lona, but then he reconsidered and became more markedly estranged from Emma, more dependent on his wife. It seemed that Lenny had been compelled to choose between his wife and his sister. Lona "won."

While their children were still young, Emma and Joe gradually became more religious. They joined an Orthodox synagogue, ate only kosher food, and observed the Sabbath in their home. Their children attended a Hebrew day school. Lona and Lenny went the other way, following a more liberal trend and observing few of the rituals. Their children attended public school and were involved in secular activities. The cousins knew each other slightly but did not ever become friendly or have a sense of belonging to the same family. The reality of their different lifestyles and separate religious pathways hammered yet another wedge into the widening distance between them. Emma and Joe initiated a family tradition with a Passover Seder at their home each year. Lenny, Lona, and their children were always invited and they would usually accept, but their presence would create enough tension to make everyone uncomfortable. Lona would complain about the arrangements, interrupt the *Haggadah* reading, and make snide remarks about the family and the food. After a few years, Emma and Joe reluctantly decided to leave them out of the Seder, adding yet another item to Lona's list of grievances.

At special moments in the life cycle of the family, Emma felt especially deprived of Lenny's presence. Impulsively, she would phone him, ask to meet him for lunch, and try to discuss the problem. At the conclusion of these meetings, she would invariably feel more frustrated and depressed. He would respond to her efforts with a hopeless shrug: "It's a long story; I can't do anything to change it." From time to time, another family member would try to intervene. One cousin arranged a meeting between Emma and Lona that ended on a sour note. An aunt also tried to bring them together but without success.

Tragedy struck Lenny's family when their seventeen-year old daughter died in a drowning accident. Emma and Joe heard of her death from Lona's brother, who phoned them in the middle of the night. Early the next morning they went to Lenny's house. Lona came to the door, impulsively hugged Emma and broke down sobbing in terrible grief. This was the only time she had ever expressed an affectionate gesture toward Emma, and it was never to be repeated. Joe and Emma came to the house frequently during the mourning week of *shiva*, but Lona never spoke with them. Whenever Emma would approach her, she would turn away.

Now, the four protagonists in this story are growing old, but not together. Each of them has married children and grandchildren, but the cousins barely know each other. There are no shared vacations or family celebrations. When they do meet, the awkwardness and tensions are palpable. Last year, the two couples attended a family wedding but Lona did not speak to Emma. Usually, Emma and Joe try to avoid these occasions.

Emma continues to phone Lenny on his birthday and on every Jewish holiday, but he rarely initiates a call to her. When Lona answers the phone, the communication is always brief and cool. Emma calls it "civil non-acceptance." Perhaps once a year, Emma and Lenny meet for lunch, but these meetings are invariably painful for Emma. At one such meeting, Emma impulsively burst out with "Oh, I really miss having a big brother!" Lenny dismissed her outburst with an indifferent wave of his hand: "Come on, you're a big girl now." Emma could barely contain her tears of pain and outrage. A few years ago, Emma wrote a letter to Lenny, reminiscing about old times. He answered with a similar letter, thanking her for writing to him. These "windows of opportunity" open from time to time, offer a spark of hope to Emma, but shut with a resounding bang, or sometimes with a whimper.

Recently, Emma and Lona came face to face at the bat mitzvah of Emma's granddaughter Miriam. Their encounter at this event was similar to all the others. Emma approached Lenny, Lona turned away, and Emma and Lenny had a brief, tense conversation. Emma made yet another attempt to bridge the distance, asking him if he would like to see her Israeli grandchildren, whom he has never met. "They're all at the table, over there. They'd love to meet you; wouldn't you like to say hello?" She allowed herself a moment of hope. But he said, "No, that's O.K.," and walked away.

At the same family event, Emma learned more about the ripples that have been set off by this estrangement, now lasting for more than four decades. Cousin Sally warned Emma that Lona would never speak with her, never forgive her, but Sally offered no other comment. At the dinner, several relatives made a special effort to greet Lona, but if they had any connection with Emma, she treated them coolly. It seems that she has made a mental note of "friends" and enemies" in the family, and responds accordingly. The cousins from the two families cut a wide berth around each other and do not speak. Lona remains a solid block of ice. Emma has made an uneasy peace with the situation. She has not given up, but she no longer expects that the conflict will resolve.

## Comments

The Gold-Fineman family provides a natural resource for studying the persistence of anger and rejection over several decades. The estrangement between Emma and her brother has been absorbed into the life of the family and festers there like an open wound. A new generation has been born, older members have died; the family life cycle moves on; the animosity remains. We do not know Lona's perception of the conflict or her version of its origins. We can only speculate about the reasons for its tenacity, its strangle hold on the family. Anger generates energy; it ignites a sense of power. Sustaining the anger keeps the sense of power alive. The feeling of outrage may be exaggerated or even pathological, but it allows the person to feign a position of strength that counteracts his fear of passivity or surrender. Whether unconsciously or intentionally, Lona may be using her anger as power, to assert control in a situation in which she somehow feels inadequate and excluded. The three-part interaction, the triangle formed by Emma, Lenny, and Lona, has retained its original jagged outlines and incessant static.

In Hebrew, one of the words for "anger" is derived from the root *kham*, meaning "heat." Anger is "hot," it simmers, bubbles up, and spills over. Heated to the boiling point, it often cannot be contained or cooled. When words are spoken in a spurt of anger, they are not "words" and not "spoken" in the usual sense of speech. "I hate you!" "Get out of my life! "You're not my son any more!" In this context, they become weapons, battering rams, poison. They are not "spoken," but spit out, slammed, vomited, exploded. Once let loose, these furious blasts cannot be taken back, denied, or ignored. In some situations, they reverberate through the family for years, sustaining the intensity of the anger and fueling the estrangement. The emotional climate perpetuates itself and the anger-driven process becomes an integral part of the family dynamic.

An estrangement can be resolved only if the protagonists are willing to address the real sources of the conflict. Or, it may be bypassed if they can agree to overlook the problems and move on. In this family, only Emma has tried to resolve the impasse. Without reciprocity on Lona's side or a change of heart in Lenny, there is little likelihood of change.

5. HANDICAP AS A PROVOCATION FOR CUTOFF.

THE FAMILY: *Esther Leff, her brother Larry and her sister Florence; their parents, Jake and Fanny, and Jake's parents.*

Esther and I are having lunch at "Café Daniel," a quiet, spacious restaurant. We first met several years ago at a professional conference and have been friends ever since. Now, we sit across the table looking at each other. We "see" in two different ways. I notice her black pants and blue top, the gray beginning to show around her hairline. I examine the items on the menu. She "sees" my voice, "reads" my mood, hears the clatter of dishes. When the waitress approaches, Esther asks for a Braille menu. The guide dog under our table suddenly gets up to stretch and Esther tells her, "Sit down, Tillie."

Esther hikes in the mountains, canoes down the rivers, goes cross-country skiing, volunteers at the old age home. She worked for many years as an educational specialist in the public schools, consulting with teachers of handicapped children and their parents. Now she's "retired," not her choice but jobs are hard to find for a middle-aged blind person, no matter how good she is at her profession. She has many friends and is learning how to access the Internet on her computer. A few years ago, she visited Israel with a group of blind young people. Last year, Esther bought a small house on a quiet street in an old residential neighborhood. She lives there alone, but not quite alone: with Tillie.

From our conversations, I know that Esther has been blind from birth. She has one brother who is sighted and a younger sister who is crippled from a birth injury. Esther comes from an observant Jewish family. She has affiliated with more than one local synagogue and has experienced various obstacles navigating the choppy waters of synagogue customs and regulations. At one place, she was told that "dogs are not allowed," not even guide dogs. At another place, when she tried to register for a class, she was told it was already full. Later she heard that they were not comfortable with a blind woman in their midst.

I had been looking forward to speaking with Esther about my book, to ask for her ideas, and share some of the stories with her. I had not anticipated her response. When I told her the topic and described the estrangement in my own family, she focused immediately on the heart of the matter. "I know a lot about that," she said. "I have a story, too."

Esther's grandparents were traditional, observant Jews. Both of their families had left Russia before the First World War, immigrated to the United States, and settled in Cleveland, where Esther's mother Fanny and father Jake were born. There were many siblings in each of their families, perhaps reflecting an effort to replace those who had been lost in pogroms and epidemics in the "old country." The families lived in the same neighborhood, and Fanny and Jake had known each other from childhood. They married when they were in their late twenties, but it was several years before they conceived their first child. When Fanny announced the impending birth, everyone was elated. However, the news of Esther's arrival was not greeted with enthusiasm by Jake's parents. The reality of her blindness was a terrible blow that turned them against the baby. From the beginning, they refused to visit her, never played with her, and treated her as an outcast. During her childhood, their infrequent visits were always tense. She remembers the rare occasions when she went to their house and was told not to touch anything. For a blind child, this was like being in a bottomless pit, with no way to get her bearings. Later, Esther wondered if their stubborn rejection could have been a deviant expression of their religiosity, since they were observant Jews who professed to obey the commandments. But how could there be a connection between obeying God and rejecting a blind child? Esther never resolved this dilemma, but it did not turn her away from Judaism, and she has continued to identify with her family's religious heritage.

Esther related these aspects of her life with deep sadness, yet with no indication of reproach or anger. At one point in our conversation, when she was recalling a particular incident, the tears came. It seems that her parents were invited to the wedding of her father's sister, who was marrying late, in middle age. There was great rejoicing in the family for this spinster woman who was finally to be a bride. Esther's parents had been told that no children were invited to the wedding, so Esther, then about twelve, stayed home with her sister and brother. When her parents came home from the festivities, her mother was furious, storming around the house. She had seen several children at the wedding, relatives as well as friends. Only Esther and her siblings had been left out.

She recalls that her mother took the check that was intended as a wedding gift and tore it up, refusing to give anything to people who rejected her daughters. It was the first time in many years that Esther had recalled this occasion. Telling the story opened some painful wounds.

Not everyone in the family had a hostile attitude toward Esther. Although her mother's parents had died when she was a young child, there were numerous aunts, uncles, and a growing array of cousins on her mother's side of the family. Most of them were living in the same city and they all related to her as a natural part of the family. To this day, she can identify each of them by name, and she knows the birth order of all the cousins. One of her mother's brothers was a watchmaker. He would frequently explain his craft to Esther and "show" her the watches in his shop. Another uncle took her to "see" a cow, and she still remembers the feel of the animal's rough tongue on her arm. These memories contrast sharply with the neglect she felt from her father's large family, all of whom joined in the cutoff from Esther and her sister. It was only after she graduated with honors from a prestigious Ivy League college that some of her father's relatives began to accept Esther as a legitimate person. Speculating about the causes of her grandparents' persistent rejection, Esther does not try to analyze or interpret their behavior, except to say, "they are not a close family."

In subsequent conversations with Esther, we discussed the aftermath of this painful aspect of her life. Although the estrangement was never resolved or adequately explained, Esther has not allowed it to destroy her sense of belonging to a family or to dampen her affection and concern for other people. Recently, she told me about a book she had read and the insight it gave her. Accessible on tape to blind readers, the book is *The Promised Land*, by Mary Antin. It is a vivid memoir of Jewish family life in a Russian *shtetl* late in the nineteenth century, before the family immigrated to America. The theme that caught Esther's attention was the fear of physical handicaps and the deep, pervasive power of superstition in the *shtetl* community. She discovered that young boys would blind themselves in one eye to escape the horrors of the Czar's army.[3] There were all sorts of magic tricks and amulets, secret prayers and lucky signs, auspicious dreams, and special spices that were used to protect the vulnerable person from such catastrophes as blindness. A certain wildflower that grew on the grassy slopes of the fields was called "blind flower," because it was said to cause blindness in the impulsive children who picked it.[4] Esther realized that her grandparents' attitudes must have been profoundly influenced by this heavy cloud of superstition. While it did not excuse their rejection, the new awareness provided a context for understanding their feelings.

**Comments**

Esther's descriptions of her parents give the impression of a substantial reservoir of strength in the family. During her childhood, both parents encouraged her independence and insisted that she participate in normal activities. Her handicapped sister was given a similar message: "You can do it!" When I asked how her father dealt with his own parents' rejection of his handicapped daughters, she replied that as far as she knows, he never confronted them on this issue. He continued to be in contact with them until their deaths. In marked contrast to their rejection, he was a constant, reliable source of strength and support to his daughters. It is tempting to speculate about the dynamics in this family. What were the historical patterns and traditions that influenced the grandparents' rejection of Esther? We can wonder if her blindness was the eruption of a genetic flaw that had been present in the family much earlier. Coming from a social milieu that valued perfection and high achievement, the extreme reaction of the grandparents may have been fueled by unbearable anxiety about Esther's future. Another possibility is that Esther served as a scapegoat for some other source of tension, a problem never articulated or resolved. Or, perhaps they were simply reacting in a selfish and hurtful way to an innocent child. Whatever the reasons, Esther has managed to accept the reality of the estrangement and create a full life of her own.

## Concluding thoughts

A family with an unresolved cutoff is like a story with no end. The issues have not been confronted, resolved, or bypassed. They remain as a haunting echo, or sometimes a lingering pestilence. Members feel as if they are caught in a war that has afflicted them for a long span of time, without victory or truce. I have observed families in which the only way to sustain connections is by criticism, snubs, or intimidation. In many stories of ongoing estrangement, we will find versions of this repetitive pattern, as if the rhythm of provocation and revenge has become a habit, an addiction.

Is there a key to reading these narratives, a method for extracting lessons from them? In the opening chapters of this book, we discussed three dimensions: family process and structure, the cultural context and historical background, and the ethical or religious foundations of family life. Each of these dimensions is reflected in the stories we have described. In some of the families, the dynamics and relationships are the prominent factors: the family as a system, its emotional climate, triangular interactions, and developmental progressions. The prolonged alienation in Emma's family highlights these elements. In other stories, the cultural, religious, and historical themes are central to the plot. The reaction of Esther's grandparents to her blindness is one example. And finally, the ultimate values, the moral and ethical basis of behavior can be seen to operate, as we shall see in two stories that appear here in Chapter 8. In every alienated family, manifestations of the three interlocking dimensions may be discerned. Some are clearly visible; others are muted and suppressed.

When we reflect on the stories of estranged families, we can trace the evolution of hostilities. We see how hidden agendas and repressed grievances lie dormant and then flare up in spurts of accusations and retaliations, or remain buried in stubborn silence. What elements distinguish these families from others who have turned away from the anger, who have moved toward repair and renewal? In more fortunate situations, new insights kindle the aspiration for change. When the protagonists begin to modify their habitual behavior patterns, they are able to see their family in a new light. The occurrence of estrangement then becomes an opportunity for growth; it can actually serve as an incentive to clarify the boundaries of relationships and redefine one's separate identity. What appeared to be polar opposites – self and others, closeness and distance, right and wrong – can be re-framed in more flexible, more constructive terms. As old animosities begin to dissolve, new modes of relating become possible. In the midst of this process, family members come to acknowledge a basic paradox of human existence: we know ourselves only in the context of living with others, and we experience relationships only in the effort to differentiate ourselves from others. The ultimate question is how a person can strengthen his or her individual identity while sustaining meaningful, mutually supportive connections with family members. Those who remain mired in anger are not able to address this question.

When the lure of money and possessions obliterates the affirmation of respect and affection between parents and their children, or between siblings, the sense of kinship is undermined and personal identity is often compromised. In the next chapter, we will explore one of the most explosive provocations for family conflict, the issue of inheritance.

# CHAPTER SEVEN

# Inheritance Feuds – Is Money the Root?

(With the collaboration of Lynn J. Benswanger, J.D., LL.M.)

## INTRODUCTION

Of the many transforming events that occur in families, death is perhaps the most complex. Every major change in the family system – birth, marriage, and divorce – requires adjustments and role modifications. These events are likely to set the family off balance until the new elements can be integrated and the emotional reactions tempered. A death in the family has a significance that is profoundly different from every other event. In contrast to births and marriages, which denote beginnings, death is a stop sign. It is the last word, the point at which choices have been made and judgments have been sealed. When a family member dies, decisions that were previously fluid, malleable, and evolving become irrevocable, engraved in stone. This sense of finality is especially relevant to the issues surrounding the inheritance.

Professionals who specialize in estate planning are familiar with the expressions of resistance that emerge during the making of a will. One of their most challenging tasks is to convince clients to consider seriously the consequences of their own mortality.

People would rather discuss almost anything else. As a result, it is not uncommon for estate planning sessions to lose focus and veer off course. Clients are reluctant to make crucial decisions regarding who will manage their affairs after they are gone, and who will be the recipients of their largesse. Much is left up in the air, as if to say, "I don't have to make up my mind about this now; there's plenty of time." Or, decisions are made and repeatedly revised. As long as things remain in flux, the decision-maker can sustain the illusion that he or she will live forever.

Despite these challenges, the results of estate planning are eventually finalized, signed and, with a relieved sigh, put away in a safe place. But in some cases, this process is transposed from the task of arranging one's affairs to the attempt to control others' lives. Rather than face the inevitable fact of her own death, the would-be testator chooses to focus instead on how to beat the system, reach out from beyond the grave to make a statement, effect a crisis, twist an arm, stamp a foot. The satisfaction to be gleaned from this kind of manipulation is two-fold. First, the manipulator is, in his or her own mind, achieving some sort of immortality. Perhaps equally important, she has the satisfaction of knowing that she will not be around to be called to account for whatever mischief she may cause.

CASE HISTORIES

Here are a few brief sketches that exemplify the "netherworld" of estate planning. A wealthy man, a lawyer, well-versed in the intricacies of probate jurisprudence, leaves a will that is deliberately ambiguous. His second marriage, to a much younger woman, had been vigorously opposed by his adult children. Perhaps he was punishing them by his divisive manipulations. During the period before his death, he informed every close relative that he had bequeathed them equal portions of his estate. In a deliberately disruptive maneuver, he told each of them that they would inherit the same properties, thus generating false expectations throughout the family. After his death, when the will was read, the family realized they had been led astray. His sons, their children, and the "wicked stepmother" all contested the will and struggled against each other in ugly legal battles that dragged on for years. By means of his manipulations, the deceased made certain that discord would be sowed by his death and the surviving family members would remember him, although he would not be mourned in the usual sense. He had achieved a certain measure of afterlife, but the flavor of gall and ashes would cling to his ghostly remains.

An elderly woman leaves a will in which she imposes specific lifestyle requirements on her youngest son, a determined rebel who is seen as the "black sheep" of the family. If he refuses to comply, he will not be allowed to access his inheritance, which his mother had placed under the tight control of his two older brothers. In this way, the deceased has ensured that the pattern of sibling rivalry will be continued after her death. With this sour legacy, it is doubtful that any of the descendants will mourn her passing. Whether or not they comply with her demands, the aftermath of this inheritance dispute will leave deep scars on the family for a long time.

Even when the person contemplating death does his or her utmost to avoid stirring up conflict, the heirs themselves often create their own rifts in the family. They may unconsciously act out previous problems in the context of a struggle over the inheritance. It is a rude awakening for any well-meaning lawyer to present a perfectly reasonable financial compromise and see his clients continue to battle, finding new pretexts to sustain their disputes in the courtroom instead of discussing them rationally in the home of their parents or siblings.

Evelyn and her brother Jeff provide an example of this type of impasse. They had always been close, especially after their father's premature death when they were teenagers. But when their seventy-year-old mother Bertha became terminally ill, Jeff just wasn't interested or capable of helping with her care. His visits to Bertha were infrequent, and he reacted angrily to Evelyn's complaints about his lack of responsibility. Eventually, it became clear that

Jeff was under strong pressure at home to devote less time to his mother and more time to his young wife and child.

As Bertha's condition worsened, she needed more care than Evelyn could provide from her own home, thirty miles away. Evelyn felt obliged to move into her mother's small condominium with her husband and two young children. Bertha had lived there for many years and was determined to die there. Although the old woman had always treated her children equally, she decided to rewrite her will to leave the condo to Evelyn as compensation for her sacrifice. But during one of his rare visits to his mother, Jeff discovered the new version of the will. He instructed his own lawyer to draft a new will that redistributed the property in his favor and, by hook or by crook, he convinced Bertha to sign it. Evelyn was angry at her brother for refusing to help care for their mother, but she was even more appalled at his manipulation of a frail, vulnerable old woman. When Bertha died, Evelyn was tempted not to inform her brother. At the last minute she did phone him, and he came to the mortuary. Brother and sister attended the funeral, but they sat apart and maintained a stony silence. The distribution of the estate was handled through separate communications with the lawyers. Additional threats and accusations were exchanged. Then, all contact between brother and sister stopped. Five years have passed since Bertha died. The rancor between Evelyn and Jeff persists, with no resolution in sight.

THE NATURE OF PROPERTY

A probate lawyer is addressing his colleagues about the nature of property.[1] He describes the elements that contribute to many of the bitter battles over inheritance. People, he says, are obsessed with possessions. We see the world as comprised of various objects, many of which are useful for our daily lives. Some are valuable as food, clothing, and adornments. Others are used as weapons; still others are essential to the production of various commodities. One thing represents the very foundation of all economic life, and that is the land on which we are born, live, work, and in which we are buried. In order to have a sense of order in the universe, all property must have an owner. It must be able to be identified as yours, theirs, or mine.

Property has two essential aspects. First, there is the thing or place itself, its visible, tangible existence. Then, there is the web of social relations that link the object to its owner. This second aspect defines the human uses of the property and the limits that are imposed on those uses. It also implies that property is endowed with emotional significance: it can be given and taken away. The manner in which property is bequeathed can express love or anger, forgiveness or vengeance, an entire spectrum of emotional reactions to others, especially to family members. The point at which the emotional attributes of property are most potent is when they become the motivation for challenging the bequests in a will.

Countless provocations can lead to conflicts over money and property. To be deprived of all or a portion of an inheritance is a particularly volatile basis for a family feud. Refusing to give an expected gift, withholding a personal possession that has special significance, reneging on a promise to provide a dowry or pay for a relative's education or medical care – any of these can set off an escalating pattern of angry claims. In such situations, is money actually the root of the problem? In many cases, it is not. Other issues, more potent and more insidious, may be hidden in the cracks, obscured by the lure of money. Among these are power struggles, turf battles, invisible loyalties, the favoring of certain relatives over others, competition for love and recognition. These issues are likely to evoke intense emotional reactions. In the context of a dispute over inheritance, any of them may serve as the provocation for a prolonged conflict.

### A silver teapot and a broken heart

A probate lawyer shared his impressions of some of the most difficult and the most gratifying cases involving inheritance disputes. The following description provides one vivid example of the extreme reactions that can be evoked by an unequal bequest involving personal possessions. Because of the lawyer's effective intervention, an ugly conflict was resolved.

At the time of her death, Bernice had two daughters, Polly and Molly, and seven grandchildren. She left small bequests to each grandchild, but one grandson was given more than the others. In addition, the older daughter, Polly, was left considerably more money than the younger one. Bernice did not specify who was to inherit her personal possessions, leaving the distribution of these objects to Polly's discretion. In a lengthy letter to the lawyer, Molly, the deprived daughter, listed various objects that had belonged to her mother. She was infuriated over Polly's stated intention to auction off such mementos as their mother's collection of English china and her silver tea set. The voluminous correspondence revealed Molly's "broken heart" over the potential loss of these objects. She had cut off all contact with her sister and was considering legal action to recover at least a portion of her "rightful inheritance." After the lawyer warned the sisters about unpleasant legal consequences should they fail to reach an agreement, Molly and Polly reluctantly agreed to a face-to-face meeting. At this meeting, the two women were able to work out a compromise about the distribution of their mother's possessions, thus avoiding messy litigation and resolving at least a portion of the hostility in the family. Cases similar to this one led another lawyer to comment on the context of many inheritance disputes. In the course of his practice, he has learned that fighting with a close relative can be "one of the basic pleasures of family life." Contesting a will is one way to punish your brother or sister for ridiculing your husband or ignoring your birthday. In a contentious family, disputes over money and possessions may provide the relatives with the only live sparks of family connection.

The solution reached by Molly and Polly is not typical of the outcome in many families who are embroiled in disputes over inheritance. More frequently, the anger persists and the conflict is not resolved. In the story of an inheritance dispute that is described later in this chapter, the outcome is vastly different and infinitely more painful.

## JEWISH ETHICAL WILLS

Every social group and religious system develops its own ways to regulate the ownership of property and to define the procedures for transferring possessions from one generation to the next. In the annals of Jewish literature, there are countless volumes that discuss the laws of inheritance, all dealing with the procedures to be followed in writing a will and carrying out its stipulations.[2] In addition to the documents that bequeath property to heirs, many Jews prepare a written statement of instructions about other matters, matters whose significance often far exceeds that of material wealth or property. This is the document known as an ethical will.

An ethical will or spiritual legacy is a statement from one generation to the next that imparts values, ideals, aspirations and sometimes, threats. Although money and possessions may be used as incentives in some of these documents, the main focus is on beliefs and expectations that are communicated from parent to child. Ethical wills are an integral part of Hebrew literature, from the Bible to the present day. The testament of the Patriarch Jacob,[3] recited orally to his sons by the dying man, is a prototype of this kind of spiritual legacy. There are numerous examples of these documents, some dating from the Middle Ages and the Renaissance. Many were written by famous scholars and rabbis; others were scribbled hurriedly by victims of persecution; still others were composed by contemporary Israelis and modern American Jews.[4] For countless families, an ethical will was and continues to be a customary practice, repeated in each generation as the patriarch or matriarch approaches the end of life. These documents are tangible expressions of a parent's spiritual legacy, personal reflections on his life as a Jew, and a summary of the precepts she wants to bequeath to her children. Often, they contain warnings of dire consequences if children do not follow the path extolled by their parent. Shortly before his death, the great Yiddish author Sholom Aleichem wrote a document that has been called "one of the great ethical wills in history." It contains ten major points. One of them is a not-so-veiled threat: "my children and children's children can have whatever beliefs or convictions they desire. But I beg of them to guard their Jewish heritage. If any of them reject their origins to join a different faith, then that is a sign they have detached themselves from my will..."[5] Another writer addresses his admonitions to his son-in-law, saying: "do not permit your children to assimilate; above all, do not permit them to marry those of another faith. Be proud of your Jewish ancestry, which is the pride and bulwark of all civilization."[6] One collection of ethical wills on the Internet includes several examples that were composed by women. Among these are the mother of college-aged sons, a terminally ill young woman, a married woman during her first pregnancy, a single mother, and a widowed grandmother.[7]

The twelfth century ethical will of Judah Ibn Tibbon, addressed to his son Samuel, is one of the most vivid examples of a devoted father's attempt to transmit his most important values.[8] This document may also be seen as an instrument for evoking guilt and remorse in the next generation. The father, a scholar, translator, and physician who was forced to leave Spain and settled in Provence, wrote this document before his death in 1190. Apparently he was worried about his young son's wayward behavior. Here is the voice of an elderly man, enumerating his sacrifices and complaining about his son's deficiencies. It is titled "In praise of learning, education and the good life." Following are excerpts from this remarkable document, which I have transposed into modern speech:

> *...I swaddled you and brought you up; I fed and clothed you; I sacrificed my sleep for you; I denied myself the usual pleasures and relaxations; I am still working to earn your inheritance.... I provided you with a library; I journeyed to the ends of the earth to find you the best teachers. Untold harm might have come to me on my travels on your behalf... But you, my son, deceived my hopes! You did not use your abilities; you ignored the books; you still depend on me to*

*rescue you from your own indolence. But soon I will die,
and then who will support you? Who will care for you as I
have done?*

*…You are still young, and improvement is possible. May
God help you to mend your ways and follow the true path.
When I am gone, devote yourself to the study of Torah; study
medicine; avoid disputes; keep your pen in good working
order and use proper ink; do not take unnecessary risks;
provide decent clothing for your family; protect your books
from damp and mice; honor your wife; read the Bible on the
Sabbath and festivals; be diligent in fulfilling my commands;
and do not destroy any of my writings or letters…*

What can be the impact of such a document on the son to whom
it is addressed? He could become angry and rebellious; he could
decide to ignore his father's warnings. But in this case, his father's admonitions apparently served as an effective alarm to
the young man. Samuel became a prolific translator of many
important works on medicine, astronomy, and philosophy. He
translated one of the most significant Jewish texts, the *Guide to
the Perplexed*, from Arabic into Hebrew, and sought the advice of
the author, the great Maimonides himself. His works established
the style of philosophic Hebrew, which was used for centuries. In
his lifetime, he earned great honor and fame. [9] One can imagine
that his father would have been proud of him. An ethical will
can serve as a source of wisdom to family members, as it did in
this case. But it can also become a vehicle for accusations and
intimidations. When the dying person uses the will to impose
impossible demands or coerce his heirs, the document is likely
to stir up lingering resentment.

DISINHERITANCE AND ITS FALLOUT

In certain situations, the act of altering wording in a document
will have weighty consequences. Changing one detail of a birth
or death certificate, erasing crucial portions of a handwritten

confession, amending specifications of a financial agreement or business contract – such acts are likely to have far-reaching effects on the persons involved. A few marks of a pen can make the difference between survival and death, wealth and poverty, gratitude and resentment. They can also undermine the status of a relationship. Modifying a will is one example of such a radical act. If a person adds a codicil that countermands previous intentions, if she changes the beneficiaries or reassigns assets, this act is likely to create massive turmoil in the emotional climate of the family.

In the following story, there was no spiritual legacy and no amicable settlement. Instead, there was a codicil to a mother's will, a gesture from the grave that caused bitter enmity between two sisters.

THE FAMILY: *Sima, her husband Moshe, Sima's sister Peggy, and their parents Gertrude and Rafael, deceased.*

## Background

Along the main streets, headlights and spotlights pierced the darkness. A terrible scene: the blinking lights of police cars, ambulances with sirens screeching, debris scattered in all directions. A terrorist's bomb had exploded in a café in downtown Jerusalem, killing several people and wounding many others. Two young people, the daughter and son of an Israeli couple, were among the dead. Ariela, age 18, had been studying in Jerusalem at a Torah Center for young women. Her brother Ron had been in New England, visiting their aunt Peggy and their grandmother Gertrude. At the end of the summer, Ron flew to Israel to spend a month with his sister. On their first evening together, they met friends at the café targeted by the terrorists. The sister and brother were killed instantly.

At the time of the tragedy, their parents, Sima and Moshe, were in France. A cousin phoned to tell them the terrible news. In deep shock, they flew home to Israel for the funeral. The following weeks and months were filled with agonizing images

208

and terrible nightmares. Their only children were dead; hopes for the future were destroyed. During this dreadful period, Sima repeatedly sought comfort from her mother but was persistently rebuffed. It seemed that Gertrude was unable or unwilling to be sympathetic, even after her daughter had suffered such a terrible loss. Three years later, Gertrude died. Sima tells this story, aided by notes and documents in a file she has labeled "Betrayal."

## Antecedents of the conflict

Sima was born in rural New England, in a house that had been owned by her father's family for three generations. He had inherited the property and its two large dwellings from his father. Sima's sister Peggy was born two years later in the same house.

When Sima was an infant, she was sent to live with an aunt and, at the age of four, to a boarding school. The same pattern was followed two years later with Peggy. Their mother Gertrude had apparently been overwhelmed by the obligations of motherhood and was seeking ways to avoid the role. To this day, Sima cannot recall any caring or affectionate response from her mother. "She never wanted us; she shouldn't have been a mother." Sima chose the word "acerbic" to describe her mother's characteristic response. "I always knew where I stood with her, except at the end."

When Sima was in her mid-twenties, she traveled through Europe with a friend. There she met Moshe, whose family had immigrated to France from Tunisia. Sima was immediately attracted to this warm, compassionate man. His strong religious commitment and fervent Zionist aspirations answered a need she had felt from her childhood, since her own family had "fallen away" from religious observance. Sima and Moshe married, lived in France for a few years, and eventually settled in Israel. Perhaps as a reaction to her mother's rejection, Sima raised her own son and daughter in an atmosphere of extravagant warmth and closeness. Their home was infused with strong religious belief and practice.

Although Sima has lived in Israel for many years, the family property in New England retained a special meaning for her. Her father had told stories about the significance of the place in the history of the family. It was a symbol of the peace and safety they had found in America after fleeing the pogroms of Poland in the previous century. The house where Sima was born was filled with family memorabilia, her father's paintings, other works of art, and antique furniture. Before they settled in Israel, Sima and her husband lived in that house for one year when their children were young. There, in the lovely New England hills, Ron and Ariela attended the local school, explored the surrounding countryside, and spent long hours listening to their grandfather's stories. Sima hoped that her children's exuberance would help to modify Gertrude's persistent grumpiness, but nothing had changed. Even the role of grandmother did not soften her attitude or lighten her characteristic petulance. Sima recalls that period in the life of her family with an ambivalent blend of sweetness and venom.

The death of Sima's children shattered the tranquility of her family. One year after the tragedy, Sima's father became ill and died. A few months later, Gertrude suffered a mild stroke. Sima, still reeling from the loss of her children, attended her father's funeral and came back to visit her mother after the stroke. Despite the old woman's increasing frailty, she insisted on remaining in her own house. Peggy, with her husband and a large brood of children, was living in the other house on the family property. As her mother became more decrepit, Peggy assumed responsibility for managing Gertrude's financial affairs and paying her bills. At that time, Sima was told that she and her sister would each inherit one half of the property.

Sima came to New England for the celebration of her mother's ninetieth birthday. During the weeks following that event, Gertrude had continued her daily walks with the dog. A month later, she suffered a severe stroke that left her crippled and deaf. On the last day, she laid down a book, partially read, and a piece of knitting, nearly finished, limped to her bedroom and died. Her death came barely one year after the death of Sima's father and two years after the terrorist attack in which Ron and Ariela were killed. The event marked the end of an era in the family and the beginning of an estrangement that may never be repaired.

When Sima's father died, he left all of his possessions to his wife, with the understanding that after Gertrude's death, everything would be divided equally between their two daughters. Sima had assumed that she and her sister would each inherit one of the houses, and the property itself would be divided equally between them. However, Peggy initiated a legal maneuver that circumvented that arrangement. Shortly after their father's death, Peggy had succeeded in obtaining a deed that transferred to her name the land on which Sima's house stood. It was only later that Sima realized the implications of this "trick."

Peggy phoned Sima in Israel to inform her of their mother's death. Sima arrived at the house a few hours before the funeral. The two sisters, with Peggy's children and other relatives, observed the traditional week of mourning together. Sima stayed on in the house to tie up loose ends and sort out her possessions. She recalls the feelings of sadness and loss that enveloped her during that week. The place still echoed with the images of her dead son and daughter. Staying in the house where her mother had lived for sixty years, surrounded by objects that had been part of her family's life for more than a century, she was able to put aside the anger she had always felt toward her mother. During that brief period of mourning, she began to see her own life from a different perspective and to recall her mother's strengths as well as her inadequacies. The house and its surroundings took on new meaning as a kind of compensation for the lack of mothering. At that time, she had no premonition that Gertrude had changed her will.

### The "betrayal"
Eight days after the funeral, Sima received a copy of her mother's final will and testament in the mail. Attached to the will was a handwritten note from her mother, composed a few months before her death. The note specified that the houses and all the

property were to go to Peggy. The terse note explained that since Sima's two children were dead, she would have no heirs and therefore "no need for the house." Sima was horrified, enraged, shocked. "It's as if I were her worst enemy!" When Sima confronted her sister with the unfairness of their mother's decision and her sense of betrayal, Peggy responded, "That's the way Mommy wanted it, so what could I do?"

Reflecting on recent and previous clues, Sima suspected that Peggy had contrived to have Gertrude's will changed in her favor. During the months before her death, their mother had become increasingly confused and forgetful. Sima is now certain that her sister exploited Gertrude's frailty for her own benefit. Searching for answers, Sima visited the family doctor to ask about Gertrude's possible dementia. Usually a warm and friendly man, the doctor was brusque, almost contemptuous: "Why shouldn't your sister get the houses?" Subsequently, he wrote a report stating that the mother had been fully capable of making her own decisions. The lawyer whom Gertrude had consulted when she decided to change her will was subsequently disbarred for reasons pertaining to a different, unrelated case. He had moved out of the area and was not able or willing to answer Sima's questions.

Sima's sense of betrayal was exacerbated by the fact that she had written a will of her own, specifying that her share of the inheritance should go to her sister's children. This piece of information did not seem to impress Peggy or soften her attitude. When Sima directed the movers to take furniture that had been hers out of the house, Peggy asked, "What are you going to do with it?" Sima recalls this remark as yet another indication of Peggy's indifference to her feelings.

Sima returned to Israel, feeling utterly defeated. After discussing the situation with her husband and her lawyer, she decided not to initiate a legal battle to challenge her disinheritance. Three years have passed since Gertrude's death, and the will has still not gone through probate. Various legal issues have yet to be resolved. There has been no direct contact between the sisters except for two brief messages from Peggy to Sima. One was an email birthday card from a commercial internet greeting card provider, which Sima promptly deleted. The other, sent after an outbreak of Arab terrorist attacks in Israel, was a brief email message from Peggy: "The whole family is worried about you." There was no signature. Sima has accepted the fact of her disinheritance and sees no realistic possibility of reconciliation with her sister.

## Comments

Several interrelated factors may have contributed to the outcome of this story: Sima's emotional attachment to the property, her problematic relationship with her mother, the tragedy of her bereavement, which served as the ostensible "reason" for her disinheritance, and one additional, unknown element, the previous relationship between the two sisters.

The story of this family highlights the tangled emotions that are implicated in disputes over an inheritance. Sima has been virtually disinherited by her mother. She has been deprived of her share of the land on which she was born, the house where she was raised, and the property that has belonged to her family for generations. Peggy has not expressed willingness to share any of the property with her sister. In this family, is money the root of the conflict? Obviously, the material property is only one element in the estrangement between the sisters. We can speculate about Peggy's position in this situation. Because she was living nearby and had full responsibility for the care of her parents during their last illness, perhaps she feels justified in claiming an extra share of the inheritance. In my conversations with Sima, she did not discuss details of her previous relationship with Peggy. We can wonder if the two sisters were ever close, or if they were constantly competing for the affection of their father and the attention of their elusive, rejecting mother. As in every family in which an estrangement has erupted, the "facts" generate other facts, and we can never obtain a complete picture. In time, perhaps the hurt will fade, circumstances will change, and Sima may decide to reconnect with her sister. Or, she may conclude that her own welfare will be better served by sustaining the separation. Whatever the future holds for this fragmented family, we can only hope that the protagonists will reach some measure of solace.

## Concluding thoughts

In this chapter, we have focused on one major provocation for conflict between family members: disputes over inheritance. This topic is extremely complex and multifaceted. Libraries contain countless volumes describing costly legal battles and prolonged struggles between relatives who are fighting over conflicting claims to property and possessions. The point I wish to emphasize is that virtually all of these battles have hidden agendas. Invariably, other provocations are more potent than the lure of money or possessions. When these conflicts erupt in the family, we can encourage the protagonists to resist the temptation to leap into battle and instead, to seek competent help to identify the deeper sources of the conflict. The process of clarifying the hidden issues and working through them can be far more gratifying than winning the battle or collecting the prize.

# CHAPTER EIGHT

# Four Families Find Solutions

The people whose stories are told in this chapter have experienced prolonged, seemingly implacable estrangements and have reached a resolution. In the process, they have achieved a new appreciation for the bonds of kinship as well as for the inevitable differences between family members – differences in terms of beliefs, expectations, and behavior. In each case, significant changes have occurred for the family as a whole and for the individual members. These stories illustrate the diverse solutions found by persons who are able to transpose the pain of alienation into new insights.

The first narrative can serve as a bridge between the stories of families who remain estranged and those who have reconciled. The experience of the Leiter family demonstrates the value of partial solutions. In this story, the conflict has not been confronted or resolved, yet despite the ongoing tensions and the vast gulf between the generations, the family remains connected.

### 1. RETURN TO TRADITION, WITHOUT PARENTAL BLESSING

"*Baal teshuvah*" is a Hebrew term meaning "those who return." In our time, it refers to Jewish men and women who decide to give up their secular way of life and adopt Orthodox beliefs and practices. The term itself is ancient. Originally it was used to describe personal experiences of profound religious transformation. Those earlier models differed from current ones in significant ways. In pre-modern periods of Jewish history, Jews were rarely assimilated into the predominant non-Jewish culture; there was no widespread secular influence in any Jewish community. A person might diverge from conventional religious practices, but in most cases his motivations would be different from those cited by contemporary youth.[1] To be a *baal teshuvah* in times past usually meant to move from a conventional, observant lifestyle to one that was more scholarly, pious, or spiritually inspired. We find accounts of such cases in the Bible and the Talmud. More recent examples are described in the pre-World War chronicles of Jewish communities in Western and in Eastern Europe.

In what ways is the current *baal teshuvah* ("*baalat teshuvah*" is the feminine form) movement unique? Who are these individuals who "return"? Often they are young, upper- and middle-class Jewish men and women who have become disillusioned with their parents' secular values and assimilated life style. Some of them have participated in anti-war protests, in the drug culture, or various other risky adventures. They are searching for a more meaningful way of life. Many have tried other religious pathways: Christian, Buddhist, Sufi, meditation, and Hindu gurus. When they discover Judaism, they feel that they have come home at last.

For some of these young people, the change is gradual, almost imperceptible. For others, it is a sudden conversion, as if they have received a message from a Divine source. Many cannot define the precise factor that convinced them to turn to Orthodoxy. Often it begins with a chance meeting, an unexpected discovery, or an intellectual curiosity that leads them to Jewish texts. Whatever the motive or the pathway, the life of the *baal teshuvah* will become radically, profoundly different. From the moment his decision becomes an authentic commitment, there will be a sharp demarcation between his old and new self. For most of us, the way we take up a particular kind of religious observance is determined by our family's pattern of observance. In the case of the *baal te-*

*shuvah*, this is not so. "Heritage…does not exist for him in the usual way…. He is like a person without parents."[2] His family's beliefs, values, and way of life no longer serve as a viable model. In the process of carving out a new identity, he may be reviving a pattern that was forsaken two or three generations ago. Perhaps he is embracing values that his great-grandfather was willing to die for. In doing so, he is separating himself from his parents, siblings, and other members of his secular, extended family. As he consolidates his new way of life, he will adopt beliefs and rituals that are totally different from theirs. The clothes he wears, the food he eats, his companions, choice of spouse, daily activities, observance of holidays – every aspect of life will be different.

Families display a wide spectrum of reactions to the presence of a *baal teshuvah* in their midst. In some situations, the parents are repelled and outraged at their son or daughter's decision. The resulting turmoil leads to an estrangement that may persist for many years. In others, one or both parents may gradually take on some, if not all, of their child's practices, joining in his observance and celebrating his new commitment. A few families manage to sustain a fragile equilibrium, with each side remaining on its respective religious track like two trains moving along a parallel course. In others, the siblings of the *baal teshuvah* are the most reactive segment of the family. A brother or sister may follow him into Orthodoxy. Or they may oppose his decision by becoming more secular and farther removed from their Jewish roots. If we could define common themes in these families, they would include adjustment, compromise, and, some would say, capitulation. Alienation and fragmentation occur all too frequently. Each family will create its own unique patterns, influenced by the individual life histories and personalities of its members.

THE FAMILY: *Joan and Henri Leiter, their son Ralph, their daughter Rina, and Rina's husband Benzi.*

This story describes how one assimilated family is responding to their *baalat teshuvah* daughter, a young woman who has chosen a radically different, devoutly religious lifestyle. My role began to emerge when a friend asked me to talk to Joan, who was determined to avoid a cutoff from her only daughter. In the first moments of our meeting, she launched into her version of the events that have caused so much turmoil in her family. For a period of three years, we have carried on a voluminous email correspondence, with long, detailed discussions of the problems and possible ways to handle them. As each new crisis erupts, I respond to her questions and offer suggestions.

**Background**

Joan, a retired actress and her husband, Henri, a photographer, live in a suburb of Los Angeles. Born in Brussels and a survivor of the Holocaust, Henri has worked as a museum photographer and recently, the producer of several documentary films. The Leiters have two adult children, a daughter, Rina, now about thirty, and a son, Ralph, who is two years younger. These children were raised in the rarified atmosphere of southern California by parents who were deeply involved in the world of art, theatre, and films. Rina and Ralph were enrolled in excellent schools with peers from similar families. The Reiters are Jewish, but they did not affiliate with a synagogue, and the children had only a superficial religious education. Although these parents have never denied their Jewish roots, they have rarely observed any religious rituals or requirements. The last thing in the world they would have expected was that both of their children would become devout Orthodox Jews.

After Rina graduated from high school, she attended college on the East coast. For her junior year, she decided to study abroad, in a developing country in Africa. Her experiences there affected her deeply. She found a culture utterly different from the one she had known. She became acquainted with people who were firmly committed to their own traditional rituals and beliefs. When they asked about her values, she had no answers. So she began to question her previous experience and wonder why her former life now seemed so empty and trivial. Because she identified with

Judaism as the religion of her ancestors, she decided to go to Israel and begin to search for her roots.

Settling first in Tel Aviv, Rina experienced a spontaneous, euphoric reaction: she felt utterly "at home." People she hardly knew welcomed her with great enthusiasm and affection. She enrolled at a religious study center for women and embarked on her spiritual journey. It was during this period of exploration that Rina met Benzi, a student from Toronto who had come to Israel on a similar quest. He had dropped out of college after two years and aspired to be a sculptor. These two young people were immediately attracted to each other. Soon they became engaged. Benzi has no family in Israel. His mother and siblings live in Canada, in a close-knit community of Jews who had emigrated from Morocco many years ago. In Israel, Benzi had been studying in various *yeshivot*, religious institutions for newly religious young men, moving every few months to seek a different approach, a more sympathetic teacher, or a new idea. Eventually, he discovered a mystical, ultra-Orthodox rabbi who had attracted a small group of students. Benzi had reached his spiritual home.

## One thing after another: the gulf widens

When Rina announced her intention to marry, her parents were perplexed and worried. They came to Israel to assess the situation and took an immediate dislike to Benzi. To them, he seemed to be a shiftless, crude young man who was exploiting their innocent daughter. Despite their opposition, the couple was married in a traditional, ultra-Orthodox ceremony in the Old City of Jerusalem. Accustomed to the chic, catered parties that are given by their friends in Southern California, this experience was the first in a long series of culture shocks for Joan and Henri. They were plunged into a foreign world of black hats, incomprehensible rituals, and frenzied dancing. After the wedding, which Rina's parents had reluctantly subsidized, the young couple moved into a two-room "hovel" in a poor neighborhood, with primitive plumbing and broken windows. Benzi set up his sculpture studio in one corner of the bedroom, using the only closet to store his tools. Within a few months Rina was expecting a baby, struggling through a painful, difficult pregnancy. One year later, her parents arrived for a brief visit and were shocked to see their beautiful, pampered daughter, nursing her baby in the midst of "squalor." To Joan and Henri, their son-in-law seemed to be loafing most of the time. Unlike many of his ultra-Orthodox peers who spend long days studying or teaching, he would sit silently in the house, "doing nothing." But Rina assured them that that she was happy with Benzi, whose spiritual quest she much admired. She vehemently insisted that she preferred her new life to any other.

During the first five years of their marriage, Rina and Benzi had four children, including one set of twins. Joan and Henri were paying for a portion of the young couple's living expenses, while they remained solidly opposed to their daughter's lifestyle. Benzi rarely sold a piece of sculpture and he worked only part time at odd jobs. During each of their annual visits to Israel, Joan and Henri tried to "talk sense" into Rina, pointing out the folly of her choices and the difficulties of her new life. She responded to their complaints by stoutly defending her husband and denying that any problems existed. Then she would ask sweetly for more money. "We're fifty dollars short this month, Mom; can you help?" And every time, Mom helped.

Last summer, Joan and Henri celebrated a special wedding anniversary and planned an elaborate party. They invited Rina, Benzi, and their children to come to California, offering to pay all their travel expenses. To prepare for the visit, Joan and Henri met with several different rabbis to ask for advice and support. According to Joan, they heard at least five different opinions about how to handle the situation. They also sought help from a psychologist, who encouraged them to accept their daughter's choices and lower their expectations. Rina, Benzi, and their children arrived for the celebration and stayed in the Leiter home. Joan had prepared the kitchen with plastic dishes and ordered kosher food from a caterer. Nearly one hundred people, including many old friends from the art world, were invited to the lavish party. Joan and Henri hoped that this vivid reminder of Rina's old life would inspire her to return to it. But the experience seemed to have the opposite effect; Benzi and Rina expressed their scorn at the conspicuous display of affluence, fancy dress, the stretch limos, and "banal" talk. Compared to their spiritual wealth, the secular world appeared to be without any real value or meaning. The young family returned to Israel, relieved to resume their chosen lifestyle.

### Another blow: the son also rebels

Rina's younger brother Ralph seemed to be heading in a very different direction. A brilliant student, he graduated with honors from an Ivy League university and won a scholarship to a prestigious college in England. But after one year of advanced study in mathematics, he decided to enroll in an Orthodox *yeshivah* in Israel. Although he did not follow his sister's path to extreme Orthodoxy, he did adopt many religious practices. Recently, he married a young woman with similar convictions. Now living in California, he is among the vast group of unemployed, educated Americans. His parents are bitterly disappointed in both of their adult children. They blame Ralph's religious commitment for his joblessness. If he had completed graduate school and applied himself to serious work, they contend, he would now have lucrative employment. As one expression of their disapproval, they removed all the Jewish artifacts from their home. They remain firmly rooted in their secular, assimilated world, with no intention to change. Soon they will embark on a radically new life course of their own. Recently retired from their professional positions, they will sell their large house and go off to explore remote parts of the world. On the one hand, this plan may be seen as an escape from the challenges their adult children have presented. On the other hand, it could be a reflection of their strength, an affirmation of their own relationship and a readiness to face new adventures together.

### Current situation

Joan and Henri continue to worry about their daughter, her heavy household burdens, frequent pregnancies, precarious financial situation, and apparently intractable religious convictions. Since Rina set out on her new course, they have repeatedly sought advice from many different sources, including rabbis, psychologists, friends, and family members. One of the most challenging problems is the question of finances. With Benzi earning barely enough to provide food for his growing family, who will support them? In the past, Joan and Henri have helped with money for crucial needs. Their most recent contribution was a down payment on an apartment. Joan was hoping that the purchase would provide extra space for the burgeoning family, but the new apartment is no larger than the previous one. It was chosen primarily for its proximity to an ultra-Orthodox neighborhood. Each person Joan has consulted advises her to reduce their financial contributions, to set clear limits and not to exceed them. These parents feel caught in a vise between the reality of their modest financial resources and their daughter's obvious needs. But more than money, they suffer from the widening gulf between her lifestyle and theirs. As the years pass, they have fewer opportunities to share experiences. The grandchildren are growing up in an atmosphere totally different from anything Joan and Henri have known. But despite these considerable obstacles, the Leiters are determined to sustain a connection with their daughter. They will continue to obtain advice from a variety of sources. They visit Rina once a year, bring gifts for the grandchildren, and try to give them a taste of the "good life." At least once a week they speak on the phone, usually about mundane matters. Joan is careful not to accuse, incite, or acknowledge her disappointment. Although these parents express love for both of their adult children and try to understand them, it is unlikely that they will ever accept or empathize with the commitments they have chosen.

## Comments

For these parents, their daughter's flight to a devoutly religious world is a harsh reality. They are unable to acknowledge the positive aspects of Rina's choices or accept her new lifestyle. For Joan and Henri, expressing love from a distance is the current solution.

It is a partial, perhaps temporary strategy, one that many of their friends and other relatives have questioned. Some people have advised these parents to adopt a new perspective and try to become more observant themselves. Others have urged them to stop all financial assistance. In many families, there are differences of opinion regarding the best or most effective solutions. Each person must listen to his or her own inner voice and choose what is most appropriate, regardless of pressures from others.

With all the dissonance that continues to reverberate in the Leiter family, significant positive effects have emerged. During this long process, Joan and Henri have strengthened their own relationship. Perhaps the insights they have gained will serve as a source of support for the next phase of their lives as retired persons. They continue to seek advice and search for ways to sustain the connection with their daughter and grandchildren, no matter how ambivalent they feel. Only time will tell how this relationship will fare and what forms it will take. In this family, the status quo is fragile and the future is uncertain.

## 2. A JEWISH PRODIGAL SON

> THE FAMILY: *Rose and Sidney Silver, their sons, Joel, Dan, and Jerry; Dan's first wife Chloe, and his second wife Fran.*

### Background

Dan Silver was the kind of child most parents would call the "perfect son." No one could have predicted the frustration and misery he would later bring to his family. Now in his late forties, Dan is the "sandwich kid" in a family of three sons. A daughter died in infancy. His mother Rose offered to share the story of Dan's uneven developmental path. Recalling his early years, she described him as an adorable child who was "the apple of his father's eye." He was funny, affectionate, close to his parents and brothers. He shared a room with his older brother and participated enthusiastically in family activities. Jerry, the youngest son, had a birth defect that resulted in various physical handicaps. Dan's response to Jerry was consistently supportive and patient. As he approached adolescence, Dan joined the Boy Scouts, earned many badges for his achievements, and became an Eagle Scout. He had a wide range of interests and many friends. His father Sidney fondly recalls a two-week vacation alone with 13-year-old Dan, canoeing and hiking through wilderness forests together. No one who knew Dan then could have anticipated the problems that emerged later, plunging the family into a crisis that lasted several years and left permanent scars.

Dan's parents were actively involved in a large Conservative synagogue. His mother was head of the Community Action committee and a volunteer in the library; his father served on the Board of Trustees in various roles. Dan attended religious school on Sundays and studied Hebrew in a small group that met after school twice a week. Rose and Sidney both had large, extended families. Dozens of relatives would gather frequently to celebrate family milestones and special occasions. At all of these events, Dan seemed to relate comfortably to grandparents, aunts, uncles, and many cousins. His *bar mitzvah* was attended by more than three hundred relatives and friends. Dan's parents owned a family clothing store in a suburban shopping mall, and Dan often did odd jobs in the store to help out. He was well-liked by the other store employees and by local storeowners who were friends of his parents. In his high school yearbook, one of Dan's peers described him as a "friendly guy who would succeed in all his endeavors." Another classmate, a bit more perceptive, wrote, "you're nice but kinda quirky."

Dan applied to and was accepted by the college of his choice, a large university in the Boston area. His first year away from home seemed to go smoothly. He excelled in his studies and made several new friends. He came home for the summer and worked part-time in his father's store. During his second year, he changed his major focus from science to philosophy. He mentioned to his mother than he had found a "mentor" in Oriental religions and was considering a move to the Far East. Rose was a bit surprised at this unexpected leap but dismissed it as a temporary late-adolescent disruption. During the following year, his parents noticed a perceptible coolness in Dan's response to them. He came home rarely, seemed preoccupied, and found reasons not to participate in family gatherings. He had begun to date Chloe, a young woman who was studying at the same university. Within a short time, they announced their engagement.

### The family tie, severed

After Dan graduated from college, he went to work in a bookstore. His parents were disappointed that he had decided not to go to graduate school. When Dan and Chloe announced the date for their wedding, Rose recalls that she was not consulted or included in any of the plans. The ceremony was small and simple, officiated by a rabbi who apparently had not known the young couple. Only the immediate families and a few close relatives attended. At the wedding, Dan's parents thought he seemed aloof, but they attributed his behavior to "wedding nerves." Dan's favorite uncle, a psychologist, remarked later that the bride appeared to be "disturbed." Rose and Sidney felt rejected by their new daughter-in-law. During the first year of Dan and Chloe's marriage, there were occasional visits and phone conversations between Dan and his parents, but the mood of those interactions was awkward and non-committal. Rose and Sidney became increasingly frustrated by their son's silence. At one point, when his parents called to wish him a happy birthday, Dan slammed down the phone. Subsequently, their cards, letters, and gifts were "returned to sender" with no explanation. They blamed the situation on Dan's wife and assumed that the crisis would eventually resolve by itself. But it did not resolve.

After about a year of silence, Dan's mother and older brother Joel went to the distant city where Dan lived, found the bookstore where he was working, and attempted to see him. Rose winced as she described the scene: Dan refused to talk with them, waved off her efforts to embrace him, turned his back and walked away. Joel became enraged and "almost hit him." His mother could only weep. They returned home, feeling defeated. At no time did Dan explain his behavior, except to say that he needed to be left alone. His parents learned indirectly that Dan and Chloe were having marital problems and had consulted a counselor who advised them to break off all contact with their families and former friends. Following this advice, they moved to a different location and became reclusive. For a period of almost two years, Dan did not communicate with anyone in the family. His phone number was unlisted. Rose recalls her agonizing thought: "If I would die, no one would know how to inform my son." During that time, Sidney had major surgery, Dan's uncle died, and his handicapped brother Jerry had a series of setbacks. Rose said it was hell to wake up each morning feeling abandoned by her son, wondering where he was and imagining all sorts of horrible possibilities.

Utterly bewildered and frustrated, Dan's parents consulted a therapist who advised them not to cut off from him, not to give up hope. "Be like the Statue of Liberty," she said. So, they continued to send notes and money to his post office box. The notes were returned but the money was kept. For a period of more than two years, Dan's endorsement on their checks was the only contact these parents had with their son.

### First signs of thawing

The first hint of a change occurred when Dan sent his parents a brief note saying only "thanks for the check." The envelope had a return address, and his parents hoped that it was an indication that their son might be willing to have some contact with them. Some weeks later, Sidney was going to a conference in the city where Dan lived. He decided to risk a visit. Sidney approached the apartment building with great trepidation, wondering if his son would again reject him. Dan came to the door wearing his coat, about to go to work. To Sidney's great relief, his son invited him to come in and they sat together and talked, not about the estrangement at all, but about mundane things such as Dan's job, Rose's recent surgery, the family dog. The meeting lasted about twenty minutes and then Dan said he had to go to work. There was no mention of future meetings and no indication that the situation had actually changed. But it *had* changed.

About two months later, out of the blue, Dan phoned Sidney and soon afterward he appeared on his parents' doorstep, greeting them affectionately. He offered no explanations or apologies and made no reference to the previous three years' separation, except one comment about the marriage counselor who had advised him to cut off from his parents: "I finally figured out that he was crazier than I was." Rose and Sidney, following the advice of their therapist, tried to accept Dan's presence matter-of-factly, asking for nothing, expecting nothing. They resisted all temptation to question him, cast blame, or evoke feelings of guilt.

Dan had separated from Chloe, initiated divorce proceedings, and was dating a woman he had met recently. For a brief time it seemed that Dan would settle down near his parents and go to work in the family business, but apparently he was not ready for such a radical change. After the brief visit, he moved to Washington and was joined there by Fran, the new girlfriend. Eventually, the couple moved to a suburb near his hometown. To his father's great surprise, Dan offered to work at the family store. He resumed his old friendly manner with the store employees and his father hoped it would be a permanent arrangement. However, after about a year, Dan decided to take a training course in technical writing and subsequently obtained a job with a local corporation.

Although they were relieved and happy to be reconnected with Dan, the comfortable relationship that Rose and Sidney longed for did not materialize. They invited the couple for meals, parties, and family gatherings. Usually, Dan came alone or not at all. On the rare occasions when they did see Fran, she seemed aloof and distracted, similar to the personality of Dan's first wife.

Rose recalls that during the months following Dan's return, she never questioned him about his personal life or asked about his plans to marry Fran. She deliberately avoided any intrusion on their privacy. She and Sidney were never invited to their apartment or included in any of their activities. One day, about three years after Dan's return, Rose got a phone call from a cousin.

"*Mazal tov*" (congratulations), she said. Rose asked, "What for?" The cousin had seen a listing of Dan's marriage in the classified section of the local paper. No one in either family had been informed or invited to the wedding. Although both Dan and Fran are Jewish and openly acknowledge their affiliation with Jewish tradition, they were married by a judge in a ceremony with no religious content at all. Dan's parents were "stunned" by the news, but neither Dan nor Fran has ever offered an explanation or expressed regret for excluding their families from their wedding.

### Partial resolution

During the past few years, the mood of the contacts between Dan and his parents has warmed somewhat. Fran occasionally comes to their home, and she seems more comfortable, more sociable. Rose and Sidney responded joyfully to the news of Fran's pregnancy and welcomed the birth of a baby girl with great pleasure. The arrival of this baby has brought about significant changes in Dan's response to his parents and brothers, although some of the old patterns persist. With Jerry, his handicapped brother, Dan is affectionate and jovial, much like the old days. With Joel, the older brother who is a partner in a prestigious law firm, Dan is more guarded and reticent. While Dan and Fran allow Rose to babysit and enjoy the fruits of grandparenthood, their visits occur only in the parents' house, never in theirs. If anyone in the family asks to visit the baby, Dan usually refuses by saying, "it's not a good idea." Dan and Fran continue to be reclusive; they do not socialize with peers and they rely on the answering machine to take all their phone calls. They seem to need to erect their own boundaries and to set the rules for all social interactions. And yet, Dan is once again a participating member of the Silver family. Despite the constraints and intermittent tensions, everyone is relieved and grateful for the turn of events.

### Comments:

Dan's journey from alienation to return resembles the traditional pattern of the prodigal son. The parents yearn for a full reconcili-

ation, but their image of "home sweet home" has not material-
ized. Dan has returned and grafted himself back onto the family
tree, ignoring or bypassing the estrangement. Neither Dan nor
his parents have confronted the issues that provoked the conflict.
Although the broken connections seem to have been repaired, the
tensions remain. The sturdiness of family bonds can no longer
be taken for granted. The prodigal son has come home, but the
emotional atmosphere of the family has been irrevocably scarred.
Each of the protagonists must adjust to the current reality and, in
the process, create a new role as a member of an altered family.

## 3. "OUR DAUGHTER IS, FROM THIS DAY FORWARD, DEAD TO OUR FAMILY."

The eruption of religious disputes causes widespread upheaval in
families. What happens when one member "marries out" of the
family's religious milieu? What is the background of the conflict,
and how do individual members react to such an event? If the
conflict is eventually resolved, what elements contribute to the
process of reconciliation? The following narrative describes the
situation in one observant Jewish family whose daughter "married out."

> *THE FAMILY: Shoshana Sorokin and her husband Berel,
> Berel's father Chaim, Chaim's sisters Leah and Fania, Leah's
> husband Boris (deceased) and their two sons.*

### Background

My understanding of this story evolved from a query I sent to the
Jewish Genealogy email list,[3] asking for descriptions of families
who had ostracized one particular member because of religious
issues. A brief sketch was sent to me by Shoshana Sorokin. In
subsequent phone conversations, she elaborated and clarified the
details. Here is her story:

Shoshana, a native Israeli, and her husband Berel live on a
kibbutz, a communal settlement in the hills overlooking the Sea

of Galilee. Berel was born in Eastern Europe around 1930. His father, Chaim, whose family was descended from a famous line of rabbis, had settled in the town of Kobrin, in Belarus. An extended family of aunts, uncles, and cousins lived in the same village. In the late 1930s, when the winds of war were sweeping over Europe, an event occurred that split the family into fragments. One of Berel's aunts, his father's younger sister Leah, shocked her Orthodox parents by announcing her intention to marry a Russian soldier. Boris, a handsome colonel in the Intelligence Corps of the Russian Army, had been captivated by the pretty Jewish girl whom he had met when his battalion was billeted in her village. Leah never converted, but they were married by the village priest sometime during the tense period before the Nazis arrived in 1941. Leah's parents were appalled and outraged at her decision to "marry out." In that time and place, her defiant behavior must have been perceived as much more serious than a daughter's rebellious act; it was the repudiation of a long and honorable religious heritage. Her parents disowned her and "sat *shiva*," a mourning ritual that signified total banishment. Berel still recalls the dreadful atmosphere of hostility and grief that enveloped the entire family when they were told they would never see Leah again.

Boris's position in the Intelligence Corps gave him access to classified information. He knew of the Nazis' intentions to exterminate the Jews. Despite the family's rejection of him, he warned his wife's parents of the impending danger and urged them to liquidate their assets and escape. They did not heed the warning to leave, but they did bury their prized silver menorah and other precious objects under a tree behind their house. Berel was then about twelve years old. With his parents and Leah's younger sister Fania, he immigrated to Palestine a few months before the war broke out. Leah's parents chose to remain behind in Belarus to care for aged relatives. After the war, when no word came from them, the family assumed that they had perished in the Holocaust. Chaim wondered if Leah could have escaped the ravages of the concentration camps. In fact, she and her husband had survived the war in Russia, but the family heard no news of her for nearly forty years.

## First hopeful sign

In the early 1970s, Chaim received a letter from a distant cousin in America, indicating that Leah was alive in Russia. As long as the Communist regime remained in power, there was no direct contact with her. Several more years passed before the family heard of her again.

During and after the war, Leah's husband Boris had done well. He had advanced to the rank of general, they had raised two sons and he had been a devoted husband and father. After he died, she was left with a small cottage in the Crimea and a government pension. No one in her family, not even her sons, knew she was Jewish. It was not until the disintegration of the Communist regime that she felt safe enough to divulge the secret of her religious past.

## Sequence of steps to reconciliation

In 1991, Leah, then in her early seventies, joined a group that traveled to Poland and Belarus. Included in the itinerary was a visit to Kobrin, the village of her birth. It was fortunate that a man in the group had a video camera and was able to capture the emotional intensity of Leah's response. Standing in front of her childhood house, she asked forgiveness from her parents, who had perished in Auschwitz. Recorded on the tape is her tearful reminiscence of how her mother and father had "sat *shiva*" for her after she married Boris. She never saw them again. During the upheaval of the war, she was "lost" to the family, as were so many others whose families disappeared in the flames of the Holocaust. The tree behind the house was gone, and the place where her parents had buried the silver menorah was obliterated by a new garage. No tangible fragment of her former life remained.

Leah's visit to Kobrin evoked memories of her past and wakened a yearning to reconnect with her Jewish relatives. She embarked on a search for the surviving remnants of her family and eventually discovered the address of her brother Chaim, living in Israel. They began to correspond. With Chaim's encouragement, she decided to come to Israel with her two sons, who were married with children of their own. The entire extended family prepared for her visit with high expectations and intense curiosity. They were uncertain about how these long-lost relatives would react to one another.

When Leah arrived, the whole family lined up to meet her. Each person had his own image of how she would look, what she would say, and, perhaps most important, how they would be able to communicate. The visit was a resounding success. The highlight was the emotional reunion with her brother Chaim, now over eighty, and with her sister Fania, the "baby" of the family. They spoke to each other in Yiddish, a language Leah had not spoken in almost fifty years. The family was amazed that Leah looked like a typical Jewish woman. She used many of the same gestures and mannerisms that they had seen in Fania, her sister. It was incredibly moving to hear them exchanging reminiscences about the village, their parents, and the experiences of their long-forgotten childhood. As they recalled the past, Leah began to connect the fragmented parts of her life. The whole family was caught up in a burst of relief and joy at finally being together. After Leah and her sons returned to Russia, her brother and his family maintained contact with her, sending money and parcels of food.

**Comments**

In the Sorokin family, the estrangement lasted for several decades and might have never been resolved. The eventual reconciliation occurred, partly because of the good fortune of Leah's survival through the war, but mainly because she was aware of her past and determined to reconnect. Leah's sons are both professionals, one a geologist, the other a pilot. With a leap of imagination, we can speculate that their respective choice of profession may have some symbolic connection with the situation in the family. The geologist son was focused on materials that lie on the earth's crust and beneath it, mirroring his mother's long-kept secret identity. The other son, the pilot, was directed upward, away from the limitations of earthly boundaries to a space where frontiers can be crossed and habitual patterns can be overcome. Both sons accompanied their mother to Israel, thus participating in her healing journey and helping to reconcile the disparate elements in the family

Various changes in the family may have facilitated the process of reconciliation. Shoshana noted that the relatives who left Eastern Europe and immigrated to Israel had rejected religious piety and turned their energies to the development of the secular kibbutz movement. Like many other Eastern European Jews, they had transposed traditional observance into the practical work of farming the land and building a Jewish state. She speculated that the secular lifestyle of the surviving family members allowed them to neutralize the toxic religious issues and move beyond them. Like every family narrative, each of the protagonists will have his or her version of the story; some elements will remain hidden. We do know that in this family, the reconciliation had a profound and lasting impact on everyone who participated in it.

4. "FOR THE FIRST TIME IN FORTY YEARS,
I FEEL LIKE I HAVE A BROTHER!"

THE FAMILY: *Jen Stern, her brother Ivan Gottlieb, and Ivan's wife, Rhonda (deceased).*

## Introduction

Jen Stern is the second daughter in a family of four girls and one boy. Now she is ninety-four but seems more like a young eighty. She has been a widow for more than twenty years. Slim, petite, and full of vitality, she wears simple clothes and no makeup. Knowing of my interest in estranged families, her son Josh had told me about the long period of alienation between Jen and her brother. When I spoke with Jen about the topic of this book, she agreed to share her story.

Jen had flown into town for the wedding of her granddaughter. We arranged to meet at an elegant restaurant in the hotel where Jen and her brother Ivan were staying. I had been expecting to hear her account and was not prepared for the scene that followed. Soon after we sat down at the table, her brother entered and joined us. Ivan is tall, robust, with a shock of white hair. He also appears younger than his eighty-three years. He is the "baby" in the family, born when his mother was forty-three. "They finally got a boy, me!" he says with a grin.

Jen and Ivan seemed quite comfortable together, but from the outset, something about their conversation was strange. They seemed to be out of sync, not in touch with each other's life or activities. As they reminisced about their childhood, Ivan would say, "I don't remember that," or "I never knew that." I realized that they actually did not know each other; they were just now getting acquainted. What had happened to alienate these siblings? As their story unfolded, I learned that they had drifted apart from inertia. They denied that any specific provocation or particular event had ignited the cutoff. But, after months and years of silence between them, efforts to reconnect felt awkward and unnatural. For nearly forty years, they had not exchanged a single word.

### Origins of the estrangement

Jen's Orthodox Jewish parents had emigrated from Russia at the turn of the century and settled in Cleveland. Except for the oldest daughter, all of the children were born in America. Abe, the father, became a "junk" dealer, selling bits of scrap metal on the street. Ivan called it "second-hand metals." Eventually the business expanded into a neighborhood hardware store where both parents worked long hours. They maintained the Orthodox religious practice they had observed in the "old world," but by the time the children reached their teens, all of them had become assimilated into the American secular culture. The parents struggled to raise five children and provide an education for each of them. Ivan was the center of attention in the family. Although the daughters were showered with affection by the parents, they all felt overshadowed by the "glory" of this only son. The Great Depression of 1929 brought multiple hardships for the family. When difficult decisions had to be made about how to allocate the limited budget, there was only enough money to send one child to college: Ivan. Perhaps this apparent "favoring" of the only son was one of the factors in the subsequent estrangement between brother and sister.

Eventually, all of the siblings married Jewish spouses, none of whom were observant or religious in the traditional sense. Jen remembers that when she and Saul moved into their first apartment, her parents refused to eat there because she did not observe the laws of kashruth. But despite the absence of Jewish ritual in the homes of their adult children, the parents did not reject or cut off from any of them. There was no precedent for the estrangement between Jen and Ivan.

Jen always felt deprived of a college education and was attracted to men who were educated. A feisty, outspoken young woman, she was determined to find her own partner. When her brother tried to introduce her to his favorite college professor, she resisted his interference, but eventually she relented. He was Saul Stern, a mature man in his thirties with a graduate degree in biology. Jen and Saul were married within a year after they met. At first, the three young people, Jen, Saul, and Ivan were a "threesome," often together, sharing ideas and plans. But this closeness was not to last. Two years later, Ivan met Rhonda; they married and moved to California. According to Jen, Rhonda was "cold," not interested in fostering closeness with Ivan's family. There was never a confrontation between Jen and Rhonda. Jen does not remember any outward sign of conflict or expression of anger. But gradually, the ties between Jen and Ivan faded. Finally, they had no contact at all. For nearly forty years, there was only silence between them.

### Halting steps toward resolution

About ten years ago, the first signs of "thawing" began to appear. Ivan was invited to the wedding of Jen's oldest granddaughter. He did not attend, but he sent a gift. Jen was annoyed. She sent off a sharply worded note, telling him they did not want his gift; he should have come to the celebration. These two communications were the first actual contact between them in more than forty years. Ivan did not respond to her rebuke. About a year later, Jen's husband Saul died. Ivan sent a note expressing sympathy but did not attend the funeral. This "low-grade" communication pattern continued intermittently for about five years. Somehow, the family grapevine served to keep them aware of important family events, but the contacts between them were always at a distance.

### The momentum builds

Last year, Jen and Ivan were both invited to the wedding of their sister's granddaughter. Everyone in the family knew about the estrangement. The relatives were buzzing about what might happen if they both came. Ivan's wife Rhonda had died a few months before the wedding. Perhaps her death would allow Ivan to break the old pattern and initiate a move. And in fact, this is what happened. Anticipating Jen's presence at the wedding, Ivan sent out some oblique "feelers." He phoned Jen's son Josh to inquire about Jen. Later, he admitted that he had been nervous, fearing a tense confrontation with his sister. Reassured by Josh that she would probably be happy to see him, he phoned Jen herself and set up a meeting. Surprised to hear his voice and intrigued by the anticipation of seeing him, she felt ambivalent and a bit anxious. They had not been together in forty years! But in the lobby of the hotel where the wedding guests were staying, they sat down together and began to mend the rift. Neither of them knew anything about the life of the other, about their children or their accomplishments. Jen learned that Ivan is a scientist who takes his work very seriously. Ivan did not know that both of his sister's sons are eminent scientists, each in a different field. His discovery of these "jewels" in her family gave an extra boost to the new bond between sister and brother. Jen says they could not stop talking. They realized how much they liked one another. They felt related as well as elated. Each of them seemed to "know" what the other would say, and they were amazed to recognize the similarities in personality and attitudes. At this meeting, they spoke primarily about their lives and families and they began to confront some of the issues that had alienated them.

## Sources of the conflict, in retrospect

My meeting with Jen and Ivan in the hotel restaurant, described above, gave me the opportunity to ask them about their long estrangement. Both of them knew that I would include their story in this book. During our meeting, I had the rare opportunity to listen to these two people, cut off for four decades, as they shared their perceptions of the past and described their ongoing reconciliation. There was no hint of leftover anger, no recriminations nor accusations. Jen acknowledged that she had envied her brother's college education and always felt that her parents had favored him, the only boy in the family. Ivan admitted that his wife had been "standoffish," and had discouraged his contacts with Jen and her family. Ivan described himself as "more than a workaholic," intensely committed to his scientific pursuits. He had treated other aspects of his life, including his family, as unnecessary distractions. In a moment of openness, Ivan confided to Jen that he worries about his only daughter; he feels that he neglected her and allowed his wife to spoil her excessively. Now he regrets his lack of interest in her development. Jen was surprised and touched that her brother was able to feel comfortable enough with her to expose this raw nerve. At various moments during the lunch, Jen reached over and put her hand on Ivan's arm, an impulsive, affectionate gesture. When I left them, they were still totally absorbed in talking and listening, sharing memories, working through the healing process.

## Affirmation of healing

The next day, I was a guest at the wedding of Jen's granddaughter. Jen sat in the front row near the *chuppah,* the wedding canopy. She looked simply elegant in a flowing silk dress, a garment infused with light and muted colors that suited her perfectly. She was intent on every detail, caught up in the mood of the traditional Jewish ceremony. At one point, the sister of the groom addressed the couple. Speaking directly to her brother, she told him, "It's a blessing to have you for a brother." At that moment, Jen, who is usually composed, began to weep. She turned slightly to look at Ivan, sitting in the row behind her. The significance of the moment was apparent to both of them, and to me.

As I left the wedding hall, the dancing was still in high gear. The music was blaring and some of the older guests were leaving. When I looked back, Jen and Ivan were standing together at the edge of the dance floor. She was leaning slightly, her head resting on his shoulder. He looked contented, a calm smile on his face. I was privileged to see this touching sight, an elderly sister and brother watching the young people leaping to the wedding music. It was a celebration for them as well, the culmination of a long journey from alienation to reconciliation.

## Comments

During the two years since their initial meeting, Jen and Ivan have spent time together on several occasions. He has visited her at home, they have met at other family celebrations, and they speak frequently on the phone. Their predominant activity is a kind of ongoing verbal excavation as they recall moments in the past and reminisce about their parents. After so many silent years, there are gaps that need to be filled and questions that remain to be answered. They do not seem to tire of this activity. Both Jen and Ivan have expressed, to me and to each other, their relief and gratitude that the blessing of healing came when they were still able to appreciate it.

CONCLUDING THOUGHTS

The stories in this chapter illustrate diverse patterns of alienation and reconciliation. The experience of each family reflects its own particular history and configuration. The contexts of their lives, the provocations that ignited the dispute, and the process of reconnecting are unique for each of the protagonists. With the exception of the Leiters, these families have experienced a clear resolution of conflict and a strong sense of gratitude for reaching closure. Their stories allow us to see the strengthening of family bonds as an outgrowth of self-understanding. Moving toward reconciliation is one vital part of the developmental process.

For the majority of the narratives in this and previous chapters, I invited the storytellers to review, correct, and elaborate my version of their stories. I am grateful for their suggestions and their generosity in sharing these painful, intimate episodes. In most instances, I have incorporated their suggestions. In a few cases, I have retained my version to protect confidentiality or to highlight specific themes.

Stories can provide a key, not only to the experience of others, but to a clearer understanding of one's own situation. By examining the elements in the process of estrangement and its aftermath, we can become more attentive to similar sequences in our own families. Let us examine these narratives more closely. First, who are the storytellers? Virtually all of them are women, speaking in their own voices. We may wonder if the same stories told by men would have a different emphasis. Perhaps they would not be the same stories at all. Rather then focusing on gender differences, it may be more useful to notice the meanings that individual men and women ascribe to the polarities of connection and separation. The case of Leah demonstrates one family's persistent yearning to be reconciled with an estranged member. Long before Dan Silver reappeared on his parents' doorstep, he had apparently begun to question the wisdom of severing ties with his family. Jen and Ivan, after four decades of alienation, seemed to be motivated by the longing to resolve old animosities and share their life stories. In each case, the meanings of connection and separateness were colored, not so much by gender as by personality factors, historical process, and family constellations.

Each of the narratives depicts a particular predicament: parents who are struggling to avoid a cutoff from their daughter; a son who severed contact from his family; a woman banished from an extended family, and finally, two alienated siblings. In every case, the entire family plays a part. Some members are passive observers; others take up a more active role in the process, either by obstructing the efforts to reconcile, or by encouraging and facilitating the connections. In a family system, every member is affected by the actions of every other member.

The family dramas in this chapter were played out on the world stage. Two families were in the same country, although they lived hundreds or thousands of miles apart. Two families were separated by wide oceans of geographical space and utterly different lifestyles. When the intention to reconnect is sufficiently strong and durable, the physical distance does not appear to be a decisive factor.

What were the factors that facilitated the process of reconciliation in these families? For the Sorokins, pivotal elements were the passage of years, the fortunate survival of key family members, and significant changes in their religious and political convictions. Jen Stern's critical response to her brother's initial efforts might have been an obstacle to subsequent meetings but he persevered, thus paving the way to their eventual reunion. Dan Silver's parents did not confront or interrogate him when he decided to return home. They were able to welcome him lovingly, a wise move at a crucial moment when the connection between them was still so fragile. Joan Leiter has learned what she can and cannot say to her daughter, what will nurture their bond, and what will exacerbate their differences. This kind of sensitivity is vital in a relationship marked by so much ambivalence on both sides.

These stories allow us to trace the sequence of the estrangement, notice how it was generated and sustained, and observe the unfolding of its resolution. In each case, we can see how the intensity of the original hostility was transposed to more constructive, more affirming emotional responses. In the next chapter, we will focus in greater detail on some of the essential elements in the process of reconciliation.

CHAPTER NINE

# Attributes of Reconciliation

*What we call the beginning is often the end.*
*And to make an end is to make a beginning.*
*The end is where we start from.*[1]

## Prelude

These lines by T.S. Eliot highlight a basic feature of the estrange-ment-reconciliation process. We have been speaking of a phenomenon in which endings and beginnings have amorphous boundaries. When did the tensions of alienation first become apparent? Was there a sudden turning point, a moment when the emotional atmosphere changed? Will the hostility ever end? In many of our stories, the early stages of conflict contain the seeds of reconciliation, and remnants of discord cling to its resolution. The past is not obliterated; it is transposed to a new reality. The end is where we start from.

The act of writing is an ongoing exploration, a continuous learning. As I write about the lives of others, I discover new dimensions of myself. Listening to the stories of estrangement and pondering their meanings, I have come to see the sequence from alienation to reconciliation as a vital opportunity for personal growth and renewal. Examining an estrangement in one's own family is a journey without a clear destination. The benefits

241

cannot be defined in terms of success or failure. It is not an event, done once and finished. Rather, it emerges as a series of stages that unfold over time, advancing and regressing in alternating progression. Similar to the musical form of a fugue, the process reverberates with themes and counter-themes, harmony and dissonance, sounds and silence. During the course of confronting, examining, and perhaps resolving a conflict, one must learn to create a sense of connection that has been lost, damaged, or broken. The process includes a renewal of oneself as well as a turning toward others. It can serve as the cutting edge for a new surge of personal growth.

**What would you do?**

In the concluding pages of Sholem Aleichem's narratives of *Tevye the Dairyman*, we find, in distilled form, some of the fundamental themes of family conflict. The reader is drawn into the vortex of the upheavals that threaten to engulf Tevye's family. Here is a description of one of the last scenes in the story:[2]

> Many years have passed. Tevye's wife is dead. His daughter Tsaytl's young husband is also dead and she has moved back to her father's house. The other daughters have vanished. The family has been depleted in some ways and built up in others. Now Tevye has grandchildren, Tsaytl's fatherless children. But suddenly, everything is thrown into turmoil. The governor has published an edict: all the Jews must leave, from every one of their villages. They have three days to sell their possessions and clear out. Tsaytl bursts into tears. Her father tries to calm her: *"We'll go where all the other Jews go – that is, wherever our two feet take us…"* But later, she is sobbing again, now for a different reason. She utters the name of Chava, the daughter who "married out" and was declared dead by her parents. Tevye is appalled: *"Hearing that name was like being doused with boiling water or clubbed on the head! What the devil does Chava has to do*

*with this?"* Tsaytl implores him to forgive Chava and allow her to return to the family.

Tevye: *"It's too late for that! Once a branch tears itself from the tree, that's the end of it. Let the fallen leaf rot where it fell...."* But Tsaytl persists: *"I'll die right here and now if you don't forgive her! She's your daughter as much as I am!"* Tevye insists: *"She's not my daughter anymore. She died long ago."*

But Chava is not dead. She has come home. When she heard about the edict, she came home. And here she is, standing in front of him. She holds out her hands and whispers a single word:

*"Pa-pa..."*

Now, how does Tevye respond? What would you do? The author brings us into the narrative; he asks us to help Tevye decide: *"What should Tevye have done? Taken her in his arms, hugged her and kissed her?... or turned a deaf ear as he did once before and said, lekh lekho – get lost and stay lost! Put yourself in Tevye's place and tell me honestly, in plain language, what you would have done."* There is no ready-made answer. We, the readers, must struggle to find the answer.

With this provocative question, "what would *you* have done?" the author highlights an essential feature of the estrangement process: the crucial choice point that determines the outcome. He asks *us*, the readers, to confront our own resistance, pride, our hesitations. He challenges *me* to put myself in the situation and imagine how I would play out this "moment of truth." What would prevent me from forgiving? If I refuse to forgive her, what will be gained, and what outcome can I expect? Is the choice only mine, or does it require a certain response from the other person? If you were in Tevye's place, what would *you* do?

## Components of the reconciliation process

Most people have a mental picture of a contented family, an image in which each person is unconditionally accepted by family members, where parents, siblings, and children can feel comfortable together much of the time. As we have seen, this image often does not correspond with reality. For many families, a more truthful image would be a shifting morass of conflicting needs, or a sticky web of plots and grudges, alliances and animosities. In these families, connections are more likely to be sustained by grievances and retribution than by affection and respect. When one branch cuts off from the others, when one person is rejected, there is invariably a sense of unfinished business. How can the family be restored to wholeness? How can estranged persons be helped to resolve the conflict and forgive each other? The effort to understand and repair an estrangement may persist for years, even decades. For some, it becomes a lifetime project. How does the process evolve? What are its essential components?

When I began to collect the material for this book, I intended to apply the principles of family systems theory and parallel theories of family dynamics to develop my own conceptual framework. As the work progressed, I realized that these theories provide only partial knowledge. To amplify and deepen my insights, I turned to religious literature, specifically to relevant themes in Jewish texts. In pondering their meanings, I have come to appreciate the power of religiously inspired viewpoints to elucidate basic attributes of conflict and its resolution. Let us examine three concepts that are central to Jewish thought. They provide a frame of reference for understanding and repairing a fragmented family.

### 1. *KAVANNAH*, INTENTION

In a religious context, the term *kavannah* refers to two kinds of activities – praying, and observing the *mitzvot* (commandments). In both of these activities, the *kavannah*, the intention, should be congruent with the act. Preparation for the act of prayer must be consistent with its purpose: to bless, praise, or entreat God. During the sequence of prayer, the *kavannah*, the proper attitude of respectful attention, must be sustained. In the second activity, obeying a commandment, the act must be taken up in the appropriate spirit. Each of the commandments – observing the Sabbath, honoring one's parents, or any of the hundreds of required acts – each of them must be expressed with the proper attitude. If the *kavannah* is lacking or deficient, the prayers may not be valid and the observance of the commandment is not fully acceptable. With the proper intention, we can aspire to approach the Divine Presence. We can come closer to the most remote, most impenetrable realms of experience.

In the context of family conflict, let us apply the notion of *kavannah* to the preparation for reconciliation. For persons who have been mired in a prolonged estrangement, the possibility of confronting and resolving the issues may seem to be hopeless. One or all of the protagonists are convinced that the rift will never be repaired; the damage is too severe. How can they begin to create an atmosphere in which positive intentions will operate?

One scholar, James Kugel, suggests that a more accurate meaning of *kavannah* is "intentness," that is, the participation of the heart in an action.[3] The first steps in the process of reconciliation are likely to falter if the intention is not infused with the proper spirit. If one's attitude is superficial or insincere, if the intention is not "heartfelt," the effort will not be effective. The resolution of conflict requires thoughtful preparation. In the beginning, there must be a readiness to change, to explore new ways of thinking and feeling. There must also be the determination to persist in the face of obstacles and possible failure. The process of seeking reconciliation is hard work. As in any serious project, one must define the objective and chart one's course. The way may be thorny and tortuous; the journey is likely to be wearying. If both partners agree to try, there is hope for a resolution. If only one partner has the intention, energy can be focused on exploring rather than resolving the conflict. By means of exploration, one person can change his role in the relationship. He can transform his own perceptions and emotions, even though the other person may not be ready to participate in the effort.

Pockets of resistance lurk in every family with an estranged member. The original unrealistic assumptions, the old expectations, contain their own feedback mechanism that serves to confirm and reinforce them. There are countless reasons why *not* to change. A father asks, "Why shouldn't I expect my daughter to honor my values?" A man insists that "it would be stupid of me to ignore my brother's insults! Then I would look foolish, as if I deserved to be put down!" A woman cannot imagine how she could ever relinquish the anger she feels toward her brother for neglecting their dying mother. In the face of these obvious incitements, why should the guilty person expect to be forgiven? What could be the incentive for forgiving someone who has wronged me? **These are legitimate questions, and here is my answer: growth, development, and change are synonymous. There is no growth without change. The alternative to growth is stagnation and rigidity. Estrangements tend to sustain stagnation and rigidity. Efforts to resolve conflict, whether or not they succeed in achieving reconciliation, will promote growth and maturity.**

## 2. *TESHUVAH*, REPENTANCE

Related to the idea of *kavannah* or intention is the concept of *teshuvah*, the Hebrew word for repentance. *Teshuvah* is a religious concept based on sacred values. The term has three distinct meanings. First, it signifies a "return," going back to God, an awakening or a renewal of one's spiritual dimension. In this context, repentance is "one of the ultimate spiritual realities at the core of Jewish faith."[4] The second meaning refers to the act of "turning around," adopting a different orientation or direction. The fundamental task of *teshuvah* is to explore the past in order to change and renew the present. It includes the willingness to assess previous acts, regret mistakes, ask for forgiveness, and grant forgiveness to others. Its significance cannot be overstated. Rabbi Adin Steinsaltz suggests that the ability to change, the willingness to rethink one's past and commit oneself to self-scrutiny, is a basic element of human existence. It reflects the vital signs, not only of our humanity but our connection to the realm of the sacred. The actualization of *teshuvah* is a "manifestation of the divine in human beings."[5]

The Jewish approach to life affirms that when a person feels complete and satisfied, he has stopped growing spiritually. Introspection, the task of searching one's soul, is one of the basic ingredients of Jewish thought.[6] The concept is as old as Jewish history itself. An ancient instance of soul-searching appears in Genesis, in the narrative of Noah and the Flood. In Noah's actions, we find all of the elements that are essential to the process of *teshuvah*: review, recognition of offense, regret or repentance, and repair. For centuries, it was the custom among the communities of Israel to set aside the eve of every new month as a day of repentance and fasting known as a "minor Day of Atonement." Even today, many people devote a few minutes each day to review their deeds and words, count their blessings, and regret their mistakes. Some people still observe a fast to emphasize the importance of soul-searching. The Jewish worldview, with its exacting code of laws and commandments, actually requires this accounting.

The third meaning of *teshuvah* is "response." In this sense, the term may be understood as the actualization of a new pattern of behavior. It requires the clarification of crucial questions: Who am I? And who are the persons around me? Authentic *teshuvah* compels me to set new boundaries between myself and others. Repentance does *not* mean giving in, losing oneself, admitting failure or defeat. It does *not* mean regression to a previous rut. Through the experience of *teshuvah*, I re-cognize myself in a new psychological and spiritual stance. I free myself from habitual behaviors and rigid patterns. In the process of changing myself, I experience a kind of "epiphany" of the other. I learn to respect and acknowledge the other person as "other," different from me, not necessarily mirroring my values or meeting my expectations. In the midst of this process, I become aware of that individual as separate and distinct, with his or her own needs, vulnerabilities, and viewpoints. In achieving this new awareness, I can re-situate myself in relation to the other person. I construct more durable boundaries and a more authentic role for myself. When the process is fully realized, I may actually feel like a new person.

Implicit in the act of repentance is the expectation of a response from the other person. When I acknowledge my mistakes and ask for forgiveness, I assume that he will appreciate my good intentions and reciprocate. But what if he does not respond? What if she continues to reject me and ignores my sincere efforts to make amends? Many estranged people replay the old hurts again and again, reinforcing their entrenched position and refusing to see new possibilities. In such a situation, I need to revise my expectations of the other. She may be unable or unwilling to reciprocate, but her refusal does not invalidate my efforts. From trying and failing to reconnect with him or with her, I may experience a different kind of reward. In the absence of a response from the other, I may come to a fuller realization of myself. Trying and not succeeding is part of growth, a step in the right direction. At a later time, when circumstances have changed, another opportunity may arise. The renewed effort will be strengthened by the previous experience and may lead to a more complete resolution.

The act of *teshuvah* also confirms the profound conviction that human beings have a measure of control over their temporal existence. How is this possible? What's done is done, we say. It is impossible to undo or alter an action after it has occurred, after it becomes a "fact." Forty years of insults and blame cannot be cancelled out. The sting of disinheritance cannot be obliterated. However, it *is* possible to change its meaning, to reinterpret it and transform its significance, for me. In a world in which time flows inexorably on, in which everything seems to progress in a cause-and-effect sequence, the act of repentance can re-structure this pattern.[7] It gives us the opportunity to re-frame a past deed and discover a new meaning, thus achieving a different outcome. *Teshuvah* becomes a form of creation.

248

### 3. *TIKKUN* – REPAIRING A BROKEN CONNECTION

The concept of *teshuvah*, repentance, is linked to another fundamental Jewish idea, the act of *tikkun*, repair. When a family connection has been broken, certain concrete acts of "equilibration"
are needed to repair the breach. For each past action that contributed to the conflict, there is a parallel act that can transpose
one's attitude and perceptions. Every insult must be countered
with a sincere expression of praise or appreciation; each act of
neglect or rejection must be balanced by the effort to affirm or
embrace the other person. The protagonists have the responsibility to identify their unique forms of "repair" and decide how
to put them into action. It may take a good deal of ingenuity to
figure out the appropriate type of repair.

A second, more difficult form of *tikkun* goes beyond correcting
mistakes and expressing regret. It is reflected in the determination to be constantly on guard against repeating destructive patterns and regressing to old habits that contributed to the original
conflict. By applying our understanding of previous conflicts to
create new forms of response, we can experience genuine *tikkun*,
that is, the durable repair of a broken relationship. This stage of
the process may be compared to a return home after a hazardous
journey or a traumatic experience. Entering your house, you feel
drained and exhausted. You unpack your bags and put everything
away. Now, you need to put yourself back together. Moving on
with your life will be a difficult challenge. Each new experience
will be lived in the light of the recent trauma. And yet, the hurt
and anxiety gradually subside. You begin to integrate those painful memories into your ongoing activities. Similar to the effort
of repairing a severed relationship, patterns that were not visible
now become apparent. You discover new insights and, along the
way, you count your blessings. This is the process of resolving an
estrangement.

A different metaphor for repair is the act of art restoration.
A rare painting has been damaged. The canvas has deteriorated,
the paint has begun to crumble. Or a marble sculpture from the

Renaissance has a missing limb, one ear broken and the face obscured by layers of dirt. The process of restoration is laborious; it takes great skill and many months before the object is restored to its full glory. Even then, it will never return fully to its original state; it will always be identified as "restored." But it will emanate light and beauty nonetheless, and enrich its beholders. A fragmented family deserves at least as much care, time, and skill as a damaged work of art. A restored family *is* a work of art.

Let's turn back to the families we spoke of in the previous chapters, those who have resolved their conflicts. How did the process of reconciliation emerge? What were the forms of repair in these stories?

In the Silver family, Rose and Sidney followed the advice of their therapist. They continued to send money and persisted in their attempts to connect with their son despite his rejection of them. When Dan returned, they accepted his presence matter-of-factly, asking for nothing, expecting nothing. They resisted all temptation to question him, cast blame or evoke feelings of guilt. The family settled into a new pattern of interactions, with more distinct boundaries and revised expectations. Over a period of years, they have learned new ways to relate to each other. Now they can accept differences and limitations with greater equanimity. The process of repair continues.

After all those years of alienation, Jen Stern and her brother began to imagine how they could reconnect. They had the *kavannah,* the intention to mend the rift but were reluctant to try. A family wedding provided the setting. Although each of them was anxious about the possibility of being rejected or criticized by the other, they took the risk and agreed to meet. The repair, the *tikkun,* came through words, talking, reviewing old times, recalling their shared past, and celebrating their newfound affection. During the period of re-acquaintance, each of them learned to appreciate their differences as well as their kinship. The process is ongoing. Everyone in the family is rejoicing in their elation.

Every person who intends to resolve an estrangement from his or her family will need to learn how to reconnect, how to build a new relationship while retaining a sense of self. The family must re-group and re-define itself in the light of the returning person. Let us examine two vastly different versions of reconciliation between alienated brothers. In the first story, we trace an old man's steps on the journey. As the narrative unfolds, we learn that the original provocations had faded with time, but neither of the protagonists had been able to initiate the task of reconciliation. In the second story, we will focus on the elements of confrontation, a face-to-face meeting that exposes stinging rage and guilt and leads to *teshuvah*, repentance and reconciliation. Each of these stories highlights crucial elements in the process.

### 1. An audacious journey to seek reconciliation

*The Straight Story* is a film documentary based on the true story of an old man, estranged from his brother for many years, who traveled hundreds of miles on a lawn mower to reconnect with him.[8] The film is a faithful depiction of the adventures of the hero on his journey. His struggles, mishaps, and eventual triumph allow us to follow the steps that led to reconciliation.

Alvin Straight was born in Montana in 1920 and brought his family to Iowa in 1973. He worked as a laborer and fathered seven children. A veteran of World War II and the Korean War, he died of heart disease at the age of seventy-five, two years after his remarkable journey. His funeral procession was accompanied by a lawn mower similar to the one he used on the trip to find his brother.

The opening scenes of the film introduce us to an ordinary working-class neighborhood in a small town in Iowa. An obese lady is sunning herself in the backyard. She hears a crash in the house next door and goes to investigate. Her neighbor, an old man, has fallen in his kitchen. Grunting and grumbling, he struggles to get up. This is Alvin Straight: a thin wrinkled face, mane of white hair, scraggly beard, persistent frown. His daughter Rose enters, upset at the sight of her father straining to lift himself off the floor. We sense that something is "not right" with Rose. Her speech is strange; she seems "slow." Because she insists, Alvin reluctantly agrees to see a doctor. In the examining room, we learn that the old man is stubborn, resistant, and fiercely independent. He refuses to comply with the doctor's recommendations and limps home, puffing on one of the cigars he keeps in the pocket of his plaid flannel shirt. His only concession is to use two canes instead of one.

In the next scene, a storm is raging. Lightning darts off the walls of the Straights' kitchen; we hear booms of thunder. The phone rings and Rose answers. We hear her halting speech: she stammers that something has happened to her father's eighty-year-old brother Lyle: a stroke. Alvin seems shocked by the news. He immediately rouses himself, mutters to Rose: "Gotta go back on the road; gotta see Lyle." How will he get there? Lyle lives in Wisconsin, hundreds of miles away. Alvin's vision is poor, he can't drive and neither can Rose. No bus goes there. Alvin's hips are bad; his legs don't work right. He can't stand up without groaning. He is seventy-three years old but looks more like ninety.

The scene shifts. Alvin is out in the yard, assembling something. We learn that he is putting parts together to construct a vehicle he can drive. Rose says "Oh jeez, Dad!" He insists, "Gotta go see Lyle, on my own."

Alvin sets out at sunrise on this strange contraption, a lawn mower pulling a small trailer. Dogs run alongside, barking. As he rumbles slowly down the main street, his cronies come out of their stores, staring, incredulous. "He'll never make it," they mutter. It is early in September. Alvin chugs along, down a narrow country road, past the lush green fields of Iowa. The vehicle gets stuck and has to be towed back to town. It can't be fixed. In a fit of frustration, Alvin takes his rifle, aims, and shoots the crippled mower. Determined not to give up, he goes in search of a new vehicle. He buys a thirty-year old John Deere mower from a garage in town and starts out again. In the trailer, Alvin has stowed the necessary equipment: his canes, some food, a rusty chair, and a grabber to pick up wood for his campfires each night. Three hundred fifty miles to go.

It takes six weeks for Alvin to reach Wisconsin on the lawn mower. Along the way, he has many adventures, meets other wanderers, seekers, and vagrants. Some are good people who help him; others ignore him and go their own way. A hitchhiker, a frightened pregnant girl, takes shelter with him one night. In their conversation, we learn a small piece of Alvin's history. She tells him, "My family hates me and they'll hate this baby." Alvin exposes an old wound: he tells her that his wife, long dead, had fourteen babies. Only seven lived. He offers no information about his surviving children. We only know about his daughter Rose, the "slow" child. Alvin gives the pregnant girl a lesson in the meaning of family. "We used to play this game," he tells her. "See this stick? Can you break it?" She does, easily. "Now look," and he gathers a bundle of sticks, holds them together, and hands her the bundle. "Now break this." She tries, but can't. "The bundle is family." End of lesson. In the morning, she is gone, perhaps to return to her family or to continue her solitary wandering.

Alvin's adventures continue. Cars, buses, trucks zoom past him; he rumbles on. After five weeks on the road, he is rolling down a steep hill when his brakes fail. Barely avoiding a collision, he steers into some bushes and sits there. A man offers to help, tows him to the next town, and lets him sleep in the barn while the mower is being fixed. Alvin turns down the offer of a ride: "Nope, I gotta do this my own way."

Our hero goes to retrieve his lawn mower from the twin brothers who have repaired it. He manages to convince them to lower the price, and in the dickering, we hear another piece of his story. For the first time, he speaks about his estrangement from Lyle. "No one knows your life like a brother," he tells the twins. "The last time we were together, we said some unforgivable things. This trip is a hard swallow for my pride. I hope I'm not too late."

The journey resumes at dawn. Sixty miles to go. The terrain is more arduous and he's been warned that the lawn mower won't make it to Wisconsin. He rumbles on, comes to a very long bridge. He's crossing the Mississippi, trying to catch glimpses of the great river below. He wobbles along, and we wonder if he'll plunge over the side. But he manages to get across and stops for the night in a churchyard, next to an old cemetery. The preacher comes out to investigate, peers at the mower and says: "Unusual mode of transport." "Yep," he agrees. Alvin asks the preacher if he knows Lyle, his brother. He does remember visiting him in the hospital, after the stroke. "He didn't mention that he had a brother," the preacher says. Alvin responds: "Neither one of us has had a brother for quite some time." Then, another piece of the story is given to us. Alvin tells the preacher, "We grew up close, on a farm. Worked hard, slept outside in summer. Talked a lot, looking at the stars, wondering if there was anybody out there. We talked through our growing up, and then..." The preacher asks him "What happened between you?" "It's old as the Bible – Cain and Abel. There was anger. Haven't spoken in more than ten years. I wanta make peace now, wanta look up at the stars like we used to do," Alvin replies. The preacher concludes: "Amen to that!"

Alvin is now on the last lap of his journey, a rocky dirt road, curving through a field. The sky is darkening. The motor dies. There is no one to help him; he sits and waits. Finally, a tractor lumbers up, a man tries to help, gets the motor going again, points "that way." We see a tiny, dilapidated shack, with overgrown bushes and broken windows. The mower lurches to a stop for the last time. Alvin gets his canes, limps toward the shack calling "Lyle!" No answer. Again: "Lyle?" Finally, we hear halting, uneven steps and an old man appears, frail, unshaven, obviously ill, limping with a walker. They stare at each other for long, silent moments. Then, a brief dialogue:

LYLE: "Did you ride that thing all the way out here to see me?"
ALVIN: "I did, Lyle."

And then we see the stars overhead, and that's all. The film ends.

**Comments**

*The Straight Story* brings the metaphor of a journey into vivid reality. Let us focus on the themes that reflect essential elements in the reconciliation process.

Alvin Straight was old and frail when he decided to reconnect with his brother. What mobilized him? The news of his brother's stroke seemed to serve as a catalyst, thrusting the old man out of his usual mood. Suddenly, he was seized by the *kavannah*, the intention to change. Is such a shock essential to initiate the process of reconciling with an estranged sibling or parent? Must a person wait for old age and approaching death to make such a crucial decision? In many fragmented families, the remorse one feels for having waited too long is more painful than the original conflict.

The quirks in Alvin's personality are vividly portrayed: he was stubborn, defiant, and self-centered. Perhaps these same traits had provoked his brother and set off the original estrangement. In many close sibling relationships, a brother (or sister) is compelled to cut off as a way of asserting his or her own identity.

Alvin announces his determination: "Gotta see Lyle." Here is a clear expression of his intention. He is aware of the obstacles but they do not deter him. He constructs a mental plan. Soon he will begin to carry it out. In the process of reconciliation, these are the basic components. First, there is the determination to act. Then, there is the readiness to create a realistic course of action, assemble the proper tools, and begin the task.

What is a suitable "vehicle" for the journey? Alvin's lawn mower is a symbol for the means to undertake the task. In other situations, the "vehicle" may take the form of a letter, a gift, an invitation to visit. It might be an awkward contraption, like the lawn mower. Onlookers may think it strange; they may warn of dangers or the probability of a breakdown. What if the effort fails? For each person, the "vehicle" will be different and the process will have its own unique shape and sequence.

During his journey, Alvin meets various people who take up different roles in his drama. Similarly, in each case of attempted reconciliation, there will be those who are supportive and others who are not. Some will discourage the effort, argue that it's foolish, futile, or demeaning. Any person who embarks on this task can expect to encounter similar challenges. Like Alvin, the seeker may sometimes find himself in the role of teacher and guide, helping others who attempt to resolve their own family dilemmas.

When Alvin refuses the offer of a ride, we see the positive side of his stubbornness. He is determined to do it his way. In his conversation with the twin brothers who repair his contraption, we learn a bit about the estrangement. "No one knows your life like a brother," he tells them. "The last time we were together, we said some unforgivable things…" Here, for the first time, we hear about the provocation that led to the cutoff. We are not told what "unforgivable things" were said. But he emphasizes that, "*We* said unforgivable things." Not "I" or "he." It is not a matter of perpetrator and innocent victim. Alvin knew that both of them were implicated in the conflict. He also understood that "no one knows your life like a brother."

Along the way, Alvin gains valuable insights. He realizes that this trip is a "hard swallow" for his pride. Somehow, he is able to overcome this obstacle, his pride. How does a person take this crucial step? What must we do to rise above our pride, to put aside our grievances? The process of reconciliation requires this kind of transformation.

As Alvin approaches the end of his journey, he meets a preacher, or an angel, or a fellow wayfarer. This meeting is more than mere coincidence. It has the quality of an epiphany, a moment in which truth is revealed. The preacher had visited Alvin's brother in the hospital, but the old man had not mentioned having a brother. Alvin's reply is a beautiful expression of insight. "Neither of us has had a brother for quite some time." Many accounts of reconnecting with an estranged relative contain a moment of vivid awareness like this one. There is a sense of awakening, a beam of light that can illuminate the pathway to a new beginning. It is one of the priceless rewards that accompany the reconciliation process.

The preacher comments on the "unusual mode of transportation." Yes, this is a remarkable journey in an unlikely conveyance. Alvin allows the past to come to the surface as he reveals more of the story. We learn that the brothers grew up on a farm, together. But then, something happened. "Cain and Abel," again. The sibling paradox, perhaps. They were similar and different, attached and separate, and "there was anger." Alvin recalls scenes of their early, shared experience, looking at the stars, side by side. Now he wants to make peace. We wonder if Lyle will welcome Alvin or turn him away. What would *you* do?

When the end is almost at hand, the possibility of failure looms. At the last minute, the motor in Alvin's contraption sputters and dies. The story could have had a different ending. Alvin could simply have given up. Or, Lyle could have died in the meantime, or moved away, or refused to see him. In the journey toward reconciliation, failure is always a possibility. In this case, the story has a gratifying conclusion. Alvin accepts just enough help to overcome the last obstacle. Lyle is able to appreciate his brother's effort and receive him. We do not know if they were able to harvest the precious fruits of reconciliation. After such a long estrangement, we hope they could recall their shared history as well as their separate lives. The next scenes are left to our imagination.

*The Straight Story* presents a portrait of one man's audacious plan to be reconnected with his estranged brother. The film concludes with their meeting, a reconciliation that occurs without heated confrontations or accusations. It seems that the old animosities were not recalled or resolved. Rather, the two men met and spoke together. Particular elements in the story can serve as metaphors for other forms of reconciliation. The lawn mower, an "unusual mode of transport," stands for any bridging device that might be used to approach estranged family members. The meanings of intention, repentance, and repair are reflected in Alvin's determined efforts to reconnect with his brother. Each milestone on his arduous journey has much to teach us about the process of change. Alvin's struggles, his persistence, and his eventual success may inspire us to embark on a parallel journey of our own.

## 2. Joseph and his brothers: Confrontation and beyond

The biblical story of Jacob's twelve sons, their rivalries, loyalties, duplicities, and eventual reconciliation, illuminates the fundamental themes of family conflict. Volumes of *midrashim* have been written, in addition to countless variations, commentaries, and fictional versions of this timeless story. Here, we will examine two examples from the literature of biblical interpretation to highlight the significance of confrontation, the most difficult phase in the resolution of hostilities. As the emotional intensity escalates, all of the ingredients in the original conflict are distilled and elaborated. In these scenes, old wounds are opened and re-pressed rage is brought to the surface. Will the tension explode into fragments, never to be mended? Or will the protagonists emerge from the fire with new insights? Let us review the events leading to the pivotal scene.

In the original biblical text, the story is played out in three separate episodes, each with its own time frame and distinct meanings.[9] First, ten of the twelve brothers come down to Egypt to purchase grain when a dreadful famine threatens their families' lives. Joseph, now the king's trusted advisor, commands them to appear before him. It is their first encounter with Joseph since they abandoned him in the pit many years ago. Unrecognized by his brothers, he speaks harshly to them and commands them to go home and return to Egypt with Benjamin, the youngest brother. The second scene presents all of the brothers in a complex interaction. Finally, they return once more to appeal to Joseph after he accuses them of lying and stealing.

In each of these scenes, we can sense the lack of symmetry between the protagonists. Joseph "knows" his brothers; he sees them for who they are. They, on the other hand, do not "know" him. He appears to be utterly foreign to them, the viceroy of the king, a man with immense power. The tension builds to a fever pitch. Threats and denunciations are hurled from one side; expressions of bewilderment, denial, and defensiveness are offered from the other side. In each of these emotionally charged encounters, we see the brothers alternately cringe in fear and then retaliate and counterattack. Joseph's accusations are calculated to bring them to realize the full meaning of their actions against him, from their murderous envy to their act of abandoning him in the wilderness. In the religious context, Joseph's treatment of them is not personally motivated. It is not an expression of revenge, but is seen as guided by a higher source. The intent is to help the brothers atone for their sins and reach an authentic state of repentance.

## An Eighth Century Poem

Phinehas HaKohen, a rabbi who lived near Tiberias in the eighth century, composed interpretations of biblical texts in the form of poetry. One of his poems presents his vision of the climactic scene in which Joseph and his brothers confront and resolve their long estrangement.[10] It consists of eight stanzas in the form of a dialogue between Joseph and Yehuda, the one who convinced his brothers not to kill Joseph but to "sell him, for he is our brother" (*Genesis*, 37:26–27). The poem replicates the setting and plot of the original text. In the opening scene, we are present in Pharaoh's palace, with the Egyptian guards as onlookers. Imagine the strained atmosphere in those tense moments before Joseph reveals his true identity. Ten of his brothers have come to buy food. Joseph, now the viceroy of the king, sees his boyhood dreams fulfilled as his unsuspecting brothers bow before him. He recognizes them, but he does not acknowledge their kinship. Instead, he speaks harshly to them, accusing them of spying. Does he intend to frighten them, punish them, threaten, or challenge them? In Rabbi haKohen's poem, as in the original text, the tensions escalate as Joseph and Yehuda come face to face. We can sense the buildup of emotion in the rhythm of alternating verses, each ending with the same phrase: *"Joseph said to them"* or *"Yehuda said to him."* The poem beautifully expresses the counterpoint of the dialogue.

In the first verse, Joseph accuses his brothers: *"You sold a brother for the price of shoes. Full of hate, you set upon him to shed his blood.... You pained your father's heart, you plotted to delude him...."* He threatens them with Divine retribution: *"Woe to you from the judgment of the Revealer!"*

The second verse presents Yehuda's response. He is astonished and terrified. He pleads with Joseph and admits their guilt. *"We are amazed to hear all this from you… Do not reveal the secrets of our past. It is our crime that has brought this trouble upon us."* And, *"your words have filled us with trembling!"*

Joseph accuses them: *"You tormented him…. Merciless, you sold him to violent men…."* He repeats the threat of divine punishment.

The dialogue continues, with expressions of guilt and regret interspersed with bitter denunciations. The scene escalates to a powerful climax, reaching almost unbearable intensity. Then, Joseph sends the Egyptian guards out of the room and stands alone before his brothers. The emotional mood is transposed to a new key as Joseph reveals his enlightened understanding of the entire sequence of events. It was God who set the plot in motion so that he, Joseph, could eventually save his people. With this explanation, he lifts the blame from the brothers and reframes the situation, allowing the positive aspects of the dispute to be seen. It was all for the good, his suffering and theirs. Finally, Joseph reveals his true self. He acknowledges the continuity between his past and present identity: *"I am Joseph."*

The brothers are astounded, speechless. Then, Joseph weeps, showing them his tender side and allowing them to express tenderness in response. The poem concludes with the powerful line from the original text: *"And afterwards his brothers talked with him"* (*Genesis*, 45:15).

*"Talked with him"*? At this moment, in the aftermath of such intense emotions, what might the brothers speak of? Do they review the past and repeat the old antagonisms? Or, are they able to "let bygones be bygones" and begin the task of repair and renewal? Do they speak of mundane matters, share news of the events that have transpired since they were last together as one family? Were they ever *together as one family*?

### The potential healing power of confrontation
Many centuries before Rabbi haKohen composed his poems,

the Sages produced dramatic interpretations of the confrontation between Joseph and Yehuda. In one collection of *midrashim*, the compiler selected excerpts from various Talmudic sources to highlight the emotional tension in this crucial scene.[11] Here is a sampling of descriptions that reflect the tone of the meeting between the brothers:

> *Yehuda let out a terrifying cry of anger... His eyes were dripping with blood. The hair on his head stiffened and pierced all five layers of his garments. He took iron bars into his mouth and ground them to dust with his teeth. He seized a stone weighing four hundred shekels, threw it to the sky and caught it, crushing it under his feet. Joseph was afraid of being killed.*
>
> *Yehuda: "You invented one accusation after another. Every time I swear I'm innocent, you accuse me of something else. I will fill Egypt with dead bodies!"*
>
> *Joseph: "If you draw your sword, I will tie it to your own neck!"*
>
> *Yehuda: "I shall stuff your mouth with a stone. I shall dye the market places of Egypt with blood!"*
>
> *Joseph: "You are dyers by profession. Didn't you dye a garment with blood and present it to your father?"*
>
> *Yehuda threatened to murder everyone in Egypt.*
>
> *Joseph asked Pharaoh to send him three hundred soldiers to prevent the brothers from destroying the country. When they arrived, Yehuda shouted so loudly that the princes in the palace fell to the ground; the animals all miscarried. The teeth of three hundred soldiers fell out and they fled, never to be seen again.*
>
> *At the height of this terrible tension, Joseph knew he must reveal his true identity.*

What is the meaning of these wild scenes? We are told that the lives of the early Sages reflected unceasing *Kiddush haShem*, devotion to God.[12] Their piety was expressed not only in their painstaking study of Torah but also in praying, working, eating, resting, relating to other people, in every facet of their lives. Why, then, would they interpret this biblical episode in such melodramatic terms? What is happening here, and what vital message did they intend to convey?

Studying their words from the point of view of a contemporary psychologist, one could suggest that the Sages had an uncanny ability to understand human feelings and behavior. They were able to portray the most sublime, and also the most abhorrent emotions. These passages can teach us not only to recall an early episode in our religious history, but also to mine the wellsprings of our own rage, fear, hatred, and love.

The descriptions in these *midrashic* texts may appear to be exaggerated beyond any credible point. But if you have ever participated in a heated confrontation with an estranged relative, overheard an encounter between enraged siblings, or received a letter of indictment from an alienated daughter, you will recognize the similarity in the magnitude of emotion. The Sages teach us the potential value of a confrontation that allows agonizing guilt and raw pain to be exposed. The Hebrew term *midda-keneged-midda* (translated as "measure for measure, in equal terms") refers to the concept that every action summons a corresponding divine response. A person is repaid by Heaven in a manner corresponding to the quality of his behavior. The reward or punishment that God brings upon a person mirrors that person's own deeds. At the time of retribution, he or she will then be aware that the disciplinary action is not a result of chance, but of Divine Providence. This concept is operative in the confrontation between Joseph and his brothers. Every aspect of Joseph's behavior, each of his accusations, is calculated to make the brothers aware of their wrongdoings, not simply for the sake of causing them anguish, but in order to expiate their sins. His actions are not motivated by malice or revenge, but rather to enable them to acknowledge their role in the conflict, admit their guilt, and open the way for authentic repentance.

The images in the biblical story and its commentaries are

relevant to an encounter between alienated brothers in ancient times, as well as to estranged members in a contemporary family. The counterpoint of voices is alternately accusative and apologetic, expressing themes and counter-themes in rapid succession. On both sides, there is justification for the escalation of rage and blame. We can empathize with the brothers' feelings of guilt, confusion, and overwhelming anxiety. We understand Joseph's urge to punish them. These dramatic interpretations may serve as a warning to estranged relatives that a searing confrontation is likely to intensify the ferocity of the conflict. Can they risk the pain of exposure, the danger that the tensions will spin out of control? Will they trust that the encounter may have redemptive power? The expression of powerful emotions can serve to cauterize the gaping wound of alienation, allowing the healing process to begin. In some situations, it can be the catalyst for enhancing one's self-awareness. Hopefully, out of the turmoil, a more wholesome, mutually supportive relationship will emerge. In the Coda of this book, you will find a description of a ferocious confrontation that opened the way to the constructive resolution of a bitter conflict.

For Joseph and his brothers, the confrontation was an essential element in the process of repairing the family, and yet it did not lead to a perfect reconciliation. Reflecting the human frailties of all families, vestiges of discord would remain as echoes in the resolution of their conflict. Even in the present day, themes from those ancient struggles continue to resonate in our own families. The past is not obliterated, but rather, it is transposed into a new beginning. *"The end is where we start from."*

### Concluding thoughts: theme and counter-theme

We have listened to the voices of persons who have been cut off, banished, rejected, and in some cases, reclaimed and reconciled. To bring these thoughts to a close, let us examine how particular themes and images can help us clarify the reality of family conflict.

When we observe the process of alienation in one family with estranged members, the sequence of their interactions may be likened to an ominous storm, gradually escalating to a climax. For another family, the conflict seems to erupt like an explosion, the fragments flying farther and farther apart. Still another would resemble a river that divides at some point, the two streams flowing in opposite directions, never to return to the original source. Or, an altered musical composition, a fugue with one voice missing, could symbolize a family with a banished member. Each of these images implies a polar opposite; one cancels out the other. We can speak of *either* storm or calm, explosion *or* tranquility, one river *or* two separate streams, sounds *or* silence, alienation *or* togetherness. But while these images may convey some facets of the estrangement process as it develops through time, they do not adequately express the reality of the phenomenon we have been exploring. A more relevant image would be a kaleidoscope, the fragments splitting and re-forming in new shapes and color combinations. In music, the same idea would be expressed by a polyphonic composition in which the individual themes emerge and combine, separate and recede, and eventually resolve in a tonic chord. These images do not require us to discard one aspect of the phenomenon while we retain the other. They help us to understand that both aspects are essential parts of one process.

In the stories of fragmented families, we have seen how the beginning of a conflict may bear the seeds of its own resolution. Some provocations evoke anger and retaliation but may also lead to self-examination and new insights. In the aftermath of a long, painful estrangement, the possibility of forgiving and being forgiven may be actualized. From an expanded point of view, we can appreciate the permutations and anticipate the changes that will bring new vitality to the situation. Most important, in viewing the process through a wider lens, we can grasp the essential connections between the apparent opposites. Attachment and separation, closeness and distance, anger and love: one does not cancel out the other. Rather, they are parts of one whole, theme and counter-theme. Andre Neher writes: "Abandonment and ingathering belong together, not because of the compensating healing effect of the passage of time, but through the inner dialectic of their inseparable relationship."[13] Estrangement and reconciliation, theme and counter-theme: they are part of the "inner dialectic" that resonates throughout the evolving narrative of life in a family.

# CHAPTER TEN

# Strategies to Explore and Resolve Conflict

## PREPARATION

In the previous chapter, we examined three components of the reconciliation process: *kavannah* (intention), *teshuvah* (repentance), and *tikkun* (repair). Here, we will suggest some concrete ways to apply these concepts to the task of exploring, and perhaps resolving estrangements.

We begin with the assumption that reconciliation is a process; it is not a single event or an endpoint. Consequently, we place the emphasis on the work of reviewing and clarifying the estrangement, pondering its impact on oneself and one's family, and developing strategies to cope with the outcome of this effort. These stages comprise the process. The task may lead to reconciliation, or it may not. In either case, the effort itself will be worthwhile.

For many people, the possibility of bridging a cutoff seems remote or completely hopeless. With a different *kavannah*, a new attitude, we can begin to construct the bridge. The following steps are meant to suggest possibilities, to provide a spectrum of ideas or a collection of tools. You may find some that are compatible with your style, or you may use my ideas to create other approaches that are uniquely yours. The crucial starting point is your intention to change old patterns. If you can create a "melting zone" in which you can begin to dissolve the frigid atmosphere of hostility, you will have accomplished the first step in the journey.

> *"In seeking wisdom, the first step is silence; the second is listening; the third, remembering; the fourth is practicing; and the fifth is teaching others."*[1]

As we approach the task of exploring an estrangement, these five steps can help us build an attitude of readiness.

### Silence

In the beginning stages of estrangement, silence is often a pervasive presence. There is the silence of passivity, of anger not expressed. There is the silence of frustration, bewilderment, and numbness. As the waves of hostility ebb and flow, silence can become a weapon, a wedge, or an expression of indifference. Let us consider how silence can be used constructively to generate change.

Andre Neher, the French-Jewish philosopher, speaks of the "desert of the word that we call silence."[2] What is the meaning of this image? "Desert" is a remote, arid space, devoid of human habitation, but swarming with winds, sand, and unseen creatures that know how to survive in such a bleak environment. In the Hebrew Bible, the desert is a place where the Jewish people wandered, waited, complained, rebelled, and eventually heard the voice of God. How can we use this image to clarify the experience of estrangement?

Search for your "desert." Search for the inner places where you feel emptiness, pain, regret, fury, despair. These are feelings that often cannot be expressed in words.

Focus on the image of being lost, blown away, left alone in the wilderness.

Allow yourself to cry, to welcome tears. Imagine that your tears will water your desert, giving sound to the silence.

Be patient until you are ready to cultivate your desert. Be silent until you are ready to speak.

Be silent until the moment when you trust that your words will be heard.

*Listening*
Listen with your eyes closed. Listen in the darkness. Listen to
  silence.
Listen to the noise, the static of ongoing hostility.
Listen to the roar of your own anger.
Listen to the words of the other, the estranged person, in your
  mind's ear.
Try to tune in to the feelings that lie beneath the words.
Listen to advice that is appropriate for where and who you are,
  now.
Imagine the estranged person, listening to you.

*Remembering*
Remember what has been useful in the past.
Remember what your mother would have said.
Remember what your wisest teacher would have said.
Remember a time when you changed a vital aspect of
  yourself.
Remember the pain of rejection.
Remember how to say, "I love you," and mean it.
Remember how to say, "I'm really sorry," and mean it.

*Practicing*
Practice telling your story to someone whom you trust.
Practice writing a version of your story with two different
  conclusions.
Practice how to ask for forgiveness.
Practice accepting the other person's idiosyncrasies.
Practice how to respond when the other person asks for
  forgiveness.
Try to replace your habitual behavior patterns with new ways
  of greeting, speaking, listening, and responding.
Practice your transformation until it becomes *you*.

*Teaching*

Tell your story to a child.

Write a version of your story from the perspective of the other, the estranged person.

Be a person to whom others can tell their estrangement stories.

Convene a support group. It may consist of only two or three people.

Compose an ethical will that will impart your wisdom to the next generation.

The steps listed above are not intended to be sequential, each done once and for all. Rather, they are like the progression of melody, rhythm, and harmony when you are studying a musical score. You may wish to play or sing the entire score from beginning to end. Or, you may repeat individual parts, or return to them after working on the other parts. My ideas are intended to be a guide, a preparation for the suggestions that follow. Think of them as a range of opportunities that you may wish to follow, modify, expand, or reject.

Now, we will move on to consider specific tools for exploring estrangements. Let us consider three modalities: prayers, questions, and rituals. Each of them is intended to promote change, expand horizons, and enhance understanding of oneself and one's family.

## 1. PRAYERS

How can we understand "prayer" as a tool? According to one interpretation from an ancient Jewish text, prayer is an expression of a person's constant awareness of the Divine. In the most profound sense, prayer is a spiritual encounter with God in which the individual experiences himself in a new light. But the act of praying can also penetrate into mundane areas of life, giving us strength, new insights, and hope. In this sense, prayer is a kind of "inner communion" that generates spiritual energy. It is "a process wherein work is really done, and spiritual energy flows in and produces effects, either psychological or material."³

The central role of prayer in Judaism becomes apparent when we examine the *Siddur*, a compilation of the prayers that are recited by observant Jews everywhere. The substance of this book encompasses the entire historical experience of the Jewish people. Its contents continue to be relevant to every stage in the lives of individuals. The *Siddur* contains many different kinds of prayers. For each one, there is a specified time, context, and focus for the act of praying. A prayer can be directed to a particular historical event, a Divine imperative, or a personal experience. Praying can take many forms. It can be an affirmation of belief, an expression of gratitude, a request for help, an acknowledgement of wrongdoing, an outpouring of praise, or an appeal for forgiveness.

The following Hasidic story reflects a view of prayer that is relevant to our task.

*One day a group of Hasidim overheard their master praying. To their amazement, he was merely repeating the letters of the alphabet. When they approached him afterward, seeking to know the mystery of this form of prayer, he explained: "Who am I to be able to find the right and adequate words to clothe my innermost feelings of adoration and praise. But God knows what I want to say and what I mean. Therefore, I merely say the letters, and let the Holy One, blessed be He, make them into the right words Himself."*⁴

Implicit in the master's explanation is the faith that his prayer will be heard and understood. He knows that the act of praying goes beyond the recitation of particular sounds or the definition of individual words. At a deeper level, prayers express the essence of the *kavannah,* the intention and concentration that the praying person brings to them. A prayer can be experienced in many ways. It can express our longing to approach the Divine Presence. It can also open new dimensions of awareness and bring us to a clearer understanding of our own thoughts and feelings. In some situations, it can serve as a springboard to a change of heart.

In the following section, we will examine the meanings of particular sequences of prayer, to see how they may be applied to the task of exploring an estrangement. Let us begin with one of the first prayers recited in the morning service, *Birkat haShachar*, or "blessings of the dawn."

> *Blessed are You, HaShem our God, King of the universe, who fashioned man with wisdom and created within him many openings and many cavities. It is obvious and known before Your Throne of Glory that if one of them were to be ruptured or one of them were to be blocked, it would be impossible to survive and to stand before You. Blessed are You, God, who heals all flesh and acts wondrously.*

The surface meaning of these words refers to the orifices and hollows of the body: the mouth, nose, and other vital openings, and the linings and separations between one body part and another. This configuration is essential to our survival; it facilitates and sustains the function of each particular part and its relation to the body as a whole. So, every morning, the person recites this prayer to thank God for preserving this fundamental balance between the open and closed portions of his or her body. Such corporeal necessities as the elimination of waste and the taking in of nutrients, so basic to our survival, are seen as gifts from the Creator. The prayer acknowledges that if one of the vital openings is blocked, or if one cavity is severed, we will not be able to stand and begin the day.

Looking beneath the surface meanings, I find that this prayer evokes thoughts about my role in the family, the quality of connections and separations between myself and others. Am I able to eliminate the "waste materials" that contaminate my relationships? Do I "nourish" the wholesome aspects? If my acceptance and respect for the other is blocked, or if the boundaries between the other and myself become clogged with unrealistic expectations or exaggerated needs, my role as a family member will be compromised. When I allow anger to dominate my responses, when I become alienated from the other, I am not able to sustain a healthy position in the family. By studying the deeper implications of this prayer and applying its teachings to my own life, I may become more sensitive to the ruptures and blockages, the dissonances and fragmentations in my family relationships.

Later in the sequence of morning prayers, there is a progression of fifteen blessings. Many of these phrases can be traced to their original biblical sources. The series is based on a section of the Talmud (*Brachot* 60b) in which the Sages teach us to acknowledge God's gift of a new day of life. Each one begins with the benediction, *"Blessed are You our God, King of the universe…"* Usually, this formulation appears once at the beginning of a unit of prayer and is not repeated. What is the significance of the repetition in this sequence? We invoke the name of God to acknowledge His Presence in these apparently mundane matters and to emphasize the distinctive importance of each one. Let us examine three of these blessings to discover how they can be applied to the task of clarifying family relationships.

The first *bracha* (blessing) in this series addresses the natural event of waking to the cry of the rooster. But this event is transposed to the realm of the sacred when we pray: *"Praised is He Who has given the cock understanding to distinguish between day and night."* Or, *"Blessed is He Who gives the heart understanding to distinguish between light and darkness."* (A note in the *Siddur* explains that the same Hebrew word (*sichvi*) refers to both "heart" and "rooster.") In the context of this blessing, "both meanings are implied: the rooster crows, but man's heart reacts and understands how to deal with new situations."[5] We may choose to recite this prayer as an expression of gratitude for the ability to distinguish between the essential, meaningful, and enduring aspects of our relationships and those that are peripheral, transitory, or superficial. Alternatively, it can help us to recognize those relationships that shed light on our lives and should be sustained, regardless of the obstacles and pain, and those that should be let go, relinquished.

The next phrase we shall consider acknowledges the Power "...*Who releases the bound*..." who frees the slave, or who gives me the means, the inspiration to liberate myself from a situation in which I am rigidly confined. When I thank God for release, I may also be expressing gratitude for new possibilities and wider horizons. Perhaps I will learn how to extricate myself from the chains of my own anger, to transform my rejection and mistrust. As I move from an enmeshed position to one of greater freedom and flexibility, I see myself in a new light. These new insights may or may not compel me to seek reconciliation with the estranged person; I will be free to make that decision.

"...*Who gives strength to the weary*..." This prayer, an echo of a phrase in *Isaiah*, (Chapter 40:29), is especially relevant to persons who are immersed in an intractable family conflict or who have been estranged from significant others for a long time. The experience can be exhausting, depriving me of energy and leaving me limp with frustration and despair. This prayer acknowledges the possibility that strength may come from a variety of sources, depending on one's own receptivity and frame of reference. Sometimes we are surprised to discover a well of hope, a novel idea, a new event that fosters vitality and constructive change in the family. When I recite this prayer, I am asking for Divine help to find these sources of strength.

It is not correct to assume that sacred Jewish texts are composed solely of references to peaceful solutions and the affirmative aspects of our experience. Prayers also teach us to beware of negative, destructive influences and to act appropriately when we encounter them. During the sequence of morning prayers, we ask God to "*distance us from an evil person and an evil companion.*" Another prayer beseeches God to "*rescue me today and every day from brazen people and from brazenness, from evil people and evil companions, an evil neighbor, an evil mishap*..." The implication is that we should recognize the difference between good and evil, between a relationship that should be nourished and preserved and one that should be terminated.

Finally, let us consider the first part of the sequence of prayer that is recited every night before bedtime. The prayer begins with a powerful statement:

> *"Lord of the Universe, I now forgive anyone who angered or antagonized me or who sinned against my body, my property, my home or against anything of mine, whether he did so accidentally, willfully, carelessly, or purposely; whether through speech, deed, thought, or notion..."*[6]

Many rabbis and scholars have pondered these words to extract their layers of meaning. Let us analyze each of these passages to see how they may be applied to the process of reconciliation.

*"Lord of the universe..."* There is some disagreement about these opening words. Some say they are of recent vintage, possibly Hasidic in origin. Others attribute them to ancient sources. Let us assume they are an integral part of the prayer, which is explicitly addressed to God. The phrases that follow are not a passing thought or a trivial remark. The salutation places it in the realm of the sacred. It is the expression of an intention that cannot be dismissed without serious consequences. The words that follow must be expressed with the utmost sincerity.

*"I now forgive anyone..."* This statement, taken alone, is far-reaching. It means any person, relative, friend, former friend, business associate, enemy, anyone. This idea is clearly stated in ancient texts: "Rabba said, Whose sin is forgiven? The sin of one who forgives sins committed against oneself" (*Megillah* 28a). In other words, I must be able to forgive others if I expect to be forgiven for my own transgressions. We will focus on the word "forgive" in the paragraphs below.

*"...who angered or antagonized me..."* Anyone who provoked me, who aroused my contempt or irritation, my rage or frustration or any of the negative emotions that can be ignited in the

course of human interactions. Even if the person caused me great pain or repeatedly caused offense, I should not take revenge (paraphrased from Maimonides, *Laws of Repentance*, 2:10).

"*...or who sinned against my body, my property, my home or against anything of mine...*" This phrase includes a wide range of sins, wrongdoing, injuries, hurtful acts that may have been inflicted, not only on me personally, but on my possessions as well. It also implies that I am willing to forgive those who have sinned against other persons in my family.

"*...whether that person did so accidentally, willfully, carelessly, or purposely...*" Each of these terms refers to the specific type of intention on the part of the person who caused me harm. It does not matter if that person planned to harm me, or if it was an honest mistake, or if it was done without the awareness that the behavior was hurtful. Whatever the other person's intention, I am required to forgive. Refusing to do so leaves me under the control of the other person; it makes me a helpless victim, mired in a pattern of rage and retribution.

"*...whether through speech, deed, thought, or notion...*" Each of these acts defines a certain type of behavior on the part of the person who provoked me. Perhaps he hurled invectives at me, cheated, or lied to me. Maybe she only thought about hurting me, or had been thwarted in her effort to attack me. I am required to focus, not on the unjust act itself, but only on my response to it. In the words of the prayer, I am required to forgive him.

We may wonder if the surface meanings of this prayer are realistic. Can I really forgive everyone who has angered me? What if the person has inflicted severe damage on me or on someone who is dear to me? If he has violated my most sacred values? What if she has no regrets about the pain she has caused? Am I required to forgive her under any circumstances?

According to traditional Jewish practice, all Jews are required to recite this prayer every evening. Imagine the voices through countless generations, vowing to forgive those who have wronged them. The act of forgiving is like a beam of light in motion. It can give renewed energy not only to me, but to the person who hears me. Hopefully, my willingness to forgive will inspire the other person to respect my effort and change his attitude toward me. As he listens to my offer, he may be able to see me in a more kindly light. The act of forgiveness is a reciprocal process; it carries the potential for change on both sides.

The last part of the prayer voices the hope that I will be able to refrain from every sin and from every evil act. So, there is the simultaneous expression of forgiveness for others and my intention to avoid wrongdoing. In other words, I can forgive others when I become aware of my own shortcomings and faults.

How can the elements in this prayer be applied to an individual predicament? The first step is to study the prayer and ponder its meanings, focusing on the relevance of each phrase to the actual estrangement in your family. Then, say it silently; whisper it, speak it out loud, slowly. Share it with a person whom you trust. Try to remember to repeat it each evening, keeping in mind the insights you have gained through study. Hopefully, you will transpose the essence of this prayer to your own feelings and responses. You will integrate its wisdom into your own life.

We have cited only a few of the prayers that are relevant to our topic. In Christian as well as Jewish liturgy, there is an abundance of sacred writings that can lead to the discovery of new solutions for old problems, or more wholesome emotional reactions to difficult situations. For some people, it is a lifelong challenge to find resources that are useful for these tasks.

## 2. QUESTIONS TO GUIDE THE WORK OF EXPLORING FAMILY INTERACTIONS

In the first section of this chapter, we outlined the steps in the search for wisdom, beginning with silence and listening. Now we will consider yet another mode of preparation – asking questions.

One portion in the Book of *Genesis* describes how Jacob prepares for the confrontation with Esau, his estranged brother. He sends angels to convey a conciliatory message, but they return with an ominous report: Esau is approaching with an army of four hundred men. The tension escalates. Jacob is keenly aware of the violence that could erupt when they meet. What does he do? He instructs his servants to anticipate the questions that Esau is likely to ask: "*Who are you, where are you going, and whose are these that are before you?*" (*Genesis* 32:19). Jacob explains how these questions should be answered. When they actually come face to face, Esau asks an additional question: "*What did you intend...?*" In this tense scene, questions serve as the bridge between the estranged brothers. As they ask questions and reply to them, the two men clarify their respective intentions and their individual identities. Then, with no actual reconciliation or confrontation, no peace treaty or declaration of war, they go their separate ways.

What? Who? When? How? Where? Why? Questions can serve to clarify the parameters of one's own family. Is this a redundant task? Asking about my own family is like asking about the air I breathe, the house where I live. I "know" my family as I know myself, perhaps even better than I know myself. I have always been "in" my family, surrounded by family, embedded in family. What is there to ask?

We ask when we do not know, or when we do not know enough. We ask in order to focus, expand, locate, identify, clarify, to confirm a hunch or correct a mistaken impression. Questions are one way to achieve new perceptions of one's own role in the family. Framing a good question is anticipating half of the answer. But questions can be risky. When we ask with the wrong intention, we may appear to be meddling or threatening. Sometimes, the responses to our questions can push us into a blind alley or put us off the track. We need to consider our questions carefully. The people who can provide the most relevant information may be the same people who are suspicious, anxious, or indifferent to our questioning. A brusque, intimidating father, a mother who is always too busy, a sister-in-law who is perpetually angry, these are the people who may have the richest storehouse of knowledge about the family. They are more likely to respond if you express interest in *their* versions of "family stories." Your *kavannah*, your intention in undertaking this task will influence its outcome. If you are genuinely curious and not judgmental, you will be more likely to succeed in gathering useful information. Ask what they remember from childhood, which relatives were most important for them and why, what events were most significant. Speak frankly about your own feelings, and intersperse your questions with references to your own experience and memories. Most important, avoid blaming anyone or making insinuating comments. Try not to analyze motives or dredge up past injustices. If tensions begin to mount, conclude the conversation calmly and try again another time.

Whether an estrangement between relatives has been long lasting or recent, the dissonance of hostility spews emotional ripples to all corners of the family. Each person has a different view of the conflict and a unique response to it. Do not be afraid to ask, but be prepared to back off if the other person is too angry or too miserable to speak to you. Your questions may not lead to simple answers; you may need to return to the same persons for clarification. Hopefully, your efforts will allow you to tune in to the mind-set of other family members, a valuable tool for distinguishing your own perspective and recognizing conflicting points of view.

In formulating the questions below, I have used categories from our previous discussion of family systems and their cultural-religious context, the dimensions that are described in the first two chapters of this book. Recognizing that each person will need to gear the questions to his or her own unique family situation, I have included only a few examples in each category. Readers may wish to compose their own categories and questions, using mine as a guiding framework. It may also be useful to frame one set of questions to ask yourself. You may be surprised to discover wide gaps in your storehouse of family information. While some of the questions are particularly relevant to Jewish families, they can all be transposed to a context that will be meaningful for families with other ethnic and religious orientations. The main point of this task is to sort out the elements that are pertinent to your family's identity and clarify your own role in the family.

## The family as a system

FAMILY STRUCTURE. Consider the size and shape of your family. Construct a diagram that will show at least three generations of immediate relatives. Include the years of their birth, death, marriage, divorce, and adoption. What was your position and role in your family of origin? That is, were you the first-born? The only girl? What was the position of your spouse in his or her family?

EMOTIONAL CLIMATE. What was the emotional climate in your family of origin? For example, how did your parents respond to your feelings of anger, grief, joy, anxiety? How did they express their own feelings? In your present family, how are feelings expressed? Which events have been the most joyful? Which ones have been the most traumatic?

COMMUNICATION PATTERNS. Who is close to whom, and who rarely communicates with family members? Does one person maintain contact with relatives who live far away? Are certain topics secret or taboo? Could you tell your father (whether or not he is still alive) what you appreciate most about him? Your mother? Your siblings? Your children? With each of these people, can you forgive them for what they did not give you?

ROLE ASSIGNMENTS. In your family of origin, how were siblings expected to behave? Were they likely to be pals or rivals? Did your parents and grandparents give labels to their children? For example, genius? loser? black sheep? caretaker? What label would you give to yourself? Who was favored, and who was rejected? How have the women defined themselves within your family? Are they breadwinners? homemakers? rebels? Who pays the bills? How do family members react if a male or female relative takes up a role that contradicts family values?

FAMILY CONFLICT. What provocations are most likely to ignite conflict? Do you have relatives who have been involved in long-term estrangements? How do other family members react to them? What is your role in the conflict? Have you ever cut off from anyone in the family? Have you been rejected? As you read the stories in this book, do you find yourself taking sides? With whom do you empathize and why?

ATTITUDES TOWARD MONEY. What was the predominant attitude of your parents regarding the proper uses of money? Have members of your family taken on specific roles in regard to the issue of money and possessions? For example, is there a gambler, miser, spendthrift, thief, or philanthropist in your family? Do you know how money and property have been passed from one generation to the next? Has anyone been disinherited? Are issues involving money discussed openly, or kept secret? Is money likely to be the provocation for conflict in your family?

## Historical patterns

MIGRATION. Is there a "historian" or a "genealogist" in your family, someone who keeps letters, photos, or other documents that reveal aspects of your family's history? Who was the first to come to this country? What motives compelled them to move? Do they tell stories about the old country? Who was left behind, and how did surviving family members cope with those losses? When and why did they settle in the places where they now live? How did they deal with the problems of finding work and learning a new language? How did the immigration experience affect the interactions between the generations? Did conflicts erupt between those who preserved the traditional beliefs and those who wanted to discard them and assimilate to the new culture? What is your role in the process of assimilation?

PERSECUTION. Do you know of any episodes of persecution in the history of your family? Do you have any relatives who are survivors of the Holocaust? Do they share their stories with family members? Have you considered how their experiences may be affecting your own life and family relationships? Can you recognize patterns of anxiety, blaming, guilt, or depression that may be traced to episodes of persecution?

SEGREGATION. Did anyone in your family live in a segregated community? Did they share stories about their lives in those places? Do you live in a neighborhood that is "mixed," or one that is mostly one ethnic or religious group? Is there a part of your family's life that is "segregated," that is, where activities are limited to one particular group of people? How do you relate to people who are "outside" of that group?

## Traditions and rituals

RELIGIOUS BELIEFS AND PRACTICES. What are the religious/ethnic affiliations of members of your family? Are there sharp differences between the religious beliefs of one part of the family and another? Do you have relatives who have married "out," either to a person with a different religion or a different way of observing the same religion? If so, how has the family responded? Has anyone in your family converted or renounced his religious identity? How does your family manage conflicts over religious issues? Do religious beliefs influence the choice of spouse, the place of burial, the names for babies in your family? Have conflicts erupted over any of these issues?

HOLIDAYS AND LIFE CYCLE EVENTS. Which religious holidays does your family observe? Do some segments of the family differ in their observance of these holidays? Are some members left out? What is the usual mood of these occasions? How does your family typically observe transitions such as weddings, funerals, baby-naming, and other rites of passage? Does your family have reunions and periodic gatherings? Do family members agree about the arrangements for these gatherings?

*YICHUS*, OR PEDIGREE. Does your family have strong attitudes toward "insiders" and "outsiders"? Are family members required to socialize and to marry only certain types of people? What kinds of penalties are given to those who do not comply? Has your family changed its status or class in a dramatic way? How did this occur? Through education? Marriage? Financial success or setbacks? How does your family respond to a member who is handicapped, deviant, or different? Have conflicts erupted because of one relative's failure to measure up to the family's standards of right and wrong?

These questions address only a portion of the issues that may be explored in the process of clarifying one's role in the family.

Each person will need to determine the approach and the questions that are most appropriate for his or her unique situation.

### 3. RITUALS AS TOOLS FOR EXAMINING AND RESOLVING CONFLICTS

In the first chapter of this book, we noted that there are no rituals to mark the occurrence of estrangement or its resolution. In the following section, we will consider the role of ritual and describe particular activities that may be useful for the task of understanding, and perhaps resolving, family conflict.

A ritual may be defined as a repeated pattern of meaningful acts. The rituals in our lives shape our experience and are shaped by it. All religious groups and cultural communities create rituals to accompany and highlight the significant events in the lives of their members. According to Erik Erikson, a noted psychoanalyst and anthropologist, rituals have a vital psychological function: they are the adult counterpart of play in childhood. Erikson considers play to be a primary formative activity during the early stages of development. In adulthood, rituals occupy an equally crucial role as a "formative activity."[7] They help to strengthen and consolidate the experiences of adult life.

The meanings of particular rituals are revealed by studies of behavior in diverse cultures. For example, anthropologists have described a wide spectrum of rituals for the acts of greeting and parting. In each case, the behavioral response depends on particular elements in the situation. Is the other person known or not? Older or younger? Same or opposite gender? Does she or he have higher or lower status? The actual behavioral manifestations are varied: shake hands, tip your hat, bow, press noses, kiss mouth to mouth, on the cheek, hand, or in the air. The persons may stand up or remain seated; they may use gestures such as a nod, a wave, or a lift of the eyebrows. There are various possible facial expressions: smile or frown, expectant or suspicious look. Verbal greetings also vary widely. They may be formal or informal, a question or a statement. For example, we say "hi," "hello," "how do you do?" or "how are you?" Others say the equivalent of "there you are" (Maori), "what news?" (Malay), or "what are the issues?" (Israeli)[8] For those who speak Hebrew or Arabic, the term for "hello" and "goodbye" is *shalom*, or *salaam*, peace. In response to the question "how are you?" Orthodox Jews invariably answer, *Boruch haShem* (blessed be the Name of God).

One author refers specifically to rituals of reconciliation, noting the language of peacemaking between alienated family members: "I'm sorry," "I forgive you," "It's all right; we'll work it out." "I love you, no matter what."[9] These are some of the phrases that are spoken and heard during the process of resolving an estrangement. The same author describes a particularly touching ritual for an uncommon meeting:

A female infant was put out for adoption immediately after her birth. Her parents were a young, engaged couple who could not face the scandal of an "illegitimate child," born a few months before their wedding. The girl was adopted by a childless couple who gave her abundant affection and a good life. Many years later, the girl's biological father initiated a search for the daughter he had never seen. He was able to locate her, and she agreed to meet him. At the end of their visit, they spontaneously enacted the following ritual: She took a piece of paper, placed his hand on it and drew around his hand and fingers with a pen. Then she gave him the pen. He placed her hand on top of the outline and drew around her hand. They put their initials side by side on the bottom of the page, dated the drawing of their entwined hands, and she gave it to him. They hugged each other, smiled, laughed, cried, and she was gone – back to her parents, her home, her separate life. This meaningful ritual marked the first, perhaps the only, face-to-face encounter of an adult woman and her biological father. The ritual vividly expressed their mutual understanding of the situation: it confirmed their connection but did not impose unrealistic expectations on either of them.[10]

**Rituals for resolving conflict**
**after the estranged person has died**

Jewish sources contain pertinent concepts and guidelines that can be incorporated into rituals for resolving conflicts when one of the protagonists is no longer alive. How can the surviving family members find solace? Is it possible to attain a sense of closure for a relationship that did not conclude peacefully? At every Jewish funeral, before the body is brought to the cemetery, there is an opportunity for anyone to approach the *mita* (platform), face the deceased, and silently apologize for any wrongdoing. The great Jewish philosopher Rambam (Maimonides), in his *Laws of Repentance*, provides a powerful example of a similar ritual that may be performed long after the death of one of the protagonists.[11]

If a person wronged another person and the latter died before he could ask forgiveness, he should take ten people and say the following while they are standing before the grave of the wronged person: *"I sinned against God, the Lord of Israel, and against this person by doing the following to him...."* A detailed confession is required, with each wrongdoing stated separately.

If you have been cut off from a family member who is deceased, whether the estrangement was initiated by you or by the other person, your perceptions of the situation can be examined and realigned. You may wish to reconsider your role in that relationship or seek a more complete sense of closure in your memory of that person. Following is a description of a ritual I used to resolve dilemmas that remained after I had reconciled with the estranged members of my father's family. This ritual helped to clarify my own perceptions and enhance my memories of my father, many decades after his death.

I began this process about one month before the *Yahrzeit* (anniversary) of my father's death. I kept a journal to record each step. During the month, I jotted down my feelings, recollections, and images of my father. I included a brief description of the conflict in our family and how I perceived it, from the beginning.

One week before the *Yahrzeit*, I reviewed my previous notes and began to compose a letter to my father. At the conclusion of the letter, I wrote a series of about twenty brief questions, accusations, complaints, requests, expressions of remorse, all the things I would say if I could speak with him.

A few days before the *Yahrzeit*, I copied each of the items onto small squares of paper, each item on a separate square.

On the evening before the *Yahrzeit*, I lit the special candle that is intended for that occasion. (Some people may wish to place an additional object near the candle, one that recalls the dead person, such as a photo or personal belonging. The purpose is to accomplish this act in the symbolic "presence" of the dead person.)

I took the first square of paper, read the question or request aloud and, holding it by a tweezer, ignited it in the burning candle. I repeated this sequence with each of the squares of paper. When I finished the task, I remained seated by the candle for several minutes, contemplating the meaning of the experience and sorting out my feelings.

Several years have passed since I enacted this ritual. In retrospect, I see that this process helped me to resolve a residue of resentment and re-frame my role as my father's daughter. The new insights were not immediately perceived but rather, they evolved over time. For those readers who wish to create a similar ritual, I offer this advice:

Be patient. During the weeks following the ritual, review your notes and decide if you have included everything that is pertinent to the situation. At a later time, you can decide if you want to repeat the process or simply recall what you have already done. The aim is to resolve any residue of anger and achieve a more affirming attitude toward yourself. Optimally, you will experience a more complete sense of closure, a readiness to accept the reality of the past and move on. As time passes, you may find that you can forgive the deceased person's transgressions and acknowledge the positive aspects of his or her role in your life.

**A ritual to express gratitude for reconciliation**

According to the *Code of Jewish Law*, specific blessings are recited to celebrate a reunion after a prolonged absence. When seeing a friend to whom one is closely attached, after a separation of at least thirty days, we say a benediction. If a separation from family members has lasted more than twelve months, a different blessing (*bracha*) is recited. *"Blessed art Thou, O Lord our God, King of the Universe, who revives the dead."* The requirement to say this blessing is considered a law, not merely a personal choice. It applies to men and to women: when a person sees his spouse, sibling, son, or daughter, after a lengthy separation, the proper benediction should be said.[12] Recalling the repetitive patterns of expulsion and persecution in Jewish history, we can assume that this law took on special significance in countless situations when family members were separated over long distances and for extended periods. In our own time, this *bracha* or blessing can be used to express gratitude for achieving resolution of a conflict. The ritual may be modified to suit each individual situation. Estranged persons who wish to celebrate their reconciliation may decide to compose their own special ceremony to mark the occasion. In the process of creating a meaningful ritual, the protagonists will become partners, moving beyond the pain of alienation toward an affirmation of their restored connection.

CONCLUDING NOTE TO READERS

Narratives of real families, biblical models, vignettes from secular literature, case studies, prayers, questions, rituals, the advice of experts: each of these resources offers a particular perspective and a different way to understand the phenomenon of estrangement. After you have read this book, perhaps you will return to certain parts and read them again. You may find one story or one idea that will strike a chord, awaken a memory, kindle a spark. Each of you will find something different. Your discovery will reflect the person you have become, your place in the family, the pain you have suffered, and the joys you have experienced in your family life. May your search be fruitful.

CODA

# Pits of Darkness, Sparks of Light

---

*"Out beyond claims of wrongdoing and rightdoing,*
*There is a field. I'll meet you there."*[1]

---

"Coda" is the term for a musical epilogue, a sequence that is heard at the end of a long composition. In music, the intent of the coda is to recapitulate the predominant themes and resolve remaining dissonances. This coda, appearing at the conclusion of this book, will restate some of the major themes, now transposed to a new key. It will suggest how a cutoff can be averted, how the rage, disappointment, and recriminations may be redirected to generate a more wholesome, more reciprocal relationship.

Up to this point, the stories in this book have focused on the past, on family conflicts that flared, persisted, and in some cases, were resolved. Writing about other families, I have taken the perspective of an observer, maintaining a degree of neutrality and distance. In my own family, the long estrangement from my sisters and brother was confronted and repaired. Then, after all the insights I had gained and the experience I had accumulated, a new conflict erupted in my life. I was on the edge of breaking the connection with my only daughter. How did this happen? And how was the crisis eventually resolved?

**Background**

A brief sketch of our family will serve as background for this story. My husband and I have been married for more than twenty years and each of us has grown children from a previous marriage. For the past decade, we have divided our time between two homes and two families: one in the States, the other in Israel. My daughter "Janet" is a lawyer in Philadelphia; she has no children. Janet occupies a unique position on the maternal branch of my family: she is the only daughter of an only daughter (me) of an only daughter (my mother) of an only daughter (my grandmother). Four generations of "only" daughters! My son "Sam" lives near Jerusalem with his wife and eight children. The dynamics in our family reflect additional divisions. During the period of his university studies, Sam formed an enduring commitment to Orthodox Judaism, a sharp contrast to the secular lifestyle chosen by his sister. Despite the divergent focus of their lives and the immense geographical distance between them, my son and daughter have sustained an affectionate relationship.

**The crisis escalates**

A few summers ago, my husband and I returned to our home in Pittsburgh after several months in Jerusalem. We were looking forward to a vacation on a lake in New England with the American branches of our family. A week before our anticipated holiday, my son phoned from Israel to tell me that one of his daughters, four-year-old "Bracha," had suddenly become ill and was hospitalized in Jerusalem. The doctors suspected a serious lung disease. After a brief discussion with my husband, I decided to return to Israel to help care for the child. The first signs of the emerging conflict with my daughter appeared when I phoned to tell her about the crisis and my decision to go. I waited, hoping to hear her spontaneous offer to come with me, but she did not offer. Her lack of response was disappointing. Apparently she was not aware of how anxious I was feeling about the child's illness. My emotional turmoil was further exacerbated by the abrupt change in our vacation plans and the conflicting claims of two families, here and there.

On the long flight to Israel, I tried to get my bearings and consider the tasks ahead, but I felt tense and uncertain. Immediately after my arrival, I plunged headlong into the unfamiliar hospital routine. As my son, his wife, and all their children rallied around the sick child and began to confront the complexities of an overburdened medical system, my anxiety escalated. Bracha was having one crisis after another and still no diagnosis, no treatment. Characteristically an endearing, spunky child, she was becoming more and more depleted and fearful. Many of the diagnostic procedures were invasive and painful. With tubes in her nose and an oxygen monitor on her finger, beeping constantly, it was difficult to find ways to distract or comfort her. One of her favorite pastimes was to "hug" my face with her cold feet, a scene that amused the nurses and other patients. During the long days in the overcrowded unit, she refused to be left alone, even for a minute. If someone from the family wasn't there all the time, she would cry and scream, getting herself more upset, worsening her condition and making her breathing even more difficult. My son and daughter-in-law were running from home to hospital, trying to cope with each new crisis while at the same time, caring for their other children, including a nursing baby. It was extremely high stress all the time.

A week passed. The child's condition continued to deteriorate, and the hospital staff seemed impotent in the face of mounting crises. We were all feeling frustrated and helpless, stretched to the breaking point. My son's exhaustion showed on his face. His wife seldom had a night's sleep or a regular meal. I was desperate for someone to intervene, to provide support and respite. The two oldest children were taking turns visiting their sister, sometimes staying through the night and sleeping on the floor beside her bed. The entire family was caught up in an escalating spiral of anxiety. I thought about my daughter back in the United States, and my anger and resentment began to build. There had been no phone calls, no email messages from her. I (*wrongly*) equated her silence with indifference, assuming that she just didn't want to get involved. In my mind, I was constructing a strong case against her, something I had frequently done in the past when she had failed to meet my expectations. There she was with "nothing to do," no compelling obligations, no children of her own. If she were here, she could comfort Bracha, listen to my concerns, help us make decisions, and give support to her brother. (*In retrospect, I realize that Sam did not have the same reaction to his sister's apparent indifference. Now I understand that his expectations of her are much less intense, less demanding than mine.*)

### Pulling apart

At the end of one especially trying day, I came home for a brief rest and the phone was ringing. It was my daughter. "Mom, we've all been trying and trying to reach you..." I sputtered an expletive under my breath and spat out, "If you're so eager to reach me, why didn't you leave a message?" (*By that time, I had re-activated my phone answering system. Before then, it was out-of-order and I had no way of knowing who had phoned during the day while I was at the hospital. The communications breakdown was just another element in the escalation of tension*). When I heard my daughter's voice, my rage exploded: "I don't want to talk to you! I don't want to talk to anyone! I'm going back to the hospital!" and I slammed down the phone. Those were the last words I would speak to her for many weeks. It was to be the longest period without contact between us since she was born. (*Much later, she would describe to me how difficult it had been for her to make that phone call, how ambivalent she had been feeling about the situation, and how she had struggled to cope with my furious outburst. But for the time being, that brief call was the fulcrum, the point at which the possibility of a cutoff became real.*)

In a crisis situation, intense emotional reactions are likely to evoke regressive, illogical patterns of behavior. This is what happened to me. I reverted to a timeworn sequence in which I imagine how I would handle a situation and then expect others, especially people in my family, to react in the same way. This expectation leads to enormous frustration and, inevitably, to disappointment. But at that tense time, I automatically shifted into my habitual pattern and the buzzing in my head turned into a full-blown tirade. With my inner voice, I hurled insults, challenges, threats, enumerating my daughter's shortcomings, her indifference, her self-centered preoccupations, on and on. I decided to keep a journal to record my feelings. (*Months later, when I reviewed my list of complaints, I noticed how totally one-sided and irrational they were. But at the time, the only thing I could do was to rant and rave. My anger was a full-blown tornado, way beyond the point of return to any sober thought or lucid reasoning. All of this turmoil was concentrated inside of me, not communicated to my daughter.*) I shared some of my feelings with my husband and a few friends, who were surprised and, I now suspect, disconcerted by the intensity of my reactions.

Almost a month after Bracha's initial crisis, her condition had improved to the point where she was out of danger and could go home. The whole family joyfully welcomed her, and I returned to the United States, completely exhausted. During the three days that remained of our vacation at the lake, I could do nothing but sleep and cry. I made no effort to contact my daughter and she did not contact me. As the weeks passed, the silence between us became more impenetrable. There seemed to be no way to break through it. Should I phone her? Write a letter? But I was unable to express my feelings in a coherent way. I did not want to accuse her, argue, or listen to her excuses or justifications. At that point, we had come to a total impasse. (*In reading my notes from that period, I recoil at the depth of my rejection. I wrote: "I find her self-centeredness disgusting, her petty concerns obscene. She is not dependable, not responsible for anyone but herself. This is a very sad fact."*)

### First steps toward resolution

After a period of blaming and rage, I began to shift gears. New insights were filtering into my anger and sober thoughts were beginning to dilute the emotional turmoil. Without calling it by name, I had embarked on a journey of intense soul-searching. My notes reflect my shifting mood: "I need to…" "I think that…"

"I am beginning to realize..." I was concentrating intensely on myself. This is what I wrote: "I need to re-think my relationship with Janet and probably with others as well. I must re-define my expectations, re-calibrate the degrees of closeness with significant others. I want to back up, pay attention to my own needs and determine how to meet them, without depending on my daughter to fill the empty spaces. Then, I must weave this new reality into my life and see how it fits there. This is a challenging task, but necessary at this point in time."

In some extreme situations, Orthodox Jewish families may decide to cut off a rebellious child by declaring her dead and ritually observing the seven-day period of mourning. They "sit *shiva*" for their living child. It is the most radical form of "banishment" from the family, usually reserved for a son or daughter who "marries out" or converts to another religion. I began to wonder if I could use a variation of that ritual to help transform my own situation. Not that I would declare my daughter "dead," but that I would enact the ritual of "sitting *shiva*" and mourn for the "dream" daughter, the one who existed only in my fantasies. This might be a way to divest myself of the false image of a daughter who would respond to my expectations, who would rush to help me in a time of crisis. Perhaps the ritual act of mourning for this wished-for daughter would help to tone down the cacophony of my anger and allow some emotional distance. But if I do recite the mourner's prayer, how would I distinguish between the "dream" daughter and the real one? Rather than mourning, maybe I should adopt the old Jewish custom of giving her a different name, as if she were deathly ill. The new name would somehow allow me to respond to her in a more constructive way. As I considered the ramifications of these ritualistic possibilities, I began to confront some fundamental questions: Who is my daughter? And who am I? Her mother or her adversary?

**Finding sources of help**
Sharing my anguish with a few close friends, I tried out the ideas of "sitting *shiva*" or giving a new name to this fantasy daughter.

Without exception, they were appalled. Each of them had a valid reason why those ideas would not work. I listened to their advice. There must be a better way.

I decided to phone my wise friend M, a retired child psychiatrist. She is a straight-to-the-mark, no-nonsense person. I can always depend on her to tell me exactly what she's thinking. She had been in touch with me during the child's hospitalization and she knew about my bitter disappointment at my daughter's failure to respond. Now M asked, "Did you invite her to come? Did you ask her to help you?" "Well, of course," I insisted. (*With my inner voice, I was replaying the old refrain: she should have known I needed help; I shouldn't have had to ask her.*) But then, I had to admit, "I'm not sure; I really don't remember; I was so angry."

M suggested that my rage might be a by-product of the estrangement in my own family. Perhaps I had not resolved all of my feelings about being an "abandoned child." Put off balance by the recent crisis, did I project the leftover fragments of anger onto my daughter? My friend asked me to turn around and look at Janet with my mind's eye. From a different stance, I might interpret her apparent indifference not as selfishness, but as anxiety. Consider the possibility that my daughter sees me as a very powerful person. She couldn't face feeling inept and awkward in that crisis situation. She is an exceptionally competent woman with many skills, but she has never had the experience of taking care of a sick child. Perhaps my expectations were not appropriate. The whole hospital scene would only serve to exaggerate her vulnerabilities. M urged me to call Janet and share the whole story, with all the details. "Meet her somewhere halfway," she said. (*Where is halfway, I wondered. Halfway between her house and mine? Or between her position and mine? I would need to search for the place "beyond claims of wrongdoing and rightdoing."*)

My search became more focused during the days leading to the solemn Jewish holiday of *Tisha b'Av*, the commemoration of the destruction of the Holy Temples in Jerusalem. It is a time to grieve, ponder, and sort out one's thoughts. At the synagogue, I heard a talk about repentance, *teshuvah*. An insightful rabbi was speaking about "senseless hatred" in the context of family. "Go home and make the phone call" was his message. "Do it now!" My husband had been giving me similar advice. How could I prepare myself to make the call? What would I say?

## Preparing for a meeting

I tried out a few opening lines, silently, to myself: "Hi Janet, it's me, the person whose voice sounds like yours but is not you..." That sounded rather silly and contrived.

Here's another: "Hi, it's me, your mother. We haven't talked in a while, and I need to do some more thinking about you and me. I'll get in touch with you again when I'm ready, ok?"

So, what would she do with that? Hang up on me? Scream at me? Say "ok"? What would she do? I phoned, but she wasn't home, so I left a message similar to the one I had planned to say. It was easier that way. She didn't have to reply immediately and neither did I.

A few hours later she sent me this email message: "ok." (*Please notice this small "ok." In the process of resolving an estrangement, a response such as "ok" is the expression of the other's willingness to confront the problems. For my daughter and me, it was an immensely significant turning point, the moment when change became possible. I will speak of it again near the end of this section.*)

I decided to send her a brief email message, no subject, no signature. I told her I was still not ready for a direct face-to-face meeting. I let her know that I planned to go back to Jerusalem for a month in September. I recalled that before the crisis with Bracha, I had talked to her about going to Israel together for the Holy Days. She had been undecided. Now, I did not want to open the question again. I could not bear to hear her refuse. I was still angry.

I sent the message.

For the next few days, nothing. No response.

In a book by Eva Hoffman, I found this passage: "Psychoanalysts talk about 'mutative insights,' through which the patient gains an entirely new perspective and discards some part of a cherished neurosis."[2] That's a useful idea. How can I discover a "mutative insight?" And, after finding it, how do I unpack it, and what do I do with it? For Hoffman, such a radical new position comes with "pinpricks of anxiety," being cast adrift in incomprehensible space, losing your moorings. It's not a simple thing.

In the same book, I found another relevant passage. Hoffman, a Polish immigrant in America, was trying to make sense of her new milieu. She described her American friends and their perceptions of their mothers. Viewing aspects of an unfamiliar culture from the perspective of an immigrant, she noticed the ambivalent nature of the mother-daughter bond. The mother appears to be extremely close and also remote, "as if she were both a vampiric incubus and a puzzling stranger..."[3] This passage seemed to be written for me. It prodded me to realize that one of the thorny problems in my relationship with Janet has been our exaggerated closeness and its counterpart, distance generated by anger. I copied the long quote, and sent it to my daughter with the signature "your mother, the vampire/stranger." I wondered if and how she would respond.

During the next few days, we exchanged brief, noncommittal email messages. Then, I received the following message:

"Mom, I don't think I see you as either a vampire or a stranger. I do see you as a complex person with needs and expectations rooted in past events that sometimes complicate or obscure the realities of the present. I see myself this way, as well. Due to the specific nature of our respective issues, when our conflicting needs and expectations find themselves occupying the same "space" at the same "time," the result can be explosive. This is completely irrespective of who is "right" or "wrong" in any given instance. I know very few people who seem to be able to perceive their mothers as having a "normal" size or shape in their lives. Of those few, none are Jewish.

Your daughter"

(*In retrospect, I think her response is a masterpiece of insight. At the time, I simply did not know how to respond to it.*)

We agreed to risk a face-to-face encounter. Janet was coming to Pittsburgh for a visit with her father. I was expecting a friend from Israel to arrive at the same time and I decided not to change the plan. So, unlike all previous visits, my daughter did not stay with us. We spoke about arrangements on the phone and I invited her to come for breakfast. I shared my anxiety with my husband, who helped me to think through what I would and would not say. I was feeling ambivalent and wary. How would I greet her?

## Coming face-to-face

At our first encounter, both of us were on guard, not knowing what to expect. We talked for more than an hour. There were some tears, a few high-pitched, angry jabs, mostly from me. I told her that I love her but do not like or respect her. That seemed like a very harsh indictment and I knew that I might have reason to regret it later, but at that moment, I felt compelled to express my feelings. I told her that she had let me down, let her brother down, that she had ignored Bracha's crisis and neglected the other children, all of her nieces and nephews. She retorted that she is not a good caretaker, never was, and never will be. She knows for sure that she couldn't have helped me take care of Bracha. I would have been too critical, as I have often been, according to her view of me. I insisted that no one has the right to refuse to respond to the needs of a close family member. She disagreed. We agreed to disagree. At that point, both of us realized that the most we could hope to get from this initial discussion was a clearer notion of each other's feelings. End of meeting.

Before the conversation with Janet, I had planned to go back to Israel for the Jewish New Year. But about ten days before departure, I began to have second thoughts. Although I was eager to see Bracha and experience the spiritual intensity of Jerusalem during the Holy Days, I had a nagging feeling that it was not the right time to go. I considered an alternative plan, to spend part of the holiday period with my daughter. By this time, the idea of "sitting shiva" or giving her another name seemed grotesque and irrational. I felt the need to communicate directly with her, to confront the issues together. After mulling over the various ramifications, the decision became clear. I would give up the plan to go to Israel. Instead, I would ask Janet if I could visit her during the week between Rosh Hashana, the Jewish New Year, and Yom Kippur, the Day of Atonement. This is the period when thoughts of repentance and forgiveness are uppermost in the minds of Jews everywhere. Perhaps it would be an auspicious time to confront some of the destructive elements in our relationship. When I phoned her to discuss this new plan, she was not enthusiastic. She needed to think about it and let me know. The next day she called to say she would be glad to see me.

At the beginning of the week with my daughter, both of us felt tense and cautious. We spoke of "neutral" topics, books we had read and recipes we had tried. After a day or two, when we were feeling a bit more relaxed, we decided to go for a long walk.

### Confronting the pits of darkness

It is a sunny morning early in autumn. Along the way, we come upon a wide meadow, quiet and inviting. We sit on the grass, face to face, and begin to confront the heart of the matter. My anger. Her relationship with her brother. My unreasonable expectations. Her apparent indifference to the crisis in the family. Her sense of never being "good" enough, always disappointing me. I ask how she could ignore the needs of a sick child. And what about *my* needs? Well, that's who she is, she tells me. My anger spurts, I accuse her of being heartless; I point out her selfish ways. It's immoral, I say; it's against every Jewish law and commandment. Too bad, she says; "that's who I am." I tell her she's still a rebellious child, still acting out old battles. She says it's her way to stand her ground, resist my intrusions. She needs to assert her own identity, separate from me. She tells me that *she is NOT ME*, not a replica of me. She remembers that I always loomed large in her life, too large. She could never measure up. I was always taking care of others, always busy with friends, always "doing good." She knew she couldn't be like me; she wanted to be different. Our voices become more strident. The fury escalates, and for a few moments, it seems to spin out of control. Sitting in the warm sun, I feel as if I am in a dark pit filled with vipers. We are locked in a bitter exchange: Janet is spitting accusations and I am alternately defending myself and then striking back with more accusations, both of us whirling in a morass of rage and recriminations.

## Sparks of light

Suddenly, in the midst of that terrible tension, I received a very clear insight. All at once, sitting on the bright green grass, with the scent of autumn in the air and the leaves falling around us, I looked at my daughter and seemed to "see" her differently. It was as if a shaft of light was beamed on her. A burst of new knowledge enveloped me. Perhaps this was the "mutative insight." In music, it would be the unexpected, extraordinary moment when the dissonance resolves to a stunning new tonic key. With complete conviction, I said to my daughter, "Jan, it's my fault."

"No," she began to defend me, "it's no one's fault." But I was certain of this fact, that it *was* my fault, if "fault" is the right word. I began to tell her about the insights I have gleaned from watching my grandchildren. I have come to see that each of them came into the world with his and her unique personality, formed and "given." I have learned that the real task of parents is to "study" their child, to learn as much as possible about this "given" personality, this created person, and then to nurture and support that person. And I told her that I had not done that for her. I had not possessed that wisdom when I was a young mother. I had not understood how to "observe" a child and nourish the emerging person. I thought the task of a mother was to put my own stamp on her, form her, twist her into my shape, impose my needs and expectations on her. And she, this stubborn daughter, came into the world with a great deal of strength and firm resistance to my efforts to mold her. So, from the beginning, we have been engaged in a mighty struggle, and I was bound to "lose." But in the course of the struggle, she, too, has lost. She has used too much energy resisting me when she could have been focusing on other, more gratifying pursuits. As we talked, I saw this pattern more clearly. In tears, I asked her to forgive me for not understanding this basic fact of parenthood, for not nurturing her personhood when she was a child.

We must have sat there for a long time, and when we finally resumed our walk, I was exhausted, but also more buoyant and relaxed. On the way home, my daughter began to share some recollections from her childhood, events long buried, when she had felt lost or frightened or overwhelmed. She expressed feelings of regret at having "wasted" time acting out her rebellion when she could have been preparing for a career or a family. And I was able to say that she had done what seemed right at the time; if she hadn't done those "wild" things, she would not have been able to grow and become the competent woman she is today. By the time we reached home, we were both very tired, but also gratified that we had come through the whirlwind. Now we could look at each other, straight in the eye, without reproach or blame, anger, or regret. We were able to hug in gratitude for the gift of truthful communication. At this point, we had not yet achieved a sense of closure, but we were on the right track.

(*A "revelation" has the quality of a re-birth. In a sense, I had given birth to my daughter again, but this time, the act of giving suck, nurturing, would be on* her *terms, not mine. She would de-termine the "formula" that could now serve to nourish her. It took us so many years to get to this spark of light. Do you remember the moment when the change became possible? when the "labor pains" began? It was the small "ok," Janet's response to my first attempt to contact her. If the other person will not, cannot say "ok," if he or she is not willing to risk the pain of the confrontation, then the possibility of reconciliation will be greatly diminished.*)

In recollecting and writing this experience, I have tried to highlight the alternating rhythms, the ups and downs, the prog-ress and the regressions. One must be ready for this emotional roller coaster ride, bouncing from a high-pressure area to a glim-mer of rapprochement, back and forth over this rutted terrain.

The disequilibrium is a frustrating but essential element in the process of reconciliation.

**Change can bring blessings**

A few days after our first long talk, my daughter and I set out again, late in the afternoon. This time, the focus was different. We were aware of still unresolved issues and unexpressed feelings on both sides. I began to reconstruct the events of the episode with Bracha. Now I included details about the crisis and my reaction to it. Janet was silent. I remembered the question my friend M had asked: "Did you invite her to come with you?" I asked my daughter, "Did I ask you to help me?" "No." I began to cry, feeling completely squashed. Then, I calmly told her the story, reviewing the entire sequence as I remembered it. She told it from her point of view. We went over each step, from both sides. I could see that during Bracha's illness, as my anxiety began to surge, it took off on its own steam. I hadn't been able to be rational, to speak calmly or ask for her help. She told me about her own pain, how she felt when she realized that I was blown away, out of reach, in a tunnel of anger she could not penetrate. In the midst of this telling, we were each able to see the other, understand, and forgive.

Dusk was falling as we entered the park. Walking along the darkening paths and through the apple orchard, we seemed to be moving together in a new way. There were clearer boundaries between us, and connecting links that were less confining, more resilient. All the necessary words had been spoken. Now there were long, comfortable silences. Each of us had a clear sense that significant changes had occurred in our relationship. Healing had been achieved.

After I returned home, I was entering my recollections into the computer when suddenly everything went blank and I couldn't retrieve any of my notes. Then, this message appeared on the screen:

"Changes have been made that affect the global template. Do you want to save those changes? Yes? No?"

I sent this message to my daughter, adding my response: "yes."

She agreed and only said "wow!"

## Afterword

More than four years have passed since this episode in our lives. The changes in the "global template" of our relationship have endured. My daughter and I continue to clarify the boundaries that separate us as we strengthen the bonds that connect us. Reflecting on this experience, I can offer this advice:

Go now, prepare to make the phone call, write the letter. Begin now.

Take these words with you:

"*I will seek the lost one, and whoever is cast out I will bring back, and the broken one I will heal…*" (Micah 4:6)

And share the lines of Rumi:

"*Out beyond claims of wrongdoing and rightdoing,
There is a field. I'll meet you there.*"

# Relevant Resources

The self-improvement sections of bookstores and libraries are crowded with books that tell us how to behave. They explain how we should talk, think, and feel. They describe the skills we need in order to live more healthfully and love more fully, to forgive those who hurt us, to manage conflicts, and to "make peace with any-one." Virtually all of these resources are advertised as "best sell-ers," "the number one self-help resource," "translated into sixteen languages." The author is invariably an "internationally renowned leader in the field of human relations." We are overwhelmed by the sheer numbers; our suspicions are aroused by the authors' exaggerated or pretentious claims. And yet, some of these books do contain valuable insights that should be digested thoughtfully and applied sparingly. With these caveats in mind, let us consider some of the resources that may be used for the task of reviewing estrangement and moving toward reconciliation. Following are brief descriptions of recent publications that are congruent with the point of view expressed in *Fragmented Families*.

GERALD JAMPOLSKY: *Forgiveness*. (Hillsburo OR: Beyond Words Publishing, Inc., 1999)
The author lists twenty reasons why it is so difficult to forgive someone who has wronged us (pp. 37–39). Among the most prominent reasons are:

1. That person really hurt you.
2. You are weak if you forgive him.
3. If you forgive, it's the same as making him right and you wrong. He may think that you agree or accept what he did.
4. Not to forgive is the best way to keep distance between you and the person who offended you.
5. Not to forgive is one kind of revenge.

Jampolsky's main point is that we can always find many convincing reasons for refusing to forgive someone who has hurt us and for justifying our resistance. He offers sensible advice for preparing to reconcile with a person who has been ostracized or who has severed himself from the family.

AARON LAZARE: *On Apology* (New York: Oxford University Press, 2004)
Dr. Lazare, a psychiatrist, analyzes various forms of apology in many different settings, from exchanges between high-ranking government officials to a friend's expression of regret for an offence committed more than sixty years ago. The author considers the relationship between forgiveness and apology and describes four possibilities: forgiveness without an apology; refusal to forgive, regardless of the apology; forgiveness that precedes apology; and apology that leads to forgiveness (pp. 231–2). His astute explanations are useful in clarifying the elements that are most likely to facilitate resolution of conflict.

BARBARA PACHTER: *The Power of Positive Confrontation.* (New York: Marlowe/Avalon, 2001)
This author presents us with the "nuts, bolts, and screws" of constructive confrontation. She outlines a sequence of steps to initiate the process of reconnecting with an estranged person. Pachter uses the acronym "WAC" to help her readers remember the steps:

1. **What's really bothering you?** The first step is to define the problem.
2. **Ask the question:** What would solve the problem for you? An apology? An explanation? A face-to-face meeting, without reference to the problem? A gift? A sincere expression of remorse?
3. **Check-in.** Try to "check in" with the other person to find out where he/she is in relation to the cutoff. Many people will not follow this suggestion, fearing the commotion or rejection that will inevitably follow. Often the offender is not willing to talk, or he becomes defensive or angry if you try to approach him. Or, *you* may be too angry to speak or write to him. If this is true of your situation, consider what Pachter says about the "other person" (spelled out in Chapter Nine). She provides detailed suggestions for dealing with specific kinds of "others" who may be anxious, resistant, or just indifferent to the problem.

NINA W. BROWN: *Children of the Self-absorbed: A Grown-up's Guide to Getting Over Narcissistic Parents* (Oakland, CA: New Harbinger Publications, Inc., 2001)
At first glance, the title of this book seems to have little relevance to our topic. A more careful reading reveals several sensible ideas for dealing with difficult people, especially if they are estranged family members. Brown focuses on the interaction between narcissistic, self-centered parents and their "victims," their children. She explains how the child of a narcissistic parent feels exploited, used, never good enough. In adulthood, such a person sustains the belief that he or she is unacceptable, no matter how hard he tries or what she accomplishes. In this type of situation, cutting off from parents may be the only way to build a separate identity.

The author outlines various strategies to "fortify" oneself, strengthen one's self-concept, and enhance self-esteem. One must learn to accept one's limitations without feeling inadequate. The adult child of a destructive, self-centered parent will find it difficult to forgive not only his parent, but anyone who insults or belittles him. Such a person holds fast to real or imagined offences and cannot let go. Even when the "victim" understands why the person did what he did, he still may not be able to forgive. Brown suggests specific writing exercises to clarify thoughts and feelings. She also describes "nonverbal expressive exercises" (pp. 121–122) to increase awareness of how emotions are reflected in body posture and movements. Persons who are estranged from narcissistic parents will recognize the patterns described in this book and benefit from the author's suggestions.

RICHARD CARLSON: *Don't Sweat the Small Stuff with Your Family* (New York: Hyperion Press, 1998).

Carlson has authored a series of self-help books geared to solving problems for specific groups. This book is focused on family dilemmas. Readers can pick and choose those ideas that are relevant to a particular problem. Carlson has a good sense of the distinction between "small stuff" and the other stuff, like life-threatening disease and war. For the "small stuff" he provides suggestions to cool down the atmosphere, try a different approach, or learn to accept limitations in oneself and others. Here is a brief list of some of his ideas, with my embellishments:

LET GO OF YOUR EXPECTATIONS (p. 41). *A crucial point in the process of resolving conflict.*

DEVELOP YOUR OWN RE-SET BUTTONS (p. 59). *I interpret this to mean that I need to work out ways to deal with myself when I over-react to another person's provocations.*

AGREE TO DISAGREE (p. 67). *Or, let well enough alone.*

CREATE A NEW RELATIONSHIP WITH SOMEONE YOU ALREADY KNOW (p. 180). *That is, give up your inappropriate assumptions and look for the positive aspects in the other person.*

TREAT THE OTHER PERSON AS IF THIS IS THE LAST TIME YOU WILL SEE HIM/HER (p. 253). *This can be a very effective strategy if it's used wisely. How would you respond to the estranged person if you knew that he/she was fatally ill? If you were on your deathbed and the person asked you to forgive him?*

Reading a long list of suggestions is rarely useful. To make optimal use of Carlson's expertise, choose two or three strategies that seem most relevant to your own experience and try them out for a limited period of time.

STEPHEN R. COVEY: *The 7 Habits of Highly Effective Families.* (New York: Golden Books, 1997).
This author has become well-known as a consultant to corporations by identifying the "habits" of highly effective, successful people. For this book, he applied his methods to the analysis of patterns that foster healthy family relationships. Covey's stated goal is to create a "beautiful family culture" (p. 20). He writes about the "spirit" of the family, the feeling, the vibes, the chemistry or atmosphere in the home. By using stories, poems, personal recollections, dialogues, and questionnaires, he creates strategies for enhancing family life. Following are brief summaries of some of the "habits":

– Become a change agent in your family.
– Develop a family mission statement.
– Build family unity through celebrating differences.

For each of these "habits," the author includes a list of references and resources that can be used to master particular skills. Covey also provides several detailed indices such as the "problem/opportunity index" (pp. 371–377), containing a list of the issues, problems, and solutions that are presented in the book. For example, how can I create change? Handle anger? Stop negative family cycles? Learn to be less reactive? What to do when family members don't cooperate? When things seem to fall apart? This book is a practical guide to resolving conflict and building more wholesome family relationships.

MONICA MCGOLDRICK: *You Can Go Home Again – Reconnecting with Your Family* (New York: W.W. Norton & Company, 1995).
The author is an experienced family therapist who takes an

eclectic approach to family issues. Rather than presenting cases with clinical explanations, she analyses biographies of famous families to elucidate patterns of alienation and reconciliation. Chapters include vivid descriptions of such disparate situations as the responses of the Kennedy family to repeated and untimely losses; the tensions that emerged from the triangle formed by Beethoven, his parents, and dead brother; the contradictory religious convictions of three generations of men in the Freud family; and the alliances and animosities in the lives of the Marx brothers, played out on a background of wild, slapstick humor. To clarify the components of estrangement, the author considers such elements as ethnic background, cultural history, sibling position, choice of marital partners, and the secrets, myths, and stories that reveal the deeper levels of family life.

LAURA DAVIS: *I Thought We'd Never Speak Again* (New York: Harper/Collins Publishers, 2002).

The problem of sexual abuse and its aftermath has been the focus of this author's work. In previous books, Davis wrote about the fallout from abuse and the subsequent relationships of victims with parents, siblings, and spouses. In this more recent book, she has expanded her scope of inquiry to include many types of damaged relationships, not only between family members but between friends, war veterans and their enemies, criminals and their victims, even Holocaust survivors and their tormentors. By extracting ideas from more than one hundred stories of estranged relationships, Davis identifies specific patterns and pitfalls that lead to alienation. Many of her insights evolved from working through a long, painful estrangement from her own mother. In conclusion, Davis presents a collection of ideas for reflection and discussion as well as a questionnaire for readers, to assess their readiness for reconciliation. Additional information and collections of stories are available on the author's website: *www. LauraDavis.net.*

Many authors have mined the vast storehouse of Jewish texts to apply religious concepts to the problem of damaged family relationships. Useful sources include:

*Consulting The Wise,* BY RABBI ZELIG PLISKIN (Brooklyn, Bnai Yaacov Publications, 1991).

This is a collection of simulated conversations with great Torah scholars through the ages, using direct quotes from their published works to address fundamental questions. In these pages, readers can immerse themselves in the ideas of such sages as the Vilna Gaon, Rabbi Moshe Chaim Luzzato, Rabbi Moshe Feinstein and the Chofetz Chaim. Some of the issues they address are: controlling anger, dealing with persons who reject your values, counteracting hatred, and making peace between two quarrelling persons.

The same author has amplified his own ideas in a more recent publication, *Harmony with Others* (Brooklyn, NY: Mesorah Publications, 2002). This book describes the "drama" of quarrels, the folly of mistaken assumptions, the value of repeated expressions of apology, and the way to sustain hope in the face of repeated failures to mend a severed relationship.

The psychologist MIRIAM ADAHAN has written several useful self-help books, all based on Torah precepts. In *The Family Connection: Understanding Your Loved Ones* (Southfield, MI: Targum Press, 1995), she focuses on the process of accepting others and expressing gratitude for their strengths. "Emotional constipation" is the term she uses to refer to one's inability to express love and caring (p. 155). She urges readers to speak of the other person with respect, regardless of the problems he imposes on us. Her motto is: "He is doing the best he can with the tools he has."

CONCLUDING ADVICE TO READERS:

Although it is certainly useful to study relevant books, articles, websites, and other written sources of knowledge, the most effective way to understand one's own family dynamics is to consult an experienced, family-oriented therapist. Persons who are involved in a long-term estrangement can benefit from the help of a competent professional who will guide them through the labyrinth of the family's sticky web. The self-awareness that emerges from intensive engagement in the therapeutic process is the ultimate reward and the most gratifying achievement.

## NOTES

### One: The Multiple Dimensions of Family

1. For example, see Alister E. McGrath, ed. *The Christian Theology Reader*, 2nd edition. (Oxford U.K. and Malden, Maine: Blackwell Publishers, 2001) This anthology of extracts from primary Christian sources provides interpretations of basic human responses to life situations. Also see V.G. Beers and R. Beers, *Touchpoints: God's Answers for Your Daily Needs*. (Wheaton, IL: Tyndale House, 1996) This is a collection of commentaries derived from Old and New Testament sources regarding such topics as anger, bitterness, responsibility, revenge, rebellion, and reconciliation.

2. Murray Bowen, *Family Therapy in Clinical Practice*. (Northvale, NJ: Jason Aronson, 1978).

3. Michael Kerr and Murray Bowen, *Family Evaluation: An Approach Based on Bowen Theory*. (New York: W.W. Norton, 1988); Dan Papero, *Bowen Family Systems Theory*. (Boston: Allyn and Bacon, 1990); Peter Titelman, ed., *The Family Therapist's Own Family* (Jason Aronson, 1987); and P. Titelman, ed., *Emotional Cutoff and Bowen Family Systems Theory Perspectives* (New York: Haworth Clinical Practice Press, 2003).

4. See Murray Bowen, *Family Therapy* (1978) 424-6 and Dan Papero, *Bowen Theory* (1990), 45-64. Also see the website: http://www.thebowencenter. org/pages/theory.html.

5. M. Kerr and M. Bowen, *Family Evaluation.*, 306-312. A slightly different diagram called a genogram," with special symbols and markings, was created by other family therapists. See M. McGoldrick, R. Gerson, and S. Shellenberger, *Genograms: Assessment and Intervention*, 2nd edition. (New York: W.W. Norton, 1999).

6. Walter Toman, *Family Constellation*, 4th edition (New York City: Springer. 1961/1993).

7. Betty Carter and Monica McGoldrick, *The Expanded Family Life Cycle: Individual, Family, and Social Perspectives*, 3rd edition (Boston: Allyn and Bacon, 1999) 37–9.

8. This phrase is the title of a useful self-help book by Harriet Lerner (New York: Harper and Row, 1985).

9. P. Titelman, ed. *The Family Therapist's Own Family*.

10. P. Titelman, ed. *Emotional Cutoff and Bowen Theory*.

11. Carol Gilligan, *In a Different Voice*. (Cambridge, MA: Harvard University Press, 1982).

12. Gilligan, *Voice*, 62.

13. *Pittsburgh Post-Gazette* June 12, 2001, 4.

## Two: Family Assets and Vulnerabilities

1. Thomas Mann (1934/1963) Joseph and His Brothers. Prelude to *The Tales of Jacob*. Trans. H.T. Lowe-Porter. (New York: Knopf), 3.

2. W.F. Nerin, *Family Reconstruction: Long Day's Journey Into Light* (New York: Norton, 1986), 37.

3. Edward H. Spicer, "Persistent Cultural Systems," *Science*, 1971, 174: 4001, 795–800.

4. Clifford Geertz, "Suq: The Bazaar Economy in Sefrou." In Geertz, C., Geertz, H., and Rosen, L., *Meaning and Order in Moroccan society*. (London: Cambridge University Press. 1979), 123–244.

5. Stephen I. Levine, *The New Zealand Jewish* Community, (Lanham, Maryland. Lexington Books, 1999).

6. See for example, Laura Varon's memoir of the Jewish community on the island of Rhodes, (*The Juderia*, Westport, Conn: Praeger, 1999) and Dan Jacobson's description of the Jews from Lithuania who settled in South Africa, (*Heshel's Kingdom*, Evanston, ILL: Northwestern University Press, 1999).

7. C. Geertz, *Suq*, 164. Geertz observed that while the Jews in Sefrou looked exactly like their Muslim neighbors, in many other ways they were totally different. The Jews were not just one more "tribe" in the Moroccan milieu, although they often appeared to be. They were not an isolated community, although they were often set apart and excluded. They spoke in Arabic and prayed in Hebrew. "Moroccan to the core and Jewish to the same core, they were heritors of a tradition double and indivisible, and in no way marginal."

8. Daniel Klein and Freke Vuijst, *The Half-Jewish Book.* (New York: Random House, 2000).

9. Many of these issues are addressed on the website: http://www.halfjew. com

10. Monica McGoldrick, "Overview". In McGoldrick, Pearce and Giordano, *Ethnicity and Family Therapy.* (New York: Guilford Press, 1996) 3–4

11. Herz and Rosen. (1996) "Jewish families". In McGoldrick, Pearce and Giordano, *Ethnicity and Family Therapy*, 364–392.

12. See the introduction to I. Metzker, ed., *A Bintel Brief.* (New York: Doubleday, 1971) 7–17.

13. Wendy Belzberg, "Jews' Families: Unhappy in Their Own Way?" *The Forward*, July 19, 2002, 19.

14. Yale Strom, *Expulsion of the Jews: 500 Years of Exodus.* (New York: SPI Books, 1992).

15. See numerous examples in Norman A. Stillman, *The Jews of Arab Lands: A History and Source Book* (Philadelphia: Jewish Publication Society, 1979).

16. Bat Ye'or, *Islam and Dhimmitude: Where Civilizations Collide* (Madison, NJ: Fairleigh Dickinson UP, 2001).

17. Huston Smith, *The World's Religions: Our Great Wisdom Traditions* (San Francisco: HarperCollins, 1958/1991) 272.

18. Genesis 2:18. This translation of the Hebrew phrase is from the Soncino edition of the Torah.

19. This translation of the same phrase is by Aryeh Kaplan in *The Living Torah.*

20. K. Kvam, L. Schearing, and B. Ziegler, *Eve and Adam: Jewish, Christian and Muslim Readings on Genesis and Gender* ( Bloomington: Indiana University Press, 1999). 17, 26–31.

21. Michael Kaufman, *The Woman in Jewish Law and Tradition.* (Northvale, NJ: Jason Aronson, 1993). See especially Part III.

22. M. Kaufman, *Women in Law*, Introduction, xxix

23. For example, see Laura Levitt, Reconfiguring Home: Jewish Feminist Identities. In T. Rudavsky, ed. *Gender and Judaism: The Transformation of Tradition* ( New York: New York University Press, 1995) 39.

24. Judith Baskin, ed. *Jewish Women in Historical Perspective* (Detroit: Wayne State University Press, 1991).

25. Sholem Aleichem, *Tevye the Dairyman and the Railroad Stories*, Trans. Hillel Halkin (New York: Schocken Books, 1987).

26. *Mishnah (Peah* 1:1).

27. See the footnote in L. Fuchs, *Beyond Patriarchy: Jewish Fathers and Families* (Hanover, NH: University Press of New England and Brandeis University Press, 2000), 71. Quote is from Louis J. Newman, ed., *The Talmudic Anthology*.

28. *Genesis* 5:1–32.

29. *Encyc. Judaica.* 7: 382. Original source in the Talmud is *Kid*: 70b.

30. "Rabban Gamliel said: There were no happier festivals for Israel than the 15th of Av and Yom Kippur, when the maidens of Jerusalem used to come out in borrowed white dresses so as not to shame those who possessed them not... and would dance in the vineyards, singing, 'Young man, raise your eyes and see what you are choosing; do not set your eyes on beauty, but set your eyes on family...'" Original source is in *Ta'anith* 4:8. See also the footnote in the Musaf Service for Yom Kippur. *High Holyday Prayer Book*. Translated and annotated by Philip Birnbaum. (New York: Hebrew Publishing Co. 1951/1979), 830.

31. Peter Farb and G. Armelagos, *Consuming Passions: The Anthropology of Eating* (New York: Pocket Books, 1980).

32. Greenberg, Blu. *How to Run a Traditional Jewish Household* (New York: Simon and Schuster, 1983), 482–495.

33. Etan Levine, The Jews in Time and Space. In Etan Levine, ed., *Diaspora: Exile and the Contemporary Jewish Condition* (New York: Steimatzky, 1986) 3.

34. Michael Strassfeld, *The Jewish Holidays* (New York: Harper and Row, 1985) 1.

35. Alan Mintz, *Banished From their Father's Table* (Bloomington: Indiana University Press, 1989), 3 (Quote is from the Talmud, *Bavli Berachot* 3a.).

36. *Proverbs*: 17:17.

37. *Psalms* 133:1.

38. *Samuel II*, 3:27.

39. *Numbers* 35:19–28; *Deut.* 19:6; *Joshua* 20:3; *Samuel II*, 14:11.

40. *Leviticus* 25:48; *Psalms* 49:8.

41. L.H. Fuchs, *Beyond Patriarchy: Jewish Fathers and Families* (Hanover,

NH: University Press of New England and Brandeis University Press, 2000), 74.

42. See Fuchs, *Patriarchy*, 74 and the accompanying footnote #9 on page 184.

43. Paraphrased from BinGorion, Micha and BinGorion, Emanuel 1990, *Mimekor Yisrael: Classical Jewish Folktales.* (Indiana University Press) 163–4. Their source is Huzin, S.B. (1890). *Maaseh Nissim*, (Baghdad), 35.

44. Rabbi Adin Steinsaltz, *The Strife of the Spirit.* (Northvale, NJ: Jason Aronson, 1988), 103.

## Three: Sources of Ultimate Values

1. Elie Wiesel, *Messengers of God: Biblical Portraits and Legends.* Trans. Marion Wiesel (New York: Simon and Schuster. 1976/1994) XIII.

2. A. Kessler, *Judaism as Religion and Culture* (New York: Vantage Press, 1997) 11.

3. Avivah Zornberg, class notes, Jerusalem, December, 2001.

4. Simi Peters, *Learning to Read Midrash* (Jerusalem: Urim Publications, 2004) 11.

5. Avivah Zornberg, *The Beginning of Desire: Reflections on Genesis* (New York: Doubleday, 1995) 74.

6. Henry Abramovitch, *The First Father, Abraham: The Psychology and Culture of a Spiritual Revolutionary* (Lanham, MD: University Press of America, 1994) 9.

7. *Genesis* 4:8.

8. Rabbi M. Weissman, *The Midrash says.* (Brooklyn: Bnai Yacov Publications, 1980) 60.

9. Elie Weisel, *Messengers* (1976) 38.

10. Andre Neher, *The Exile of the Word* (Philadelphia: Jewish Publication Society, 1970/1981) 95.

11. Robert Graves and Raphael Patai, *Hebrew Myths: The Book of Genesis* (Garden City, NY: Doubleday, 1964) 85–88.

12. Eli Wiesel, *Messengers*, 44.

13. Nechama Leibowitz, *Studies in Bereshit/Genesis.* Trans. Aryeh Newman. (Jerusalem: Publishing Department of the Jewish Agency, 3rd edition, 1976) 40.

14. Three versions of the same theme: see Graves and Patai, 91–92; Nechama Leibowitz, 39; Eli Wiesel, 48–51.

15. Elie Wiesel, *Messengers* 41.

16. See Graves and Patai, *Myths* 92 and the note on page 283. This interpretation is derived from an aprocryphal *Book of Adam*, preserved in an Armenian text. A similar idea is found in Rabbi M. Weissman's *The Midrash Says,* 63. The original source is in Bereshit Rabbah, kaf bet.

17. *Genesis* 4:9.

18. N. Leibowitz, *Bereshit*, 49–50.

19. *Genesis* 4:14,16

20. Graves and Patai, *Myths*, 93. (See footnote #9 and the source listed on page 283. This list of afflictions is attributed to *Adamshriften* (1900).

21. Graves and Patai, *Myths*, 108.

22. *Genesis* 16:4–5 "…her mistress was despised in her eyes."

23. N. Leibowitz, *Bereshit*, 155.

24. N. Leibowitz, *Bereshit*, 156–7

25. See Graves and Patai, *Myths*, 156–59.

26. A. Zornberg, *Beginning*, 134–5.

27. Bialik and Ravnitsky, *The Book of Legends (Sefer Ha-Aggadah)* Trans. William Braude. (New York: Schocken, 1992) 39.

28. *Genesis* 25:9.

29. F.E. Peters, *Children of Abraham* (Princeton University Press, 1982) 197–8.

30. *Genesis* 25:22.

31. *Genesis* 25:25.

32. *Genesis* 26:35.

33. *Genesis* 27:19.

34. A. Zornberg, *Beginning,* 169–179.

35. A. Steinsaltz, *Images*, 46–7.

36. *Genesis* 27:45.

37. N. Leibowitz, *Bereshit/Genesis*, 289, Quote is from Benamozegh, (1822–1900), an Italian Jewish commentator: "Rebecca said: one will be no more, slain, and the other, the murderer, will be detested by me as an enemy and stranger. Cut off by one, and lost to the other, I will be bereaved of both my sons." The earlier source is *Em Lemikra*.

38. Rabbi Adin Steinsaltz, *Biblical Images*, 43–44.

39. *Genesis* 33:15.

40. N. Leibowitz, *Bereshit/Genesis.* 345–350.

41. *Genesis*: 33:4.

42. N. Leibowitz, 374. The textual basis of this interpretation is the rare appearance of scribal dots that appear in the Torah above the word for 'and he kissed him,' which is nearly identical to the word for 'and he bit him.' This led the ancient Sages to infer the ambivalence of Esau's 'affection.'

43. Benno Jacob, quoted in N. Leibowitz, *Bereshit*, 377.

44. *Genesis* 35: 29.

45. Thomas Mann, *Joseph and his Brothers* (New York: Alfred A. Knopf, 1948) Foreword, v.

46. *Genesis* Chapter 37.

47. *Genesis*. 37:27.

48. Zornberg, *Beginning*, 290.

49. Zornberg, Class notes, Jerusalem, January 4, 2002.

50. Zornberg, *Beginning*, 280–281. A similar version appears in Graves and Patai, 271–2.

51. Zornberg, 283.

52. *Genesis*: 46:29.

53. Comments by Cyril Brill. *Quintessential News* (Jerusalem, February, 2001) 7.

54. *Genesis* 46:30.

55. *Genesis* 49:1.

56. Zornberg, *Beginning*, 360–364.

57. Zornberg, *Beginning*, 360.

58. E. Wiesel, *Messengers of God* (1976) xii.

59. Excerpted from an article on "herem" by Haim Hermann Cohn in *Encyclopedia Judaica* vol. 8, 355.

60. Cited by Abraham Hirsch Rabinowitz in *Encyclopedia Judaica*, vol. 10, 935. The original source in the Talmud is *Ket.* 28b.

61. Norman Stillman, "The rabbis of Aleppo pronounce a ban of anathema upon Sabbath desecrators. (1906), *The Jews of Arab Lands in Modern Times.* (Philadelphia: Jewish Publication Society, 1991) 223–4.

62. Der Nister (Pinhas Kahanovitch) *The Family Mashber.* (London: Fontana Paperbacks, 1948/1989).

63. Der Nister, *Mashber*, 384–395.

## Four: Images of Family Conflict in Secular Literature

1. Sholem Aleichem, *Tevye the Dairyman and the Railroad Stories. Trans.* Hillel Halkin (New York: Schocken Books, 1987) 3–131. The story was first published in 1914/1916.

2. Sholem Aleichem, *Tevye*, 53–69.

3. In *George Eliot, Collected Poems.* Edited by Lucien Jenkins (London: Scoob, 1989). 84–90.

4. Frederick. R. Karl, *George Eliot: Voice of a Century* (New York: Norton, 1995) 8.

5. Karl, *Eliot*, 254.

6. Dinah Birch, *Introduction to The Mill on the Floss* (Oxford/New York: Oxford UP, 1996) VII.

7. George Eliot, *The Mill on the Floss*, 484–5.

8. Eliot, *Mill*, 521–2.

9. Karl, *Eliot*, 644.

10. This is an insight derived from Christine Downing, "Sisters and Brothers Casting Shadows," in Connie Zweig and J. Abrams (eds.) 1991. *Meeting the Shadow.* (Los Angeles: Tracher, 1991) 65.

11. Vimala Pillari, *Scapegoating in Families* (New York: Brunner/Mazel, 1991).

12. J.K. Rowling, *Harry Potter and the Sorcerer's Stone* (New York: Scholastic Press, 1997) 1.

13. Geoffrey S. Proehl, *Coming Home Again: American Family Drama and the Figure of the Prodigal* (Madison NJ: Fairleigh Dickenson UP, 1997) 53.

14. *New Testament, Luke* 15:11–32. King James Version.

15. See examples in Ruth B. Graham, *Prodigals and Those Who Love Them* (Colorado Springs: Focus on the Family Publishing, 1991).

16. G. Proehl, *Coming Home*, 80. The quote is by Tom Cheesman: "The return of the transformed son: a popular ballad from a complex cultural history, Germany 1500–1900."

17. Alan Mintz, *Banished From Their Father's Table: Loss of Faith and Hebrew Autobiography* (Bloomington: Indiana UP, 1989) 3.

18. Shirley Jackson, "Biography of a story". *Come Along With Me,* edited by Stanley Edgar Hyman, 1979. No publisher given. 221–235.

19. S. Jackson, "Louisa, Please Come Home," In *Come along with* me, 163–179.

20. Judy Oppenheimer, *Private Demons: The Life of Shirley Jackson* (New York: Putnam, 1988).

21. Oppenheimer, *Demons*, 15.

22. Shirley Jackson, *Louisa*, 179.

23. Philip Roth, *American Pastoral* (New York: Vintage Books, 1998).

24. Roth, *Pastoral*, p. 86.

25. Roth, *Pastoral*, 423.

26. Thomas Wolfe, "A Portrait of Bascom Hawke," *The short novels of Thomas Wolfe*, C. Hugh Holman, ed. (New York: Charles Scribner, 1961). 4–71.

27. David H. Donald, *Look Homeward: A Life of Thomas Wolfe* (Boston: Little Brown, 1987).

28. David H. Donald, *Look Homeward*, 74.

29. Wolfe, *Hawke*, 56.

30. Wolfe, *Hawke*, 57.

31. Harold Clurman, Biographical notes in *The Portable Arthur Miller* (New York. Viking Press, 1971) vii.

32. Martin Gottfried, *Arthur Miller: His Life and Work* (Cambridge Mass.: Perseus/Da Capo, 2003).

33. Gottfried, *Miller*, 46.

34. Gottfried, *Miller*, 392.

35. Lawrence Fuchs, See Chapter 9: "Immigrants and their children, 1880–1920" and Chapter 10, "The Americanization of fathers," *Beyond Patriarchy: Jewish Fathers and Families* (Hanover, NH: UP New England, 2000). 101–139.

36. Arthur Miller. *The Price*. In *Arthur Miller's Collected Plays*, Vol. II (New York: Viking, 1981) 329.

37. Tamara K. Hareven, "Family Time and Historical Time," *Daedalus*, 1977, vol. 106: 57–70.

38. Jonathan Root, *The Betrayers: The Rosenberg Case – A Reappraisal of an American Crisis* (New York: Coward-McCann, 1963) 32.

39. Ilene Philipson, *Ethel Rosenberg: Beyond the Myths* (New York: Franklin Watts, 1988) 113.

40. The historian Paul Lyons, quoted in Philipson, *Ethel,* 105.

41. Philipson, *Ethel,* 123.

42. Philipson, 198–9.

43. Philipson, 210.

44. Philipson, 345.

45. R. Meeropol, and M. Meeropol, *We Are Your Sons.* (Urbana and Chicago: UP Illinois, 1986).

46. Sam Roberts, *The Brother.* (New York: Random House, 2001).

47. Roberts, *Brother,* 298.

48. Roberts, 158.

49. Aram Saroyan, *Last Rites: The death of William Saroyan* (New York: Morrow, 1982) 27.

50. David S. Calonne, *William Saroyan: My Real Work is Being* (Chapel Hill: UP North Carolina, 1983) 58.

51. Saroyan, *Rites,* 14.

52. Saroyan, *Rites,* 21–22.

53. Saroyan, *Rites,* 10–14.

54. Lawrence Lee and Barry Gifford, *Saroyan: A Biography* (New York: Harper and Row, 1984).

55. Saroyan, *Rites,* 34.

56. Saroyan, 119.

57. Saroyan, 161.

58. Saroyan, 165.

59. Saroyan, 175

60. Saroyan, 167–8.

61. Peter R. Stillman, *Families Writing* (Cincinnati: Writer's Digest Books, 1992) and Tristine Rainer, *Your Life as Story* (New York: Tarcher/ Penguin Putnam, 1998). Also see the classic text by Thomas Mallon: *A Book of One's Own: People and their Diaries* ( New York: Penguin 1986).

## Five: My Family – Estrangement and Reconciliation in Retrospect

1. Various examples of this process are described in a collection of articles on Bowen Theory. Peter Titelman, ed. *The Family Therapist's Own Family* (Northvale, NJ: Jason Aronson, 1987).

2. Ellen G. Benswanger. "Strategies to explore cutoffs," In P. Titelman ed. 1987. 191–207.

## Six: Five Families, Still Estranged After All These Years

1. "People say that tales are for going to sleep to, but I say that, through tales, people can be shaken from their sleep." Ora Wiskind-Elper, *Tradition and Fantasy in the Tales of Reb Nachman of Bratslav*. (Albany: State University of New York Press, 1998). Quote is from *Hayyei Moharan* 5a:23. Footnote 220, 286.

2. Andre Neher, *The Exile of the Word*. (Philadelphia: Jewish Publication Society, 1981) 13.

3. Mary Antin, *The Promised Land: The Autobiography of a Russian Immigrant* (Cambridge, MA: The Riverside Press. 39th impression, 1911/1963) 14.

4. Antin, *Land*, 82.

## Seven: Inheritance Feuds – Is Money the Root?

1. J.P. Straus, (1982) "Preparation, Probate, and Prophecy,". *The Probate Lawyer* (Los Angeles, CA, The American College of Probate Council, 1982). Vol. 8. Summer. 3.

2. D.I. Grunfeld, *The Jewish Law of Inheritance* (Oak Park: Targum Press and Jerusalem: Feldheim, 1987).

3. *Genesis*: 49.

4. Riemer, J. and Stampfer, N., eds., *Ethical Wills: A Modern Jewish Treasury* (New York City: Schocken Books, 1983).

5. Riemer and Stampfer, *Wills*, 151.

6. Riemer and Stampfer, *Wills*, 154.

7. www.ethicalwill.com/examples.html

8. Nahum N. Glatzer, ed., *The Judaic Tradition*, (West Orange, New Jersey: Behrman House, 1969). An alternative source is: "Ibn Tibbon's ethical will: a father's admonition," *Internet Medieval Sourcebook. Jewish Ethical Wills, 12th and 14th Centuries.*

9. *Encyclopedia Judaica*, 15: 1129–30.

## Eight: Four Families Find Solutions

1. M.H. Danzger, *Returning to Tradition: The Contemporary Revival of Orthodox Judaism* (New Haven: Yale UP, 1989). 13–22.

2. Rabbi Adin Steinsaltz, *Teshuvah: A Guide for the Newly Observant Jew* (Northvale, NJ: Jason Aronson, 1996) 58.

3. www.jewishgen.org

## Nine: Attributes of Reconciliation

1. T.S. Eliot, *Four Quartets* (New York: Harcourt, Brace and World, 1943/1971) 58.

2. Sholem Aleichem, "Lekh-Lekho," the last story in *Tevye the Dairyman and the Railroad Stories*. Trans. Hillel Halkin (New York: Schocken Books, 1987) 116–131.

3. James Kugel, (1990) *On being a Jew.* (San Francisco: Harper and Row, 1990) 130.

4. Rabbi Adin Steinsaltz, *The Strife of the Spirit* (Northvale, NJ: Jason Aronson, 1988/1996) 102.

5. Steinsaltz, *Strife*, 102.

6. Steinsaltz, *Strife*, 9–23.

7. Steinsaltz, *Strife*, 102–3.

8. *The Straight Story*, Dir. David Lynch, actors Richard Farnsworth, Sissy Spacek. Walt Disney Pictures, 1999.

9. *Genesis*, 42–45.

10. Phinehas haKohen. "Joseph reveals himself to his brothers," T. Carmi, edited and translated., *The Penguin Book of Hebrew Verse* (New York: Penguin Books, 1981) 233–4.

11. See references to the original Talmudic sources compiled by Rabbi Moshe Weissman, *The Midrash Says: The Book of Bereshis* (Brooklyn Benei Yakov Publications, 1980) 417–423.

12. Weissman, *Midrash*, Foreword, xii.

13. Andre Neher, *The Exile of the Word*. Trans. David Maisel. (Philadelphia: Jewish Publication Society, 1981) 235–6. Quoted by Avivah Zornberg (1995) *Beginning: Genesis*, 141.

## Ten: Strategies to Explore and Resolve Conflict

1. This phrase is attributed to the eleventh century Spanish poet and philosopher Solomon ben Judah ibn Gabirol, *The Choice of Pearls*. Trans. Rev. A Cohen. ( New York: Bloch Publishing Company, 1925).

2. Andre Neher, *The Exile of the Word*. Trans. David Maisel. (New York: Jewish Publication Society, 1981) 149.

3. William James. *Varieties of Religious Experience*, Lecture xx. (Cambridge: Harvard UP, 1985) 382.

4. Cited by Rabbi Bernard M. Casper in *Talks on Jewish Prayer* (Jerusalem: Popular Torah Library, 1963) 40.

5. *Complete Artscroll Siddur* (Ashkenaz) 1984/1991, See note, 18.

6. *Artscroll Siddur*, 289.

7. Erik H. Erikson, *Toys and Reasons: Stages in the Ritualization of Experience* ( New York: Norton, 1977) 113.

8. Raymond Firth: "Verbal and bodily rituals of greeting and parting," In LaFontaine, J.S. *The Interpretation of Ritual* (London: Tavistock, 1972) 1–38.

9. Robert Fulghum, *From Beginning to End: The Rituals in our Lives* (New York: Ivy/ Ballantine, 1995).

10. Fulghum, *Rituals in our Lives* 76.

11. Maimonides, *The Laws of Repentance* (*Hilchot Teshuvah*), Chapter Two, *Halachah* 11.

12. *Code of Jewish Law* (*Kitzur Shulchan Aruch*) Compiled by Rabbi Solomon Ganzfried, trans. Hyman E. Goldin. (New York: Hebrew Publishing Company, 1993) Volume Two, Chapter 59:20.

## Coda:

1. Paraphrased from Rumi, a thirteenth-century Sufi poet, *The Book of Love: Poems of Ecstasy and Longing*. (San Francisco, Harper. 2003) 123.

2. Eva Hoffman, *Lost in Translation* (New York: Penguin Books, 1989) 104

3. Hoffman, *Lost*, 265.

# REFERENCES

Antin, Mary. (1911/1963). *The Promised Land: The Autobiography of a Russian Immigrant*. Cambridge, Mass: Riverside Press. 39ᵗʰ impression, 1911/1963.

Baskin, Judith, ed. *Jewish Women in Historical Perspective*. Detroit: Wayne State UP, 1991.

Bat Ye'or. *Islam and Dhimmitude: Where civilizations collide*. Madison, NJ: Fairleigh Dickinson UP, 2001.

Belzberg, Wendy. "Jewish families: unhappy in their own way?" *Forward*. July 19, 2002, 19.

Benswanger, Ellen. "Strategies to explore cutoffs." In P. Titelman, ed. *The Family Therapist's Own Family*. Northvale, NJ. 1987, 191–207.

Bialik, H.N. and Ravnitsky, Y.N. *The Book of Legends (Sefer Ha-Aggadah)*. Trans. William Braude. New York: Schocken, 1992.

BinGorion, Micha and BinGorion, Emanuel. *Mimekor Yisrael: Classical Jewish Folktales*. Indiana UP, 1990.

Bowen, Murray. *Family Therapy in Clinical Practice*. Northfield, NJ: Jason Aronson, 1978.

Calonne, David S. *William Saroyan: My Real Work is Being*. Chapel Hill: UP North Carolina, 1983.

Carter, Betty and McGoldrick, Monica, eds. *The Expanded Family Life Cycle: Individual, Family and Social Perspectives*. 3ʳᵈ edition. Boston: Allyn and Bacon, 1999.

*The Complete Artscroll Siddur.* (Sefarad) Scherman, N. and Zlotowitz, M. eds. Brooklyn: Artscroll Mesorah Series, 1985.

*Code of Jewish Law. Kitzur Shulhan Arukh* Compilation by Rabbi Solomon Ganzfried. Trans. Hyman Goldin. Rockaway Beach: Hebrew Publishing Company, 1993.

Danzger, M. Herbert. *Returning to Tradition: The Contemporary Revival of Orthodox Judaism.* New Haven: Yale UP, 1989.

Der Nister (Pinhas Kahanovitch). *The Family Mashber.* Translated from the Yiddish by Leonard Wolf. London: Fontana Paperbacks, 1989.

Donald, David H. *Look Homeward: A Life of Thomas Wolfe.* Boston: Little Brown, 1987.

Eiseman, Moshe. *Beginnings: a study of some of the topics that make up Parashas Bereshit.* Baltimore: Pub. Rabbi M. Eiseman, 2002.

Eliot, George. *Collected poems.* Edited by Lucien Jenkins. London: Scoob, 1989.

Eliot, George. The *Mill on the Floss.* Introduction by Dinah Birch. Oxford/New York: Oxford UP, 1996.

*Encyclopedia Judaica.* Jerusalem: Keter, 1997 and CD Rom Edition 1.0.

Erikson, E.H. *Toys and Reasons: Stages in the Ritualization of Experience.* New York: W.W. Norton, 1977.

Farb, Peter and Armelagos, George. *Consuming Passions: The Anthropology of Eating.* New York: Pocket Books, 1980.

Firth, Raymond. "Verbal and Bodily Rituals of Greeting and Parting," J.S. La Fontaine, ed. *The Interpretation of Ritual.* London: Tavistock, 1972, 1–38.

Fuchs, Lawrence H. *Beyond Patriarchy: Jewish Fathers and Families.* Hanover, NH. UP New England and Brandeis UP, 2000.

Fulghum, Robert. *From Beginning to End: The Rituals in our Lives.* New York: Ivy/ Ballantine Press, 1995.

Geertz, C., Geertz, H., and Rosen, L. *Meaning and Order in Moroccan Society.* London: Cambridge UP, 1979.

Glatzer, Nahum N., ed. *The Judaic Tradition.* West Orange, NJ: Behrman House, 1969.

Gottfried, Martin. *Arthur Miller: His Life and Work*. Cambridge, Mass: Perseus/DaCapo Press, 2003.

Graves, Robert and Patai, Raphael. *Hebrew Myths: The Book of Genesis*. Garden City: Doubleday, 1964.

Greenberg, Blu. *How to run a traditional Jewish household*. New York: Simon and Schuster, 1983.

Grunfeld, D.I. *The Jewish Law of Inheritance*. Oak Park: Targum Press and Jerusalem: Feldheim, 1987.

Hareven, Tamara K. Family Time and Historical Time. *Daedalus*, 1977, v. 106, 57–70.

Heilman, Samuel. *When a Jew Dies*. Berkeley: UP California, 2001.

Hoffman, Eva. *Lost in Translation*. New York: Penguin Books, 1989.

Holtz, Barry W., ed. *Back to the Sources: Reading the Classic Jewish Texts*. New York: Summit Books, 1984.

Ibn Tibbon, Judah. "In Praise of Learning, Education and the Good Life." Glatzer, Nahum N. *The Judaic Tradition*. Boston: Beacon Press, 1969, 347–352.

Imber-Black, Evan. *The Secret Life of Families*. New York: Bantam Books, 1998.

Jackson, Shirley. "Biography of a Story," *Come Along With Me*. Edited by Stanley Edgar Hyman, 221–235. No publisher given, 1979.

*The Living Torah*. Translation by Aryeh Kaplan. Brooklyn: Maznaim Publishing Corp, 1981.

Karl, Frederick. R. *George Eliot: Voice of a Century*. New York: W.W. Norton, 1995.

Kaufman, Michael. *The Woman in Jewish Law and Tradition*. Northvale, NJ: Jason Aronson, 1993.

Kerr, Michael E. and Bowen, Murray. *Family Evaluation: An Approach Based on Bowen Theory*. New York: W.W. Norton, 1988.

Kessler, Aaron. *Judaism As Religion and Culture*. New York: Vantage Press, 1997.

Klein, Daniel and Vuijst, Freke. *The Half-Jewish Book*. New York: Random House, 2000.

Kugel, James. *On Being A Jew*. San Francisco: Harper & Row, 1990.

Kvam, K.E., Schearing, L. and Ziegler, V. *Eve and Adam: Jewish, Christian and Muslim Readings on Genesis and Gender*. Bloomington: Indiana UP, 1999.

Lee, Lawrence and Gifford, Barry. *Saroyan: A Biography*. New York: Harper and Row 1984.

Leibowitz, Nehama. *Studies in Bereshit (Genesis)*. Translated by Aryeh Newman. Jerusalem: Publishing Dept of the Jewish Agency, 3rd edition, 1976.

Levine, Etan, ed. *Diaspora: Exile and the Contemporary Jewish Condition*. New York: Steimatzky, 1986.

Mann, Thomas. *Joseph and his Brothers*. New York: Knopf, 1934/1948.

McGoldrick, M., Gerson, R., Shellenberger, S. *Genograms: Assessment and Intervention*. 2nd edition. New York: W. W. Norton, 1999.

McGoldrick, Monica, Giordano, Joe and Pearce, John, eds. *Ethnicity and Family Therapy*. New York: Guilford Press, 1996.

Meeropol, R. and Meeropol, M. *We Are Your Sons*. Urbana and Chicago: UP Illinois, 1986.

Metzker, Isaac, ed. *A Bintel Brief*. New York: Doubleday, 1971.

Miller, Arthur. *The Price*. New York: Viking Press, 1968.

Mintz, Alan. *Banished From Their Father's Table: Loss of Faith and Hebrew Autobiography*. Bloomington: Indiana UP, 1989.

Neher, Andre. *The Exile of the Word*. Trans. David Maisel. New York: Jewish Publication Society, 1981.

Nerin, W.F. *Family Reconstruction: Long Day's Journey into Light*. New York: Norton, 1986.

Oppenheimer, Judy. *Private Demons: The Life of Shirley Jackson*. New York: Putnam, 1988.

Palazzoli, M.S., Boscoli, L., Cecchin, G.F. and Prata, G. "Family Rituals: A Powerful Tool in Family Therapy." *Family Process*. vol. 16, No. 4, December, 1977. 445–453.

Papero, Daniel. *Bowen Family Systems Theory*. Boston: Allyn and Bacon, 1990.

Peters, F.E. *Children of Abraham: Judaism, Christianity, Islam*. Princeton UP, 1982.

Peters, Simi. *Learning to Read Midrash*. Jerusalem: Urim Publications, 2004.

Philipson, Ilene. *Ethel Rosenberg: Beyond the Myths*. New York: Franklin Watts, 1988.

Phinehas Hakohen. "Joseph Reveals Himself to his Brothers." In Carmi, T., ed. and trans. *The Penguin Book of Hebrew Verse*. New York: Penguin Books, 1981. 233–4.

Proehl, Geoffrey S. *Coming Home Again: American Family Drama and the Figure of the Prodigal*. Madison NJ: Fairleigh Dickenson UP, 1997.

Riemer, J. and Stampfer, N., eds. *Ethical Wills: A Modern Jewish Treasury*. New York: Schocken, 1983.

Root, Jonathan. *The Betrayers: The Rosenberg case – A Reappraisal of an American Crisis*. New York: Coward-McCann, 1963.

Roth, Philip. *American Pastorale*. New York: Vintage Books, 1998.

Rowling, J.K. *Harry Potter and the Sorcerer's Stone*, 1997. New York: Scholastic Press.

Rudavsky, T.M. ed. *Gender and Judaism: The Transformation of Tradition*. New York: New York UP, 1995.

Saroyan, Aram. *Last Rites: The Death of William Saroyan*. New York: W. Morrow, 1982.

Sholem Aleichem. *Tevye the Dairyman and the Railroad Stories*. Trans. Hillel Halkin. New York: Schocken, 1987.

Spicer, E.H. "Persistent Cultural Systems." *Science*, New Series, vol. 174, Issue 4001, November 19, 795–800, 1971.

Steinsaltz, Rabbi Adin. *Biblical images: men and women of the book*. New York: Basic Books, 1984.

Steinsaltz, A. *The Strife of the Spirit*. Northvale, NJ. Jason Aronson, 1988.

Steinsaltz, A. *Teshuvah: A Guide for the Newly Observant Jew*. Northvale, NJ: Jason Aronson, 1996.

Stillman, Norman, A. *The Jews of Arab Lands: A History and Source Book*. Philadelphia: Jewish Publication Society, 1979.

Stillman, Norman A. *The Jews of Arab Lands in Modern Times*. Philadelphia: Jewish Publication Society, 1991.

Strassfeld, Michael. *The Jewish Holidays: A Guide and Commentary*. New York: Harper and Row, 1985.

Straus, J. Pennington. "Preparation, Probate and Prophecy," *The Probate Lawyer*. Los Angeles, CA. The American College of Probate Council. vol. 8. Summer. 1982.

Strom, Y. *Expulsion of the Jews: 500 years of Exodus*. New York: SPI Books, 1992.

Titelman, Peter, ed. *The Family Therapist's Own Family*. Northvale, NJ: Jason Aronson, 1987.

Titelman, Peter, ed. *Emotional cutoff: Bowen Family Systems Theory Perspectives*. New York: Haworth Clinical Practice Press, 2003.

Toman, Walter. *Family Constellation*. Fourth edition. New York: Springer, 1961/1993.

Weissman, Rabbi Moshe, ed. *The Midrash Says. Selected and adapted from the Talmud. and Midrash*. Brooklyn: Bnai Yakov Publications, 1980.

Wiesel, Eli. *Messengers of God*. Trans. Marion Wiesel. New York: Simon and Schuster, 1976.

Wolfe, Thomas. "A Portrait of Bascom Hawke," Holman, C. Hugh, ed. *The Short Novels of Thomas Wolfe*. New York: Charles Scribner's, 1961. 1–71.

Zornberg, Avivah. *The Beginning of Desire: Reflections on Genesis*. New York: Doubleday, 1995.

Printed in the United States
69986LV00004B/83